Global Logistics

by SOLE – The International Society of Logistics

John J. Erb, DML, and Sarah R. James, DML, Editors

Global Logistics For Dummies®

Published by: John Wiley & Sons, Ltd., The Atrium, Southern Gate, Chichester, www.wiley.com

This edition first published 2017

© 2017 by John Wiley & Sons, Ltd., Chichester, West Sussex

Registered Office

John Wiley & Sons, Ltd., The Atrium, Southern Gate, Chichester, West Sussex, PO19 8SQ, United Kingdom

For details of our global editorial offices, for customer services and for information about how to apply for permission to reuse the copyright material in this book, please see our website at www.wiley.com.

For general information on our other products and services, please contact our Customer Care Department within the U.S. at 877-762-2974, outside the U.S. at 317-572-3993, or fax 317-572-4002. For technical support, please visit https://hub.wiley.com/community/support/dummies.

Wiley publishes in a variety of print and electronic formats and by print-on-demand. Some material included with standard print versions of this book may not be included in e-books or in print-on-demand. If this book refers to media such as a CD or DVD that is not included in the version you purchased, you may download this material at http://booksupport.wiley.com. For more information about Wiley products, visit www.wiley.com.

A catalogue record for this book is available from the British Library.

Library of Congress Control Number: 2017952101

ISBN 978-1-119-21215-7 (pbk); ISBN 978-1-119-21216-4 (ebk); ISBN 978-1-118-98765-2 (ebk); ISBN 978-1-119-21219-5 (ebk)

Printed and Bound in Great Britain by TJ International, Padstow, Cornwall.

10 9 8 7 6 5 4 3 2 1

Contents at a Glance

Table of Contents

Introduction

There are many good reasons to consider expanding your successful domestic business into a new foreign location. There may be a new market in which to sell or distribute your product. There may be manufacturing cost savings by locating closer to either new consumers or to your product's raw materials and components. Or, you may have determined that you can achieve labor cost savings in order to meet the expanding demand for your product. However, in spite of all the economic advantages you may have perceived, be aware that the physical and cultural challenges of your new location may far outweigh any potential cost savings. In this book, we will assist you in identifying — and, hopefully, avoiding — these challenges.

About This Book

The book has four major focuses: the logistics involved in establishing and sustaining a "global" manufacturing operation (Part 2), the logistics related to globally marketing and distributing your products (Part 3), providing logistics services to or for global clients (Part 4), and the unique aspects of providing humanitarian and disaster relief logistics (Part 5). Finally, in The Part of Tens (Part 6) we highlight ten companies that have been successful in their global expansion; examine ten companies that made significant missteps in their global expansion (although some of those companies adjusted their approach and are very successful today); and provide ten suggestions for resources you may consider when conducting your due diligence to make your ultimate decision to "go global."

We also use the following conventions throughout the book to make the world of global logistics even easier for you to venture into:

>> New terms appear in *italics* and are closely followed by an easy-to-understand definition. In a few instances, *italics* are also used for emphasis.

>> **Bold** text highlights the action parts of numbered steps.

>> Web addresses appear in monofont. (Some URLs may have broken across multiple lines as we laid out this book, but rest assured we haven't added any spaces or hyphens. Just type in the address as you see it.)

Foolish Assumptions

Because the world of global logistics can be daunting, this book is based on the premise that you already are part of a business or organization that has a solid logistics foundation; one that is considering expanding its domestic logistics operations — whether manufacturing, selling product, or providing some form of logistics services — into a new and foreign market.

While the basic "language" of logistics may be familiar to you, the "world" of humanitarian and disaster relief (H&DR) may be totally foreign. There are an almost overwhelming number of governmental and non-governmental agencies that become involved in a natural or man-made disaster. Because we didn't want your introduction to H&DR logistics to thoroughly discourage you from participating in disaster relief efforts, we limited our focus to discussing just the major elements and agencies of the United Nations (UN). We apologize in advance for the detail of the discussion, but hope that you'll see value in becoming part of relief initiatives in spite of the UN's organizational complexity.

Finally, we understand that your understanding of logistics may be more limited than that of the authors. When SOLE – The International Society of Logistics (SOLE) talks logistics, it speaks to the entire enterprise that is "logistics," and not just a single aspect (such as supply chain management). Accordingly, in Part 1 we introduce you to what we mean when we speak of "whole enterprise" logistics.

Icons Used in This Book

As you may expect, this icon highlights important points you won't want to forget.

REMEMBER

This icon clues you in to some tips that can help you along the way and potentially make your life a little easier.

TIP

When you see this icon, read carefully. It marks potential pitfalls and helps you steer clear of frustrating and time-consuming mistakes.

WARNING

Beyond the Book

In addition to all the great information provided within this book, you can also find a handy online Cheat Sheet that provides both an overview and summary of the hurdles in mastering the logistics of global manufacturing, marketing, and distributing your products; providing logistics services to foreign customers; and an introduction to the logistics of providing global humanitarian and disaster relief. To get this Cheat Sheet, simply go to www.dummies.com and enter "Global Logistics For Dummies" in the Search box.

Where to Go from Here

While you may only be interested in one particular aspect of global logistics, we recommend you spend a little time reading through the other parts because some of the nuances of one aspect of the global logistics environment may also be relevant to your global plans.

1

Taking Your First Global Steps

Discover both the history and evolution of global logistics, as well as how SOLE – The International Society of Logistics defines the elements of the total logistics enterprise.

Understand not only the role of logistics in global manufacturing and sales, but also how geopolitical and social operating environments affect a company's decision to "go global."

Explore a framework for providing logistics services in a foreign environment as well as the types of companies that provide logistics services.

Gain a perspective on the critical need for global humanitarian and disaster relief logistics support, to include an appreciation of the costs and impacts of providing such support.

Chapter **1**

Getting Started in Global Logistics

"The line between order and disorder lies in logistics . . ."

This succinct observation about the importance of logistics was made over 2,500 years ago by Sun Tzu, the Chinese philosopher and general whose work on military strategy significantly influenced both Western and Eastern philosophy.

The requirements for large-scale manufacturing, purchasing, and distribution were mostly found in support of war campaigns, since an armed force without adequate supplies and transportation was doomed to fail. History's great military leaders Hannibal, Alexander the Great, and the Duke of Wellington are considered to have been logistical geniuses. Alexander's military campaign from Greece to India (334–324 BC) benefited considerably from his meticulous (and occasionally ruthless) attention to the provisioning of his army. And, in 218 BC, Hannibal's march of elephants from Spain to Italy over the Alps loaded with his troops and supplies might easily be considered to be history's first recorded supply chain!

Understanding the Evolution of Global Logistics

As populations grew and trade routes were established and expanded beyond country borders, manufacturing started to ramp up. The British and American industrial revolutions (1760–1870 AD) brought about the capability to produce in larger volumes to meet the growing demand. Often the local repositories of raw materials had become inadequate or totally depleted, which forced manufacturers to expand their sourcing beyond national boundaries.

World Wars I and II significantly increased the need for commercial logistics in order to meet the heavy demands of the fighting forces. Following both wars many of the factories that used to manufacture combat items shifted production not only to meet the growing demand for consumer items but also (and probably more importantly) to remain in business.

As global distribution infrastructures matured, manufacturers realized that profit could be generated from sales beyond one's own region and nation, and started marketing their products to a more global market. This marketing expansion was made possible both by the development of modern communication technologies and networks, and the deliberate political choice of many nations to open markets to international trade and finance.

The history of organized logistics support to international humanitarian and disaster relief operations is a fairly recent phenomenon. Until the 1970s humanitarian and disaster relief (H&DR) was the sole responsibility of the affected nation; any international support (if it occurred at all) was primarily financial. It has only been in the last 40 years that international manpower and logistics support to augment an affected country's capabilities has become more prevalent.

Finally, with the establishment of the World Trade Organization (WTO) in 1995 — which replaced the General Agreement on Tariffs and Trade (GATT) of 1948 — the many individual free-trade agreements that were negotiated between countries were governed under specific rules of international trade. It was through the negotiation and establishment of numerous multinational and regional trade treaties that the world's "global supply chain" emerged.

Introducing SOLE – The International Society of Logistics

SOLE – The International Society of Logistics was founded in 1966 (originally as the Society of Logistics Engineers) as an international nonprofit professional association. Since then, SOLE has served academia, business and industry, and logistics professionals around the world through its certification and designation programs, training, forums, publications, and thought leadership.

Since its inception, SOLE has been regarded as a highly valued organization that serves the entire spectrum of logistics, focusing on the entire logistics enterprise. The association is perhaps best known for its certification and credentialing programs that recognize the professional expertise and accomplishments of logisticians within commerce, industry, defense, government agencies, academia, and private institutions. In addition to its certification and designation programs, SOLE has long provided other critical avenues for professional support, education, and advancement for logistics practitioners.

SOLE's many accomplishments include the following:

>> Recognition as ethical, objective, and expert consultants to the highest levels of government and industry. As such, SOLE has helped US federal agencies like the National Aeronautics and Space Administration (NASA) and the Department of Defense (DoD) to plan, host, manage, and facilitate forums on topics ranging from human capital development, to emerging logistics technologies, to the impact of extreme space weather.

>> Selection by the US Department of Labor (DOL) as the default commentator as regards expert assessments of the logistics services industry as a whole.

>> The conferral of over 2,500 Certified Professional Logistician (CPL) and Certified Master Logistician (CML) credentials.

>> The conferral of over 25,000 Designated Logistician program credentials since 2005.

>> Development and delivery of unique educational programs in the United States and abroad, including logistics body-of-knowledge overview classes, local and regional professional development forums on an array of technical topics, and customized training programs and academic curricula for industry and higher education.

>> Establishment of the SOLE Press, which has published four volumes on logistics principles, integrated logistics support, and quantitative measurements of logistics.

>> Since its inception over 50 years ago, support of logisticians in over 50 countries around the world.

Getting Started: Some Basic Logistics Concepts

The term "logistics" has undergone numerous attempts to be defined and re-defined over the past 50 years. Today, there are literally thousands of companies around the world that have the word "logistics" in their name, in their logo, or in their description. For some, "logistics" is simply the movement of goods from one place to another. Others — when they use the term "logistics"— are actually only describing an element of the whole logistics enterprise, that aspect of the supply chain that includes the functions of procurement, storage, and distribution.

SOLE views logistics as an integrated, whole logistics enterprise that begins with the integration of logistics engineering and support considerations into a product's design and use, and ends with the system or item's disposition. Specifically, SOLE considers *logistics* to be "The art and science of management, engineering, and technical activities concerned with the requirements, design, and supplying and maintaining resources to support objectives, plans and operations." It is a whole enterprise view, as depicted in Figure 1-1. This definition of logistics provides for an integration of the many elements of logistics that mirrors a product or service life cycle from start to finish (or, from "birth to death" — hence, the logistician's use of the term "product life cycle").

The world of logistics is, therefore, broad in scope but can generally be depicted by five functional domains, as shown in Figure 1-2.

The Logistics Enterprise

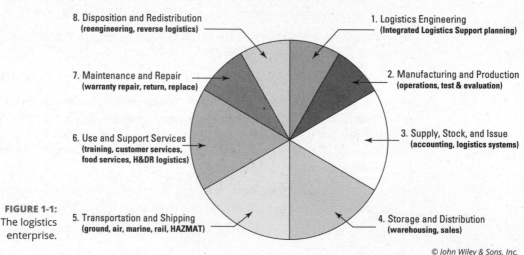

8. Disposition and Redistribution (reengineering, reverse logistics)

1. Logistics Engineering (Integrated Logistics Support planning)

7. Maintenance and Repair (warranty repair, return, replace)

2. Manufacturing and Production (operations, test & evaluation)

6. Use and Support Services (training, customer services, food services, H&DR logistics)

3. Supply, Stock, and Issue (accounting, logistics systems)

5. Transportation and Shipping (ground, air, marine, rail, HAZMAT)

4. Storage and Distribution (warehousing, sales)

FIGURE 1-1: The logistics enterprise.

© John Wiley & Sons, Inc.

Logistics Functional Domains

Logistics Engineering	Supply Management	Maintenance Management	Distribution & Transportation	Logistics Services
Those activities that deal with product design and development. Includes planning, development, implementation and management of an affordable, comprehensive and effective product support strategy.	Those material management activities, from procurement through disposal, that ensure the integration of multiple sources and processes to meet both production and customer requirements.	Those activities involved in the planning for and execution of maintenance—both scheduled and unscheduled, at multiple levels—of not only products but also production lines and distribution assets.	Those packaging, cargo scheduling, dispatching, and material and personnel movement activities and support services in response to production and customer requirements.	The specified provision of personnel, equipment, or facilities (any or all) in support of logistics planning, management, and execution.
Elements may include:	*Elements may include:*	*Elements may include:*	*Elements may include:*	*Elements may include:*
• Configuration management • Environmental engineering • Safety engineering • Spares requirements and Level of Repair Analysis • Warranty program development • Obsolescence management • Identification of special tools and test equipment • Quality management • Failure Modes and Effects (Criticality) Analysis • Maintainability Planning and Allocations • Life Cycle Modeling • Computation of Total Ownership Costs • Performance of Task and Skills Analysis • Technical data management	• Identification and establishment of production inventory • Demand forecasting & analysis • Development of integrated supply concepts • Provisioning planning • Spares calculations • Establishment of end product stockage and safety levels • Source analysis and selection • Inventory procurement and accountability • Receipt and issue of inventory • Management of stock-outs • Quality control and inspection • Inventory security and control • Disposal or destruction of expired or damaged inventory • Re-accession or redistribution of customer returns • Supply data management	• Reliability Centered Maintenance Analysis • Computation of Mean-Time Between Failure • Identification of levels & types of maintenance & repair • Management of reparable items and components • Scheduling and conduct of preventive maintenance • Spare parts management • Maintenance technical documentation • Management of an operational float for repair and return, or critical items • Testing and performance evaluation of end items and components • Conduct of unscheduled repairs • Maintenance data management	• Identification and management of intermediate unit & end item packaging • Selection of transportation mode(s) and route(s) • Scheduling & dispatch of cargo or personnel movements • Management, storage, shipment, and security of controlled, hazardous or regulated items • Receipt of shipments & submission of discrepancy or damage reports • Identification & management of fleet requirements & assets • Permit completion and customs declarations submissions • Management & execution of reverse logistics program • Transportation & shipment data management	• Development & management of logistics operational, data or information security plans & metrics • Provision of 3PL/4PL/5PL contract logistics services • Medical logistics management • Food services management & dining facility operations • Development of logistics data information systems and networks • Development or conduct of logistics training • Provision of unique logistics services (for example, graves registration or laundry) • Provision of humanitarian and disaster relief logistics support (domestically or internationally)

© *John Wiley & Sons, Inc.*

FIGURE 1-2: The functional domains of logistics.

Logisticians rarely work alone. Rather, they are critical players in the whole logistics enterprise that manages an integrated process that is defined for each product or service at its inception. The *Integrated Logistics Support (ILS) Plan* (as depicted in Figure 1-3) is a plan that's developed by the logistics community, working closely with the product designers and systems engineers; and that provides a technical basis for integrating all support elements in order to maximize the product or system's availability while optimizing the costs of logistics support throughout the life cycle.

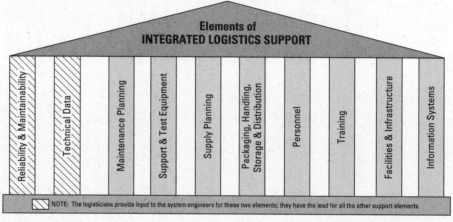

FIGURE 1-3: Elements of Integrated Logistics Support (ILS).

© John Wiley & Sons, Inc.

Life cycle support is viewed as the composite of all considerations necessary to assure the effective and economical support of a system throughout its programmed life cycle. It is an integral part of all aspects of system planning, design and development, test and evaluation, production or construction, consumer use, and system retirement. Over time, integrated logistics support planning has evolved to include the following major elements:

>> **Reliability and maintainability:** The logistics engineering elements of reliability and maintainability impact all other product aspects because a life cycle support-centered design is one that minimizes the logistics footprint while maximizing reliability. Such a design ensures that maintainability is user friendly and effective, and addresses the long-term issues related to obsolescence management, technology refreshment, modifications and upgrades, and usage under all operating conditions.

>> **Technical data:** This includes product production designs and instructions, operating and maintenance instructions, inspection and calibration procedures, facilities information, drawings, and specifications that are necessary

for not only the performance of the product but also its associated maintenance functions.

» **Maintenance planning:** This includes all planning and analysis associated with the establishment of requirements for the overall support of a system throughout its life cycle. Maintenance planning starts with the development of the maintenance concept and continues through the product's design and development, the procurement or acquisition of support items, and through the consumer use phase when an ongoing system/product support capability is required to sustain operations.

» **Support and test equipment:** This category includes all tools, special condition monitoring equipment, diagnostic and checkout equipment, metrology and calibration equipment, and maintenance stands; and the identification of the servicing and handling equipment required to support all scheduled and unscheduled maintenance actions associated with the system or item.

» **Supply planning:** Supply planning addresses all spares (for example: units, assemblies, and modules), repair parts, consumables, special supplies and inventories needed to support the end product, related software, test and support equipment, transportation and handling equipment, training equipment, and facilities. Supply planning also covers provisioning documentation, procurement functions, warehousing, distribution of material, and the personnel requirements associated with the acquisition and maintenance of spare and repair part inventories at all support locations.

» **Packaging, handling, storage, and distribution:** This element of logistics results in the articulation of the requirements for any special provisions, containers, and supplies necessary to support packaging, preservation, storage, handling, and transportation of the product; associated test and support equipment; spares and repair parts; personnel, technical data, and mobile facilities.

» **Personnel:** This category includes the identification of the personnel required for the installation, operation, evaluation, handling, and maintenance of the product and its associated test and support equipment.

» **Training:** This category includes not only the initial product familiarization training for users and support personnel, but also refresher training when new users and support personnel are exposed to the product or system. Safety is a major element of all training.

» **Facilities and infrastructure:** This refers to all buildings and real estate needed for product production, product distribution, and the performance of maintenance functions. Since infrastructure costs can be a significant factor in the production and maintenance of a new product, a cost analysis is normally included with this category.

>> **Information systems:** This facet of support refers to all computer equipment and accessories, software, program databases, and any peripheral equipment or data systems used during the manufacturing, maintenance, sales, and distribution functions. The element also includes both condition monitoring systems and maintenance diagnostic aids.

Deconflicting Some Unique Language of Global Logistics

Sounds simple, right? Hopefully, as you go through the various parts of this book you will see that the whole logistics enterprise is a complicated one — one that will become exponentially more complicated when the enterprise goes global.

TIP

Because there are so many logistics-related terms to keep track of, we have provided a listing of terms that are used throughout the book. You can find it in the Glossary after Part 6.

Earlier we discuss how SOLE defines "logistics" as the higher-taxonomy level domain, under which operate the functions of logistics engineering, supply chain management, maintenance, and numerous other logistics services (such as food and mortuary services). With these basic logistics concepts outlined earlier, it becomes clear that SOLE has always considered logistics to be more than supply chain management. Accordingly, when we talk to the "whole logistics enterprise" we include *all* the functionalities and domains of logistics.

Having said that, we need to call special attention to one concept in particular — that of *sustainability.* When we use terms relating to sustainability with regard to global humanitarian and disaster relief (see Part 5), we are using the concepts set forth in the globally accepted definition that was articulated in the Bruntland Report of 1987. Specifically, "*Sustainable development* is development that meets the needs of the present without compromising the ability of future generations to meet their own needs."

However, those of you in the field of logistics — particularly those of you who may be working as part of a country's military-industrial complex — may be using the term "sustainability" primarily either as an adjunct to or in place of the technical terms "reliability, maintainability, and supportability"; or the concept of product, system, or operational "survivability." (For example, the US DoD uses the phrase "life cycle sustainment" in describing the end result of providing "life cycle support.")

If that weren't confusing enough, in many companies and organizations the term "sustainment" is all about keeping the company itself financially healthy and operationally viable (that is, "staying alive")!

Identifying the Need for This Global Logistics Discussion

We have started this discussion based on the premise that you are part of a successful business or organization that is considering expanding your domestic logistics operations — whether manufacturing, product sales, or the provision of some form of logistics services — into a new, foreign market.

There are many good reasons to consider exporting your successful domestic business to a new foreign location. There may be a new market in which to sell or distribute your product. You may achieve manufacturing cost savings by locating closer to either new consumers or to your product's raw materials and components. Or, you may have determined that you can achieve savings in the cost of the labor required to meet the expanding demand for your product. However, in spite of all the economic advantages you may have perceived, be aware that the physical and cultural challenges of your new location may far outweigh any potential cost savings.

You are not alone. Hundreds of companies every year — small, medium, and large — look to expand their operations on a more global basis. And, generally, less than 30 percent of them are successful at their first attempt.

The reasons for being unsuccessful are many and varied, but most often relate to not having a *complete* grasp of the proposed foreign location's people, customs, culture, laws, and regulations. In this book we describe many of the pitfalls that may be encountered when venturing into a new foreign location. Our hope is that — with the knowledge of what lies ahead — you can make the right decision for you and your company.

It should be noted that while the global expansion of manufacturing, sales, and product distribution has been and continues to be a growth area — especially due to the rise of the Internet and electronic commerce — logistics support to global humanitarian and disaster relief operations is predicted to grow even faster.

Accordingly, the book has four major focuses: logistics related to manufacturing "overseas" (Part 2), logistics related to global marketing and distribution (Part 3), providing logistics services globally (Part 4), and the unique aspects of providing humanitarian and disaster relief logistics (Part 5). While you may only be interested in one particular aspect of global logistics, we recommend you glance through the other parts, as some of the nuances of that segment of the global logistics environment may also be relevant to your global plans.

Finally, in The Part of Tens (Part 6), we include chapters on ten companies that have been successful in their global expansion; ten companies that made significant missteps in their global expansion (although some of those companies adjusted their approach and are very successful today); and ten resource suggestions for you to consider when performing the due diligence necessary to make your final decision about "going global."

Welcome to the world of global logistics!

Chapter 2

Understanding the Role of Logistics in Global Manufacturing and Sales

Now that you've successfully mastered the logistics necessary to profitably design, manufacture, sell, and recycle your product in your domestic market, you're weighing the decision to expand your operations into foreign markets.

As shown in Figure 2-1, logistics plays a significant role in the successful design, manufacturing, sales, and disposal of all products. The term *life cycle* is used to identify the major elements in a product's "life," from its conception (that is, its initial design) to its ultimate disposal.

In this chapter, we provide an overview of those aspects of your current manufacturing life cycle that you may need to adjust or redesign when establishing your foreign manufacturing operations as well as the associated distribution chains (as addressed in Parts 2 and 3).

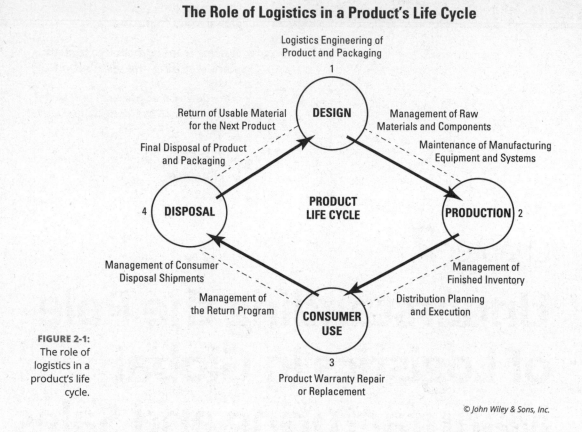

The Role of Logistics in a Product's Life Cycle

Logistics Engineering of
Product and Packaging

1

DESIGN

Return of Usable Material
for the Next Product

Management of Raw
Materials and Components

Final Disposal of Product
and Packaging

Maintenance of Manufacturing
Equipment and Systems

4 **DISPOSAL**

**PRODUCT
LIFE CYCLE**

PRODUCTION 2

Management of Consumer
Disposal Shipments

Management of
Finished Inventory

Management of
the Return Program

**CONSUMER
USE**

Distribution Planning
and Execution

3

Product Warranty Repair
or Replacement

© John Wiley & Sons, Inc.

FIGURE 2-1:
The role of
logistics in a
product's life
cycle.

Finally, we conclude with some additional thoughts regarding the influence of world affairs on global operations, as well as a discussion of the impact of *e-commerce* (that is, the electronic sale of items over the Internet) on global logistics.

Manufacturing in a Foreign Location

In Part 2 we explore both your decision-making process and the ultimate establishment of manufacturing options in a foreign location. In relationship to Figure 2-1, this discussion starts with the production of a product that has already been designed and is currently being manufactured in your domestic location(s).

Chapter 5 covers the setting up of manufacturing operations in a foreign location. There must be clear corporate goals, a comprehensive business plan (one that includes additional emphasis on security and the protection of intellectual property, which is discussed in detail in Chapter 9), and an informed foreign manufacturing strategy in place when determining the location of your foreign operations. The chapter also explores the decision to use either internal (that is, domestically-based corporate assets) or external (that is, contracted out) logistics support for both the physical production facility and the new supply chains associated with your foreign operations.

Chapter 6 includes a discussion on the inventory levels of raw materials and components needed to support foreign production, with a particular emphasis on how those levels may be different than those in your domestic operations due to the establishment of local foreign supply chains. The chapter also provides aspects to consider when establishing the warehousing and distribution locations associated with the foreign production facility; shipping foreign-manufactured product back to your domestic market (if that is desired); and managing returns of your foreign-manufactured goods.

Chapter 7 considers eventual consumer use and focuses on the additional environmental considerations of product and packaging, establishment of the foreign physical facilities, and distribution chain management. It includes a discussion on the need for ensuring a corporate culture of environmental stewardship sensitive to your foreign presence, as well as an exploration of the various components that make up "green manufacturing." Finally, it offers several "green" best business practices, such as the development and execution of an environmental management plan.

In Chapter 8 we explore the establishment and use of operational readiness levels and production metrics for your foreign manufacturing and distribution operations. We also provide an analysis of potential production stoppages and present recommendations for risk reduction and recovery options should stoppages occur.

Chapter 9 discusses risk, with the focus on the inherent dangers to your intellectual property (specifically product designs and corporate "trade secrets") and logistics data resulting from long-distance management of remote supply chains. The chapter closes with a detailed discussion on how to prevent and (if necessary) recover from the loss or compromise of such intellectual property and data.

Dealing with Foreign Distribution Chains

Whereas Part 2 addresses your company's establishment of foreign manufacturing operations for either the production of existing products or for new product lines, Part 3 speaks to the sale and distribution of your products — whether made domestically or in a foreign country — in the global marketplace.

Chapter 10 is all about selecting the transportation system and modes that best support your global operations. It explores not only the various options for and selection of the optimum movement method (via land, air, or sea) but also discusses how to determine the optimum mix of transportation modes for each segment of the distribution chain. This determination is based on the outcome of any decision you make about operating your company-owned fleet of transport vehicles or contracting out the movement of all — or any portion of — your supply and distribution chains. In our discussion of the pros and cons of each course of action, we explore the role of freight forwarders to assist in the movement of your raw materials or finished products.

In Chapter 11 we discuss both protecting your cargo against loss or damage, and investigating and responding to threats in your distribution chain should that protection fail. The chapter includes a warning about piracy, now a real and major concern on many land and sea routes. Further, since your global operations likely ship across international borders, we provide a discussion on the responsibilities to ensure compliance with shipping laws and regulations designed to help prevent the flow of contraband between countries.

Chapter 12 explores the establishment of your foreign points of sales; adjusting your current product configuration or packaging to enhance product acceptance by your foreign customers; and creating a profitable global sales strategy. Finally, the chapter discusses how logistics can help in gaining and keeping customer loyalty to your brand.

Chapter 13 wraps up the section on foreign distribution chains and focuses on dealing with losses, theft, damages, and returns. All companies routinely encounter these situations, but they can be much more significant when your distribution chains are operating in a foreign market. We provide suggestions both for how to minimize the risk from these incidents and how to recover when they occur. Because it has been proven that customer returns tend to occur more frequently in foreign markets, the chapter addresses the need to be prepared to either modify your domestic return policies and procedures or develop new ones that are foreign-market specific. The chapter concludes with a hard look at the large — and constantly growing — issue of counterfeit products and its impact on both original product manufacturers and the global economy.

Anticipating the Impact of Geo-Politics and Social Change

We would be remiss if, after the discussion of the chapters in both Parts 2 and 3, we didn't call your attention to those underlying aspects of global logistics that are critical to the success or failure of any decision to expand your domestic operations to the global arena.

Society has changed significantly in the past 50 years. Technology advancements have resulted in a level of information capacity and product capability that has significantly impacted not only our daily lives but how governments manage. Countries not only have opened their borders to foreign goods but also often encourage foreign businesses to establish local production facilities. As the flow of information has become more sophisticated and more available, the demand for many existing and new products has increased. International trade organizations have been formed to provide protocols and procedures for conducting commerce across borders. As a result, the focus of marketing efforts has become far more international.

That said, there is still much uncertainty that impacts the conduct of foreign trade. Issues such as having to manage an influx of large numbers of refugees (whether generated by political unrest or natural disaster); increasing national debts and currency fluctuations; and a resurgence of nationalism affect business on a daily basis. Foreign trade agreements are often in flux, as a result of political pressures concerning the balance of trade between nations. Currency valuation — while normally fairly stable — may change dramatically as the result of local, national, and international issues. The work environment and cost of labor in many developing countries is becoming more legislated. Concerns over ecological issues are forcing change in the design, production, and disposal of many types of products. Further, the export of raw materials, as well as some highly technical products with possible military implications, is becoming more controlled.

REMEMBER

When you make the decision to "go global," multiple world conditions can affect your foreign operations far greater than they might your domestic operations. Those global impacts include man-made events such as wars, border disagreements, or even labor disputes that delay shipments or close critical transportation nodes. They also include natural disasters such as earthquakes, typhoons, or floods that have the same effect on your supply and distribution chains.

The unpredictable theft of goods during shipment is also an ever-increasing concern when manufacturing or selling in foreign markets. While nations have worked together to try to reduce the number of incidents, the criminals have also developed sophisticated capabilities that enable them to more easily target high-value shipments.

Adapting to the Logistics of Global Internet Sales

The advent and growth of the Internet and its cyber technology saw the emergence of e-commerce. And, with the rise of e-commerce has come a reassessment of the traditional "brick and mortar" storefront with its supply, warehousing, and distribution processes.

The Internet has become the most significant factor in the way business is conducted globally. The number of worldwide Internet users grew an estimated 918 percent between 2000 and 2016, and, by some estimates, now reaches over half the world's total population. Even in Africa, where the percentage of users is the lowest at slightly less than 30 percent, there are still a reported 340 million–plus users.

In business, the Internet has expanded the marketplace at its most rapid rate in history. According to multiple statistical sources (such as Statistica.com or e-Marketer.com), in 2015, alone, Internet retail sales reached over $2.2 trillion with sales projected to continue to grow an estimated 10 percent annually.

Because of its availability to consumers 24 hours a day and resulting increase in product demand, the Internet has forced businesses to streamline not only their retail operations but also their production and sales distribution systems. In many cases that streamlining results in the elimination of physical storefronts, which then eliminates the associated expense of in-store and warehouse theft.

However, e-commerce brings with it many new challenges for companies. The percentage of goods that are purchased in a traditional store and then returned is approximately 8 percent, while an estimated 25–30 percent of goods that are purchased on the Internet are ultimately returned. This is causing a new emphasis on the need for the rapid inspection of returned items so they can quickly be returned to inventory. It is also creating the need for more durable packaging.

Internet-related theft and fraud are major concerns for both businesses and customers. A business's intellectual capital can be stolen if not protected adequately.

Consumers risk identity theft or the theft of credit-card information. Accordingly, increased and improved online security is not only expected but demanded from merchants and e-commerce service providers. Consumers expect the deployment of countermeasures such as firewalls and anti-virus software to protect e-commerce networks.

In a variation of "high seas piracy," there has been an increase in the Internet ransom of businesses and individuals, where a business or personal Internet site is "held captive" until the site owner pays to get its data restored. *Phishing* (that is, the attempt to fraudulently acquire sensitive information by email) is another danger, where consumers are fooled into thinking they are dealing with a reputable retailer when they have actually fed private information to a system operated by a malicious party. Denial of service attacks continue to be a risk for merchants, as are server and network outages. Further, the thefts by hacking of tens of thousands of customer records from retailers' on- or off-line corporate databases are growing in alarming number and frequency.

Finally, the sale of counterfeit goods is yet another critical area that has seen an increase because of e-commerce. Now that consumers have the ability to compare prices between Internet sites, they are often inadvertently encouraged by applications or websites that consolidate unvalidated web-listed prices to purchase from sites that sell counterfeited versions of the products being sought, at a reduced price. Unfortunately, neither the customer nor the product manufacturer has any recourse if the purchased item is counterfeit. The customer may lose his money (since the "real" manufacturer won't refund or replace a counterfeit item), and the manufacturer loses not only a sale but also a small portion of the brand's image.

TIP

Having provided an overview of the logistics involved in both establishing a foreign manufacturing operation (Part 2) and the global distribution of your manufactured products (Part 3), in Chapter 3 we explore the world of providing logistics services to foreign customers (which we will further expand on in the chapters of Part 4).

Chapter **3**

Providing Global Logistics Services

I n Chapter 2 we preview both Part 2 (setting up your new manufacturing opera-tions in a foreign location) and Part 3 (understanding the modifications that may be needed for an effective and efficient foreign distribution chain).

In this chapter we provide an overview of providing global logistics services (the focus of Part 4). We start by addressing the many tasks that can comprise logistics services for a foreign customer, as well as defining the types of organizations that provide those services. Our focus is on the workforce — the options you have when it comes to providing logistics services, either for your own operations or for a foreign client — and all the rules and regulations that you must consider. Additionally, we address how to protect your investment by obtaining the insurance and licenses required when operating in another country.

We close this chapter with a discussion of the *absolute* requirement not only to understand and appreciate but also accommodate the culture of the country and its residents. We also shed light on the additional challenges faced when providing global logistics services under a government contract.

Defining Logistics Services and Logistics Service Providers

While no one list of global logistics services is all-encompassing — that is, most lists do not reflect the full scope of the logistics enterprise — the list used by the United Nations Economic and Social Commission for Asia and Pacific provides a basic supply chain–centric platform and includes the following:

>> Transportation services (both people and things)

>> Logistics information services (including order tracking and tracing)

>> Warehousing

>> Freight consolidation

>> Customs requirements and other order administration

>> Selection and integration of multiple carriers

>> Packaging, assembly (or kitting), and processing of goods

>> Technical testing

>> *Localization* (that is, the process of adapting a product or marketing program for a specific region or language by adding locale-specific components and translating text)

>> Quality inspection

>> Logistics consulting and supply-chain design

>> Management of a supply chain

>> Operation of a supply chain

>> Procurement and contracting

>> Financial services (such as collateral management)

>> Aftermarket services (such as reverse logistics and returns)

>> Maintenance and repair

>> Call-center operations (for example, technical and warranty inquiries)

Although the preceding list is a good start, it doesn't include food service support or mortuary services support (both of which are included as part of the services provided by many countries' military logisticians). Also not included on the list are logistics engineering services, which are an integral part of our definition of the logistics enterprise.

As for who provides logistics services, there are several options. First, the services can all be provided in-house, by the company that manufactures, directly sells, and services the product. This is known as a *first party logistics provider (1PL)*. This type of original manufacturer logistics was much more prevalent when products were produced only for a local market.

If the manufacturer does not perform all its own logistics services, then the remaining services requirements must be contracted with other companies specializing in one or more of the required services. These companies are characterized as one of the following:

>> *Second party logistics providers (2PLs)* is the term for companies hired by the manufacturer to serve as either a carrier, a warehouse manager, or a logistics engineering firm for the operational execution of any clearly defined logistics task. The management and oversight of the service provided remain the responsibility of the manufacturer. The manufacturer's relationship with the logistics provider is often only cost-driven and short-term, with the provider delivering what the client requires and being paid accordingly.

>> *Third party logistics providers (3PLs)* are used when the manufacturer outsources a grouping of transport and logistic activities. The 3PL service provider organizes those activities and may act as a broker and — in turn — subsequently hire additional companies for task execution. The 3PL service provider often interfaces not only with the manufacturer but also with the actual provider of the service. The manufacturer often enters into a long-term partnership with the 3PL provider in a cooperative environment. The manufacturer retains enough expertise in order to measure, evaluate, and, if necessary, correct the logistic performances of not only the 3PL service provider but also the task subcontractors.

>> *Fourth party logistics providers (4PLs)* provide support on an even higher level of logistics system integration. The manufacturer outsources not only the organization of its logistic tasks but also the full management thereof. 4PL providers often manage an entire, singular supply chain. The 4PL's role requires a heightened involvement in the business operations of the manufacturer, because the manufacturer has not only contracted for the execution but also the monitoring of all the company's specified logistic processes. In effect, the 4PL serves as a member of corporate-level staff. Short-term relationships established by collaboration agreements that are based purely on cost-related criteria are replaced with long-term partnerships, where quality of the service plays the primary role and risks and benefits are shared jointly. Further, 4PLs now have to address the management and security of multiple electronic interfaces between supply chain providers with enormous databases.

>> The emergence of *fifth party logistics providers (5PLs)* is relatively new. A 5PL provider guarantees the management of *networks* of supply chains, or even

the entire logistics enterprise — in effect, serving as the company's corporate chief logistics officer (CLO). The manufacturer hires 5PLs for the development of strategic and innovative logistical solutions and concepts. A 5PL service provider develops and implements, preferably in close consultation with the client, the best possible logistics solutions. The term "5PL" is often linked with e-commerce.

Providing Global Logistics Services

Now that we've identified the possible providers of global logistics services, let's take a look at the various discussions in Part 4 of the various specifics providing global logistics services.

Chapter 14 sets the stage for a comprehensive discussion of perhaps the most critical aspect of providing global logistics services. Businesses that plan to provide global logistics services using a foreign workforce must understand what is important to that workforce. The barriers to such an understanding can include both language issues (written and spoken) and the cultural issues that may affect everything from work hours, to the gender or age of the workforce, to the food in the lunchroom. The chapter also warns that the workplace climate and company loyalty may be at odds with those of your domestic operations and corporate headquarters. The chapter concludes with details on identifying and dealing with social or political uncertainty or upheaval.

So how do you go about trying to protect your interests? Chapter 15 identifies some of the nuances of operating in a foreign country. It discusses some of the various types of insurance that may be necessary and that may not be available through the insurer of your domestic operations. The chapter also details how to establish your company's intellectual property rights protection plan, as well as what protection is available under the World Trade Organization (WTO) Agreement on Trade-Related Aspects of Intellectual Property Rights (TRIPS). The chapter finishes with a section concerning how to obtain and retain your business licenses to operate in a foreign country.

Chapter 16 goes into detail about the various options you have when you are ready to staff your new location. These options include both internal as well as external hires. The chapter describes the differences between local nationals, expatriates, and third-country nationals; and when each type of staffing is appropriate or advantageous. Depending on both the host country where you operate and the country where your domestic headquarters is located, each country may have rules and restrictions that affect your hiring options. The chapter also discusses the pros and cons of hiring independent contractors instead of using your own paid workforce.

In Chapter 17 we examine many of the labor laws that you may have to comply with. This includes an overview of the resulting impact on and cost of workforce scheduling, accommodating restrictions, and your ability to successfully fulfill your logistics services support contract. The chapter includes a section that highlights some of the issues you may encounter in various foreign locations when hiring females and minors. Also included is a section on complying with foreign national and regional requirements and prohibitions for work hours, overtime, and vacation time, as well as providing examples of how the rules vary significantly between countries. Similar variances are discussed with respect to potential host-country requirements concerning the compensation of any mix of workforce you intend to employ.

Culture, Culture, Culture

According to multiple industry analysts, as many as 70 percent of companies fail in their first attempt at expanding successful domestic operations into the global marketplace. (Having said that, the estimate may be low since there is a reluctance in many cultures to openly admit to failure.) While the reasons for failure are many and varied, most failures are built upon an ignorance of cultural and societal differences between domestic and foreign markets.

While improvements in global information systems have helped companies gain a better awareness of culture and their religions, traditions, and ideologies, it is still common for businesses to ignore the information that is available to them. Instead, they fall back on the same policies, processes, and procedures that made them successful in their domestic operations.

WARNING

This lack of appreciation of people — whether they are your foreign customers, new government regulators, or your own new workforce — is almost certainly a fatal mistake in any attempt at a global expansion.

In Part 6 we include a chapter on ten businesses that have been successful in their global expansion efforts, and another chapter on ten businesses that initially fell short. In all cases the understanding of the culture in the foreign locations was a critical factor in success or failure.

Working for Government Clients

Many companies, large and small, provide logistics services for government contracts operating in foreign locations. The work is normally performed under contracts that range from one to five years, depending on the contracting rules of the client government. The work can be done at the government's own facilities, at the client's facilities, or at a third-party location determined by the contract.

Foreign support can include providing logistics services to a host nation's government — for example, providing fuel sample inspections for an oil producing country. Foreign support could also be the provision of logistics services for your own nation's operations in a foreign country — such as providing a vehicle repair capability for one or more of your country's embassies abroad.

REMEMBER

Whatever the circumstances, working for a government client can be much more complicated than working for a nongovernment client.

It is entirely possible that between the time the contract specifications and requirements were published, bid, and won, the original foreign government contacts have been replaced by a new group with completely different requirements, needs, and expectations. This situation can lead to disagreements between you and your government customer, especially if the type of contract your company bid and won can't easily or quickly be modified by the mutual agreement of both parties.

Many times the government contract is very specific concerning the education level or technical licenses required of all your employees. This specificity can cause significant challenges when an employee suddenly resigns and you have to go back through a new visa process to get an acceptable replacement in-country. Oftentimes the contract requires you to provide a specific number of hours of technical support, which causes you to have additional personnel cleared and available when an employee takes extended vacation or is sick.

As we've already pointed out, foreign labor laws frequently change. Often your government customer either may not be aware of the change or doesn't appreciate your immediate responsibility to adjust your workforce based on the change.

Ultimately, most government contracts are awarded to the company able to meet all the requirements at the lowest price. As such, this often dictates a high element of risk-taking by those companies bidding on the contract. This results in bidding low profit margins (compared to similar work for nongovernment contracts), while hoping that nothing goes wrong that further reduces the margin of profit.

It is obvious, then, that your decision to provide logistics services globally — regardless of the customer — is one that requires having a corporate team that fully understands the financial, legal, and human-resource risks of failure.

Chapter **4**

Supporting Global Humanitarian and Disaster Relief Efforts

Once your company becomes more comfortable with its global logistics operations, it is highly likely that at some point in time you may be asked to provide humanitarian and disaster relief (H&DR) logistics support services. As the world's population continues to grow, each disaster that occurs has an increased chance of affecting a significant number of people.

Disasters can be natural, man-made, or a combination of both causes. Some of the largest natural disasters in recent history — listed in descending order of lives lost — include the 1976 Tangshan earthquake in China that killed an estimated 450,000 people, the 1970 Bhola cyclone (in what is now Bangladesh) that killed an estimated 375,000 people, the 2004 Indian Ocean earthquake and tsunami that killed an estimated 280,000 people, and the 1991 Bangladesh cyclone that killed an estimated 139,000 people. Even periods of excessive heat and drought can be devastating, as evident in both the 2003 European heat wave that killed an estimated 70,000 people, and the 2010 heat wave and resulting wildfires in Russia that killed an estimated 56,000 people. But the largest loss of life in a 20th century natural disaster was the Great Chinese Famine of 1958–1961, where scholars have estimated between 20 million and 43 million people perished — in part due to the political climate in China and the government's unwillingness to seek international aid.

As horrific as the number of deaths due to natural disasters are, man-made disasters — that is, disasters resulting from political upheaval or industrial accident — have caused far greater losses of life or property. World War I (1914–1918) accounted for up to 21 million deaths, and World War II (1939–1945) resulted in an estimated 65 to 85 million deaths. It was during these wars that many of the well-known, nongovernmental humanitarian organizations were first formed — including the International Red Cross and Red Crescent Societies, which was awarded the Nobel Peace Prize on three occasions (1917, 1944, and 1965) for its work to protect the life and dignity of the victims of international and internal armed conflicts.

Deaths and injuries are not the only impact of disasters. Due to not only the requirement to rebuild critical infrastructure but also a disaster's potential impact on a nation's global trade, the costs of recovery and reconstitution continue to mount long after the initial event. As reported by the World Bank, the following disasters have been the most costly, and all have occurred in the last 25 years. (Note that the figures do *not* include loss of life, but only reflect damage to property and infrastructure.)

>> The 2011 earthquake and tsunami in Japan (including the resulting shutdown of the Fukushima Nuclear Power Plant) cost in excess of $300 billion.

>> Hurricane Katrina and subsequent failure of the levies in New Orleans, United States, in 2005 caused approximately $130 billion in damage.

>> The 1995 Kobe earthquake in Japan destroyed an estimated $102 billion of property.

>> Hurricane Sandy devastated the Northeast United States in 2012, with costs of nearly $60 billion.

>> The California earthquake of 1994 caused estimated damages of $42 billion.

>> The damages incurred during China's 2008 earthquake in Sichuan were estimated at $28 billion.

Directing and Managing International Disaster Relief Efforts

The government of the affected country is responsible for the response to any disaster. In most cases, such as regional floods or storms, the affected country has sufficient resources to deal with the situation. In those situations where the disaster is too great for the affected country to handle alone, it may activate pre-established support arrangements with other countries in the region.

At the point that a country can't direct and manage its relief efforts by itself or with a regional partner, the affected country then turns to the international relief community — led by the United Nations (UN) and its partner agencies — for help. As of the end of 2016, the international relief community was involved in providing relief support to the following geo-political disasters:

>> **Iraq:** The surge in violence between armed groups and government forces has displaced an estimated 3.1 million people and left millions of people in need of assistance.

>> **Syria:** 13.5 million people, nearly half the population, are in need of humanitarian assistance. An estimated 6.3 million people have been displaced inside the country.

>> **Yemen:** Armed conflict has spread rapidly since March 2015, with devastating consequences for the civilian population. Aid groups estimate that 4 of 5 Yemeni require some form of humanitarian protection or assistance.

In addition to those major disasters identified, the international relief community continues to support ongoing relief efforts in the following countries:

>> **Haiti:** The country was devastated by Hurricane Matthew in October 2016, while still dealing with the aftermath of its 2010 earthquake.

>> **Ethiopia:** Back-to-back seasons of poor or nonexistent rainfall in 2015 were exacerbated by the strongest El Niño phenomenon on record in the same year, which led in 2016 to the worst drought in decades.

>> **Nigeria:** The conflict in Nigeria's northeast provoked by Boko Haram has resulted in widespread population displacement, violations of international humanitarian and human rights law, protection risks, and a growing humanitarian crisis.

>> **Central African Republic:** Since 2012 the country has experienced a major political crisis that has resulted in violent conflict affecting the entire population, as well as leaving nearly 2.3 million people (over half the population) in dire need of assistance.

Organizing for H&DR Logistics Support

With the preceding as background, Part 5 is designed to provide you and your company not only an introduction to the world of H&DR logistics support but also explores the various options available to you in providing support to local, regional, or international relief efforts.

Chapter 18 both describes today's global H&DR environment and defines the critical role of logistics in H&DR operations. The types, levels, and scope of disasters are defined, and we identify the major international relief providers and the roles of each. The complex lines of command and control are discussed, so as to provide an understanding of the critical role logistics plays in all international H&DR efforts. Finally, we explain the planning, preparation, and infrastructure that have to be in place so that your company can be prepared to successfully respond to a UN call for international H&DR support.

In Chapter 19 we examine how a company can participate in international H&DR logistics operations, beginning with the corporate decision to provide financial assistance, donate goods, or provide personnel to support the relief efforts. We detail the process of determining the specific corporate response to a call for participation, including activating and preparing your logistics team (and their families) for the upcoming deployment. Finally, we discuss the absolute need to develop corporate and team systems, protocols, procedures, and metrics to ensure successful logistics contributions.

We continue in Chapter 20 by discussing the provisioning and deployment of your logistics support team. Significant emphasis is placed on interacting with the thousands of relief personnel and hundreds of external organizations already in-country. We also provide a discussion on the criticality of operating in a multinational, multicultural environment that often appears unstructured and disconnected. We conclude Part 5 by identifying the steps required in closing out the team's mission and bringing it back from the affected country.

Providing Logistics Support to H&DR Events: Dangerous but Rewarding

In the previous chapters of Part 1, we outline how different and difficult it can be when establishing and conducting logistics manufacturing, distribution, or service support operations in a global environment. Once successfully established the operations can run as smoothly as those in your domestic location, as long as your company continues to monitor the geo-political environment in your foreign locations.

Providing logistics support to H&DR operations is much more difficult! Disaster events are always catastrophic and chaotic. While organizations like the UN and the International Red Cross and Red Crescent Societies have worked hard to establish a set of basic processes and protocols to support disasters, events "on the ground" never go exactly as planned.

When responding to earthquakes, your H&DR logistics team often has to operate in an environment of aftershocks that can cause significant further damage to the infrastructure. Dams can break in flooded areas (much like what happened in Hurricane Katrina in New Orleans) and devastate a much wider area. Severe droughts can cause entire populations to evacuate.

But nothing is more chaotic or dangerous for disaster response teams than those disasters that are man-made. These disasters often affect an entire country or region. Depending on the circumstances, coordination with the affected country's government may be difficult or impossible, as can be the coordination with other disaster relief organizations or the military. Pre-approved disaster relief routes can suddenly be compromised, and even the relief teams come under fire. There is likely no clearly identified (or agreed upon) end to the disaster — and that alone often results in significant emotional turmoil to the relief teams and their families. The logistics response teams — and the companies and organizations — that provide logistics services under those circumstances are truly heroic.

2
Manufacturing in a Global Environment

Discover how setting up your global manufacturing operations can be significantly different from or more complicated than your domestic operations.

Find out what aspects to consider when determining both your foreign inventory types and levels, and the warehousing and distribution locations required to support your company's foreign manufacturing operations.

Consider the additional environmental factors in establishing foreign manufacturing operations and physical facilities, adapting product and packaging, and setting up and managing your company's supply and distribution chains.

Explore the establishment and use of both operational readiness levels and production metrics for foreign manufacturing and distribution operations, as well as recommendations for reducing the risk of stock outages.

Identify the inherent dangers to your intellectual property and logistics data resulting from long-distance management of remote supply chains.

Chapter **5**

Making Your Product and Establishing Your Global Supply Chain

Once you've decided to enter the global market, what's next? First, you have to establish a presence in the countries in which you plan to operate. You also have to decide whether to support your global operations from your home location, or build an out-of-country logistics support infrastructure. If you decide not to set up an out-of-country support network, then you have to manage the global logistics operations remotely.

In this chapter, we delve into the decisions you need to make early on, the challenges to the various approaches you can take, and the questions you need to ask yourself along the way.

Establishing Your Presence

For any global manufacturing initiative you have to establish operations in a location that not only ensures an economical and efficient supply of raw materials to the factory, but also provides all the production logistics support necessary to manufacture and distribute the finished goods to the customers. If this sounds familiar, it's probably because you went through this same process when you first set up your domestic operations.

While making that location decision isn't that much different than the one you made for your in-country manufacturing, expanding operations out-of-country brings a new set of unique logistics challenges that have to be considered.

Before embarking upon the journey with both feet, do some basic high-level, 30,000 foot level planning. Make a list of what you know and don't know. Then leverage what you know to help you find the resources you need to market, manufacture, and deliver your product(s). With sound logistics planning you should be able to get from here to there, and have a successful global logistics effort.

Shifting politics, unstable economies, lack of basic infrastructure, and limited technologies within developing countries provide the enterprise logistician with plenty of challenges. The global market can be very unpredictable. You need a primary strategy as well as additional backup plans and alternative strategies for unique and unpredictable markets.

As your business grows, you need to know when to rely on local partnerships and how to form global supply chain relationships to assist with integrating logistics efforts. Along with having several contingency plans, you also need an exit strategy in case the venture doesn't pan out.

WARNING

With an emphasis on constant growth and the pressures of meeting financial targets, emerging into global markets often becomes inevitable. Companies that take a "one size fits all" approach to expanding into foreign markets may be setting themselves up for failure.

There are risks, but risks can be reduced to manageable levels with sound planning and by aligning global expansion plans with the larger business objectives.

TIP

Consider having multiple supply chains, with each one tailored to the specific needs of individual regions and communities. Each supply chain must be supported by local capabilities and manpower talent, and flexible enough to accommodate corporate growth and change.

Decentralizing operations can allow your company to effectively deal with the challenges of crossing borders, taxes, geographical obstacles, political roadblocks, varying technologies, and discrepancies in the labor market. A company has to be very dynamic, with the resiliency to be able to shift from one alternative plan to another to adapt to changing conditions.

Keeping your corporate business model in mind

Corporate business models must reflect the operations chosen for each of the global sites considered. Questions to ask yourself include the following:

>> What unique market characteristics require the need for specialized logistics?

>> What logistics capabilities are critical to delivering our customer value?

>> How can we leverage existing or shared logistics capabilities to serve the new markets?

>> How can we improve our logistics efforts to become more competitive and be a market leader?

REMEMBER

When developing a global logistics plan, it should always be subordinate to and reflect corporate objectives.

Before applying for permission to do business in a foreign country, have a solid business plan. Keep it as broad as possible, to allow the company to operate within whatever restrictions are imposed by government and regulatory agencies. You want to be a "good neighbor" by integrating seamlessly into your host country's culture, as well as providing reciprocal benefits for being allowed to operate there.

TIP

Find a good mentor who can assist with the details that can allow you to learn from others' successes and failures. An expert such as a reputable international corporate lawyer can help overcome business and cultural differences in foreign markets. Banks are also a great resource. Many have an international presence, and may already do business with the firms that you might include in your global supply chain. Having someone who understands import/export regulations and the maze of paperwork is not only essential but critical.

Comprehensive strategies should be in place to build and retain out-of-country talent while taking advantage of the home country values and traditions. Companies must be able to find and develop the right employees within geographical areas of operation. Who else can better understand the nuances of specific markets and culture?

REMEMBER

People are always a company's greatest asset. Decisions you make about out-of-country recruiting will have an enormous impact on your business.

Developing a realistic foreign manufacturing strategy

Always consider global manufacturing opportunities when expanding competitive strategies that want to take advantage of unique market opportunities. Companies often must significantly reduce production costs to compete with existing lower-cost foreign competitors. Global manufacturing operations can also be established to gain penetration into foreign markets. The worldwide manufacturing network must then be integrated into the company's overall operations. A sound logistics plan is essential to the overall corporate global marketing and manufacturing success strategy.

REMEMBER

Logistics often determines the overall success or failure of strategic manufacturing efforts.

Acquisition logistics provides the raw materials and in-process inventory needed for production. Production logistics controls the flow of materials through the manufacturing process. Distribution logistics delivers the goods once they leave the factory. All of these logistics activities are directly related to basic organizational processes, layout, production planning and inventory control and must be integrated both with each other as well as all the company's other non-logistics departments.

In assessing the impact of entering the global marketplace, you also must take into consideration the logistics and costs of global operations. Some multinational manufacturing companies are export or import firms. These companies are engaged in producing and selling domestic goods abroad. A company in the United Kingdom that exports to Germany is a multinational company. So is an American firm that imports from Germany. Foreign currency exchange rates affect both types of firms. A company that expects payment in dollars may have to make payments in Euros.

Multinational manufacturing firms engage in business with foreign countries in different ways. All multinational businesses deal with currency exchange rates, buying and selling foreign currency as part of their daily business. These companies face foreign exchange risk every day, because there is a real possibility of losing money from unexpected fluctuations in exchange rates.

Domestic firms can be involved in the production of goods in foreign countries in a variety of ways. Here are three types of strategies to consider:

>> **International strategy:** While the company's objectives relate primarily to the home market, the company may have objectives that require overseas activity to gain a competitive advantage.

>> **Multinational strategy:** Firms involved in markets beyond the home country need distinctive strategies for each market. Customer demand and competition may be different in each country. Competitive advantages are determined separately.

>> **Global strategy:** A firm may treat the world as one market and one source of supply with little local variation. Competitive advantage is developed on a global basis.

Creating partnerships to support your manufacturing effort

Product innovation when operating "solo" is often not enough in the fiercely competitive global marketplace. Partnerships spread the manufacturing risks common to organizations, and collectively leverage each other's strengths.

Why consider a partnership?

Partnering with a company that already has a global presence simplifies the process. Partnerships should be considered as part of the overall business decision-making strategy. Although partnering companies may be in competition with each other, a partnership needs to be a win-win situation for all. Define the metrics of success for all partners. But also determine the mutual costs (monetary and intrinsic) necessary to achieve success. All potential partners need to create a single, synergistic plan where the results are greater than doing business alone.

Partnerships sometimes require a serious financial commitment to work. Estimates of the effort required — along with estimates of the investments that need to be made — have to be fairly robust. Perform a cost/benefit analysis to determine whether the predicted business results are worth the effort and investment. Set aside a dedicated budget for the initial investment, along with earnest money to get the team effort off the ground.

TIP

Successful partnerships should produce expanding results over a longer period of time. Monitor the progress of the partnerships often, and look for business opportunities to enhance and expand the partnerships. This could even eventually lead to a merger among partners. Evaluate, reinvent, and reinvest in the partnerships whenever goals change.

Understanding the types of partnerships that may benefit you

Development partnerships can eliminate operational inefficiencies; manufacturing partnerships can eliminate the need for new equipment and capital; engineering partnerships can eliminate expensive engineering staff; and logistics and distribution partnerships can eliminate infrastructure set-up costs required to penetrate a new market. Land, distribution, and facilities partnerships can dramatically improve business margins, even in the most constrained markets.

TIP

Corporate objectives must be balanced with short and long-term trade-offs. Consider how the business can operate more productively, efficiently, and at a higher economic margin with less risk with a partner. But, if the business is such that you must go it alone, have a stable of trusted non-competitive consultants to draw assistance from.

REMEMBER

Sometimes the partnership doesn't work out, or the benefits no longer exceed the costs. When that happens, it's time to make a clean break rather than let the partnership linger or suffer a slow death. This is the time to review the successes and failures, and to figure out what lessons you've learned.

Be polite, be courteous, and don't "burn any bridges" that you may want to use to support you in the future. Celebrate successful logistics partnerships, and learn from their failures.

Testing the waters: Starting small

Once you validate that great idea for producing a product in the global marketplace, you are hopefully on the road to success. Now you need to start planning to make it a success. Not every global venture is going to generate millions of dollars. In fact, some may intentionally initially operate at a loss just to get a foot into those global markets.

Begin with a solid business plan. That plan is your road map for moving forward. Without it, you will quickly get lost. A solid business plan that is based on lessons learned from previous successes (and failures) and that has been drafted by all stakeholders significantly lowers the risks. To minimize financial risks a company usually plans to start small. If the venture fails, then losses should be in the acceptable range of the larger corporate financial planning.

The business plan should also have schedules and time limits as to how long and how much capital expenditure is acceptable during the initial test phase. Every company has its own threshold of pain. Sooner or later, the rewards have to meet the corporate expectations as outlined in the plan.

TIP

Allow sufficient time for the business to prosper in the foreign market, but no more.

Once established, you can then strategically grow the company through vertical integration up and down the supply chain.

Integrate forward by setting up operations closer to customers, such as by establishing manufacturing operations closer to retail stores. Direct sales to customers can drastically reduce costs by reducing or eliminating retail sales locations.

Integrate backward by moving manufacturing closer to sources of raw materials. Manufacturers need specialized raw materials as a major component of the end product. The company may decide to acquire these vendors to gain better quality control and eliminate the risk of not having raw materials.

Eliminating the middleman in both directions is integrating both forward and backward at the same time. Getting direct access to vendors and customers can be a huge benefit. This is the major reason for operating within the global market-place: to operate where the logistics paths to the customers are shortest.

Deciding How to Support

Logistics is often used to describe support and supportability, that is, a measure of the amount of support provided. Your company is going to need logistics support. Whether your company provides that support itself or has that support provided by an outside provider (in other words, outsourcing) can be an important decision.

Assessing internal versus external logistics support

Logistics involves the acquisition, movement and flow, management and storage of materials and goods from the point of origin to the point of consumption. When combined, the individual linking of all these processes from beginning to end makes up the "supply chain." Each link in that chain is as important as any one of or all of the others. When a link fails, the right materials may not get to the right destinations, at the right time, in the right quantities, for the right customers, for the right cost, or in the right condition. The process of providing these services is known as *supply chain management* (SCM).

A well-managed supply chain establishes and maintains relationships with suppliers, distributors, and customers to optimize the process, increase efficiency, and reduce cost. Logistics provides accountability, traceability, tracking, and visibility of everything that moves throughout the production and distribution processes.

Logistics includes the movement of raw materials and finished goods as they enter, move through, and exit the production facility. *Production logistics* consists of those logistics operations that support the manufacturing process. They are usually always handled internally, using company resources.

Shipping in raw materials and shipping out finished goods can be handled by company-owned assets. But what if the company doesn't have the resources to do so? Would it be advantageous for a company to acquire the assets, or should it partner with an external company that can provide volume discounts on this service?

REMEMBER

Deciding to use either internal or external logistics requires sound business planning, and knowing the risks and rewards of each.

Looking at internal logistics

Internal logistics is performed when a company needs or wants total control. For instance, if the company owns the source of the raw materials or in-process materials; or the manufactured items are very expensive, contain intellectual property, or are competition sensitive, then owning the transportation equipment may not be an option.

When a company uses its own assets it must take total ownership of the equipment's life cycle costs. These include licensing, insurance, operator training, and maintenance management (scheduled and unscheduled maintenance) of those assets.

Another solution may be to lease the equipment and use that company's employees as operators. Leasing companies sometimes offer operator training and maintenance agreements as an added service. Construction companies often lease equipment, for which the leasing company provides maintenance services during periods of downtime.

Equipment in foreign markets may have controls on the opposite side of the vehicles, or somehow function differently than those commonly used in the home country. Local operators familiar with the equipment can significantly reduce losses from mishandling or neglect, damage to property, and injury to workers.

Looking at external logistics

External logistics companies are in business to help you move materials between your suppliers, your factories, your distribution centers, and your customers. It is their business to know what transportation modes to use when, what paperwork has to be completed, which routes to use, and how to move the materials or product economically and on schedule.

The use of external logistics companies can optimize transportation costs by sharing the load. There are times when the cheapest way to ship does not result in optimal results. Cost must be weighed against schedules to ensure timely and efficient delivery. The optimum footprint of materials and goods to have on hand, as well as the costs associated with having inventory versus inventory *stock-outs* (in other words, having no inventory on hand), must all be addressed in the decision-making process.

Choosing to use your own (internal) logistics capabilities or hiring someone to do it (external) involves looking at the life cycle costs, determining whether any special transportation and warehouse requirements exist, and working the details into the overall company business strategy. If the choice is to outsource some or all of the logistics support, then decisions have to be made as to which type(s) of logistics can provide the best efficiency, economy, and service. And, finally, choosing which providers to use has to be determined based on the location of the market(s), the types of services required, and the types of services offered.

Establishing in-country manufacturing and supply chains

It's an exceptional company that can manufacture a product entirely on its own, beginning with the mining of raw materials out of the ground. Most companies must operate with a network of suppliers and partners to help them produce their products. Some of the primary reasons for manufacturing within the global marketplace are to leverage the advantages of having local supplies and having a shorter customer pipeline.

To have a stable supply chain, manufacturers must know the status of their partners and suppliers, and establish good business relationships with them. Failures in the supply chain caught early can mitigate potential disruptions and financial manufacturing losses. To avoid those losses, verify that vendors and suppliers are doing well in their own business as well as in the business relationships you have with them.

WARNING

If you are considering expanding your business organization into another country there may be additional international issues (for example, legal, financial, cultural, and so on) with or within your supply chain that you may not have encountered in the past that could add significant risk or expense.

Building and maintaining in-country relationships takes dedicated time and energy. These relationships have established boundaries and modes of interaction that may be different than those "at home." Open communication paths are vital, as is mutual understanding and respect. The better your relationships with your supply chain vendors are, the more likely the vendors will help look for ways for both of you to succeed. Solid relationships are most critical during those stressful times when challenges put a strain on your business. This is when true partners in business will shine.

Having comprehensive and detailed contracts with vendors and suppliers is crucial. They can provide price and supply guarantees, establish priority in shortage and back-order situations, and require early notification of process changes. Establishing good contracts upfront allows practicing the business details when things are easy. That practice and the resultant closer business relationships that develop may come in handy when the unexpected happens.

REMEMBER

Building supply chain relationships requires a mutual understanding of long-term goals and objectives.

It is easy to exceed budget when operating outside of your home territory. Consider all costs that will be passed on to the customer, including changes in inbound, outbound, and especially inter-facility logistics costs. Decisions should not be based on standard fixed or variable costs but on true cost history. The global marketplace will most likely operate by a different set of financial rules than those of your home country.

Factor in the total manufacturing and supply chain costs from raw materials to end customer. Also evaluate the effect on existing manufacturing and distribution infrastructures. Avoid outsourcing opportunities that promise savings but can't deliver. And reevaluate your business strategy often. Establishing global manufacturing and supply chains should trade off domestic capabilities for international ones, and create greater economy and efficiency from your global business operations.

Making sure your decision supports the larger corporate goals

How good is your organization at making and executing decisions? What are the strengths you can build on and what are the weaknesses that prevent you from doing better? One way to find out is to rate your organization's decision-making ability against corporate goals. Decisions must be made at the right level of the organization. And the company's culture should encourage people to make the right decisions for the customers.

>> Are individuals clear on how to make critical decisions?

>> Do people with decision-making authority have the skills and experience required?

>> Does the company encourage fast decision-making and execution?

You must have clear growth priorities. Know what your company's most important capabilities are (the things it does well) and how they relate to the strategic objectives.

Deploy the costs appropriately by spending money on the essential items. Make sure that staffing levels in different parts of the organization are appropriate. Your highest-priority initiatives should get more attention than legacy programs that have less impact on the bottom line.

Organizations must be nimble to move and adapt before your competition wins the business. Information must be readily available to the people who need it. Ensure that decisions that have a long-term impact are in keeping with the organization's long-term business plans.

REMEMBER

Success depends on how well the entire global trade process is streamlined across all departments and functions.

Some companies streamline their operations by continuously improving their efficiency and effectiveness. This strategy focuses on developing the capabilities that define the company's goals. Successful programs for growth include the following:

>> Set clear strategic priorities.

>> Invest in the capabilities that allow you to deliver your products.

>> Optimize costs to optimize resources appropriately and efficiently.

>> Establish a nimble, well-aligned organization that can adapt to changing corporate priorities.

Focus on corporate priorities to build the capabilities that help to distinguish your company and contribute to its success.

Managing Your Global Logistics Operation

It is essential to expand your managerial "tool kit" to succeed in the global market. Import/export regulations, language barriers, currency exchanges, regional laws, and local social customs complicate meeting corporate goals and complying with contractual requirements, all the while controlling budgets and schedules.

Global trade continues to increase with an estimated 30 percent of the world's gross domestic product currently moving across national borders. It is a way for businesses to expand and grow that is necessary to survive in a global competitive market. Worldwide trade is more complex and riskier than domestic trade, so management strategies have to adapt.

The move into the global arena affects every aspect of the business and is not limited to a "shipping and receiving department" challenge. A cross-functional, system-wide view of global trade is needed to streamline the process. This includes everything from the initial marketing efforts, taking orders, and to the delivery of the products and the follow-on customer support. Global trade management is essential to obtain goods and services, sell products, and establish offices and manufacturing capabilities within foreign countries.

Inadequate planning, execution, and synchronization of all business functions can lead to costly business challenges, including:

>> Shipment delays (see the sidebar "Mistakes can be expensive")

>> Increased inventory, shipping, and warehousing expenses

>> Higher accounting costs (for example, accounts receivable)

>> Fines and penalties

>> Lost sales

MISTAKES CAN BE EXPENSIVE

One company with years of experience in international trade had a shipment to be delivered to a customer in Botswana in Africa. All the equipment was loaded onto a cargo aircraft which stopped in Miami to go through customs. All the paperwork was complete and passed the customs' inspection except for one item — a briefcase-sized battery charger that had been purchased from an Australian company. The company did not have the papers needed to re-export this one item. As a result, the aircraft sat at the Miami airport for three weeks while the necessary paperwork was completed. The added rental cost of the aircraft consumed a significant part of the profit that was made on the contract.

Integrating domestic and foreign logistics elements and practices

Government regulations have a significant effect on logistics operations. These regulations vary from one country to the next as do taxes, licensing, and subsidies. All modes of transportation require some assistance from the governments. They build roads and airports, maintain channels to docks, and provide personnel and services such as air traffic controllers and security agents. In some countries some modes of transportation — such as the railroads — are fully government owned and controlled.

Logistics functions are typically centralized in facilities at strategic locations to improve the flow of freight and materials. These can be very large facilities with locations that permit the flow of goods between regional and long-distance modes of transportation. Freight distribution connects sources of raw material to the manufacturing and production locations. Large-scale goods flow through major gateways and hubs such as large shipping ports, major airports, and warehouses near highway intersections.

By combining and integrating the best practices that both the home and out-of-country logistics providers bring to the table, the most cost-effective and efficient solutions to support your global manufacturing efforts will be realized. Accordingly, it is essential to know both the logistics strengths and shortcomings of the foreign market areas.

Adjusting logistics operations to national and regional requirements

At its most basic level, logistics is the process of moving goods from where they are to where they are needed. There are options in the transportation modes that offer trade-offs between speed, cost, and capacity. Intermodal transportation has become common in global logistics. Don't focus solely on managing logistics costs as affected by the shipment process. By embracing the value of broader global trade and its management, your logistics department will be looked upon to provide leadership in understanding and adding value to the entire manufacturing operation, to include the following:

>> Purchase order management

>> Total landed cost modeling

>> Insurance and claims

>> Import/export compliance

>> Security regulations

Leveraging foreign logistics service provider capabilities

Corporate strategies and business plans assist in the decision to either develop embedded logistics capabilities, or contract for those services required. One privately-owned supplier for a major manufacturer managed its own trucking fleet because the owner considered the trucks and trailers "rolling billboards" that provided advertising and brand placement. Cost and expertise become significant factors when a company has to make the same decisions in the international market.

TIP

In-country logistics providers can bring value by being familiar with local transportation modes, laws, routes, and customs.

By using existing foreign logistics services providers, a company can reduce the following:

>> Operating costs, in distribution, transport, procurement, and staffing

>> The need for working capital, because inventory is reduced and order cycles are shortened

>> The need for fixed capital as the network becomes more flexible and asset utilization is increased

All these factors provide the opportunity to enhance product quality, availability, and customer service performance while increasing profitability and shareholder value.

Chapter **6**

Stocking and Distributing Your Products

The questions of what items you need, how much of those items you need to keep on hand as inventory, where to locate and warehouse your inventory, how to move your inventory along the production line, how to manage inventory so you can meet demands, and what to do if you run out of an item are the many aspects of inventory management that we'll address in this chapter. Being able to manage the "whats" and "hows" effectively at any stage in your manufacturing process is both an art and a science, and requires the consideration of additional elements when manufacturing in a foreign country.

Building and Managing Your Inventory

Raw materials and *work in progress* (that is, partially fabricated components of your products) used during your manufacturing processes must be collected and stored before use. The amount to keep on hand must be adequate to avoid shortages, but not so much as to cause excessive cost and space. During manufacturing, decentralized storage must be maintained near the assembly process for efficiency. After manufacturing, finished goods must be stored before shipment to wholesalers, retailers, and customers. The physical location of the inventory must also allow for the efficient movement to and from the storage site.

Inventory consists of raw materials, work in progress, and finished goods. Items may need to be stored during any part of the manufacturing process. The shipping, handling, and storage of these items requires continuous and controlled inventory management to effectively and efficiently maintain them.

It's important to safeguard the inventory, track it, and manage it so that you know how many new items are being added, how many items are being removed (or consumed), and how many items you have on hand at any given point in time.

While small inventories may be tracked in one's head or on a simple spreadsheet, many specialized inventory companies make it their business to develop and market inventory management software systems. For companies that manufacture many different products, have multiple warehouses, or complicated supply chains — especially involving multiple countries — inventory management is sometimes contracted out to third-party inventory management specialists.

TIP

Store what you need and need what you store. Ensure that the items are properly accounted for and remain in a condition such that they can be used when required.

Establishing and maintaining the proper inventory

The first step in establishing your inventory is to determine how much stock you need to have on hand at any given point in time. While you will need to consider many factors (such as recurring and nonrecurring requirements, time between ordering and receiving stock items, and so on), ultimately an inventory is based on supply and demand. That is, how fast will you receive the material you need, and how fast will you then use it? Inventories must also include an additional amount — that is, a safety level — to serve as a buffer to cover delays in stockage receipt or to accommodate surges in production. As you consider entering into the global marketplace, it is critical for you to plan and adjust your inventory levels to cover the inevitable delays that occur in an expanded supply chain.

An inventory must also be reflective of and responsive to the demands for your finished product. A customer's monthly ordering of your product generally will make it harder to forecast production inventory levels than will daily ordering.

REMEMBER

Have just the right amount of inventory on hand, plus enough to cover unexpected delivery delays or increased inventory requirements.

A good inventory management system will be well organized such that the storage location for each item is assigned and managed to ensure that items can be found quickly when needed. This often means using the latest technology to label, barcode, or tag the inventoried items, bins, shelves, aisles, rows, rooms, and storage facilities.

There are a number of factors that may dictate how you can store the inventory. Height and weight restrictions, inventory packaging, special inventory characteristics (such as hazardous or volatile, high dollar value, environmental impact) will all affect how and where you store your inventory. Employees need to manage all the special inventory characteristics to ensure the inventory isn't damaged or degraded in storage, while management needs to ensure that the risk of injury to workers is minimized or eliminated.

Deciding how much inventory to stock

Having "just the right" inventory on hand is the ultimate goal of inventory management. Other considerations — such as the risk and cost of stock-outs — can cause the inventory manager to hedge on the side of caution. But excess inventory also comes at the price of floor space and may cause items to decay or degrade in place, decrease or increase in price, and may not serve to contribute to the generation of revenue (that is, the item is never used).

The amount of space available for inventory storage will dictate the size and breadth of your inventory. Mathematical models that compute requirements and stockage levels — such as those determining an item's *economic order quantity* (that is, the amount ordered that minimizes the total cost of shipping, handling, and storage), reorder point, and safety level — can provide simple, high-level solutions to optimizing inventory stockage. Other factors may require the use of a linear programming model, or reliance on demand history. By keeping accurate records over time, you will be able to accurately forecast the optimum levels to maintain for both normal and unusual demands.

However, most models rarely take into account the risks of outside influences. For example, something as simple as unexpected road construction can delay inventory shipments either to or from the warehouse. A geo-political situation involving two or more suppliers' countries can freeze inventory anywhere in the supply chain. The shutdown of a port or distribution hub — either because of a natural disaster or a labor disagreement — will wreak havoc with either the receipt of production inventory or the release of your finished product.

REMEMBER

While scientific modeling is helpful in establishing inventory stockage levels, planning for the unexpected and understanding the historical fluctuations in and operational characteristics of your supply chain are critical.

Managing stock-out risks

So, what happens if you suddenly find yourself running out of inventory? If you've managed correctly, the risk of running out will be low for both cost and schedule. During periods when risks and the consequences of stock-out are higher, more inventory should be kept in stock, even if it means having to occasionally dispose of spoiled or time-sensitive goods.

Can you accurately predict the demands for the items in inventory? Are the items used as part of a planned activity or can demands be determined with some sort of a monitoring program? What is the probable peak "one-time" demand? Or what is the maximum number of items needed during a single demand event? To minimize stock-out risk, set your minimum value based on this probable peak demand, rather than average demand.

The risk of having stock-outs is significantly increased by holding minimum levels of stock — or, as it is often called, operating a "just-in-time" inventory. However, remember that holding high levels of inventory will not eliminate your risk of a stock-out. Ideal inventory levels are not always stable. If outside influences are known, then fluctuations can be predicted. Seasonal items may need to be ordered and stocked months in advance, but the dates of those events are usually well known.

REMEMBER

Determine the consequences of stock-outs, manage their risks, and have a backup plan.

Warehousing and Distributing

Manufacturing is rarely flexible enough to account for the ups and downs of customer demand, so warehouses are designed for the short-term storage of manufactured products. The location of warehouse and distribution facilities is critical in achieving the efficient handling and movement of both inventory and manufactured goods into and out of the facility.

Identifying your warehousing and distribution locations

It is often not practical to have the manufacturing facility right at the point of sale or consumption, so warehouses temporarily store and distribute the finished products. Depending on the product and distance from the factory to the end user or consumer, several warehouses may be involved. One may be close to the factory to absorb fluctuations in manufacturing output, and another close to the customer to allow for fluctuations in demand. As you decide to enter the global marketplace, you must take into consideration a number of elements in establishing warehouse and distribution locations. Some — but not all — that you need to address are local security, the ability to hire skilled warehouse employees, the ability to integrate your domestic and foreign information technology equipment and systems, and the state of the local transportation infrastructure.

Distribution warehouses are used to receive and consolidate many different products — often from different manufacturers — and route them to common locations. For instance, a retail chain will use distribution warehousing to assemble a multitude of products for delivery to each of its stores to restock shelving. Items do not stay long in a distribution warehouse: 24 hours is typical. Bulk items come in, get reassembled into desired loads for specific destinations, and then quickly exit the facility via the appropriate modes of transportation.

It is not uncommon for companies trying to establish themselves in a new foreign market to rely on the use of a distribution warehouse until they are sufficiently established to build their own facility.

Warehouses offer safe storage and flexibility. Distribution centers offer product mixing and transportation efficiency.

Setting up your storage facilities for maximum efficiency

Maximize your warehouse space for efficiency. Storing stock and items on an angle can be more advantageous than having to take sharp 90 degree corners with the material handling equipment. Height and load weight (that is, the maximum weight the warehouse floor can handle) should also be considered, especially as a safety measure when storing items in earthquake-prone areas. Bulky and oddly shaped items generally will require more floor space.

Items that aren't going to be consumed or issued within a reasonable amount of time should be moved to less trafficked areas. Manufacturing storage is not long-term storage. Redesign the storage layout when necessary to improve the use of space and material handling equipment; reduce product handling damage, the labor requirement, and housekeeping; and ensure employee safety.

Designing for the capabilities of the material handling equipment is as important as maximizing the use of shelf and floor space.

Measure the space you have to work with and plan how you can maximize its use. Identify all fixed obstacles such as walls, stairs, doors, tight clearances, and docks. Define different storage condition zones for items with unique storage (such as refrigeration or controlled humidity) and handling requirements (like hazardous materials and gasses). Consider stacking items when feasible, but only to heights that can be reached safely and efficiently. Be flexible when storing bulk items that don't easily fit together.

REMEMBER

The more varied your inventory and finished products are, the more storage space and types of storage you will need to use.

Creating an efficient distribution flow

Storing items efficiently is only part of the effort. The items must also be placed and picked efficiently. To best plan on where to place items, the capabilities and efficiencies of the material handling equipment must be considered. When that "equipment" is human labor, you must apply the science of ergonomics to prevent or reduce injuries. Items must be easily identifiable and easy to reach.

A simple rule is to make the most used or issued items the most easily picked. All items should be in discrete locations with proper labeling to avoid confusion in picking. Reduce the travel time to and from frequently used or issued items, and position your high-dollar-value items in a location that is both visible and has controlled access. Generally, it costs more to pick items vertically than horizontally. Place slower moving items higher up than faster moving ones.

In areas where the picking density is greatest (more demand for units), aisles should be wider to reduce traffic congestion. Develop a traffic flow so that material handling equipment is all moving in the same direction and not waiting for one piece of equipment to vacate an aisle before another can occupy it.

Keep a record of how long it takes to store and retrieve individual items. Experiment with small adjustments to tweak the efficiency. Use technology such as software applications to help make improvements. Are all your warehouse workers communicating while in motion? Handheld radios will allow orders to be changed mid-pick and help find "lost" or missing items.

REMEMBER

Measure efficiencies and routinely make small adjustments and alterations to find optimum solutions.

Shipping and Receiving: From Beginning to End

The movement of your inventory and finished products may — or may not — take the same routes or use the same modes of transportation. The movement of raw materials and inventory to your manufacturing facility entails the shipment from the supplier, often through an intermediate location or process (such as a port and customs), to your warehouse or manufacturing plant, where the shipment is received and either accepted, or rejected and returned.

If accepted, the materials then need to be shipped internally to the right locations within the manufacturing facility. If rejected, the shipment is returned to the supplier. After manufacturing, your goods need to be shipped out, received by the next link in your distribution chain, and ultimately received by your customer.

Getting your raw materials to your manufacturing location

Raw materials may come in "pieces and parts," or they may come as partially processed or assembled items. For instance, a manufacturer of juice products may buy concentrated juice that arrives from the supplier in truck or train loads. If at all possible, the manufacturing facility should be close to perishable sources of raw materials, or at least be sensitive to the time it takes to obtain them.

Obtain a primary source of supply for the raw materials that meets both budgetary and assured delivery requirements. If your raw materials are not located in the country in which you've built your foreign manufacturing plant, then you will either have to find a source from another foreign country or decide to import them from your domestic operations. Recognize that the supply chain you initially establish may later change as your foreign operations become more robust.

Ensure that the infrastructure at the source of your raw materials and at your manufacturing locations will efficiently support delivery of your raw materials to consistently meet all scheduled demands.

TIP

Keep secondary sources as backup, especially when the raw materials are coming from another country. Plan for multiple orders from multiple secondary sources to ensure delivery on time and on quantity.

Moving your materials and products along the manufacturing line

Production logistics has unique requirements of its own. Raw materials often require "just in time" delivery to the manufacturing line. Planning for some level of in-plant safety stock or built-in holding delay time during throughput is advisable to account for small fluctuations and disturbances in the assembly process.

Secure, reliable, and timely connectivity between computerized, mechanized, and automated manufacturing machinery along with material flow plans and production schedules is critical, and should accommodate variations in assembly times. When and if required, consider the use of *expeditors* (that is, individuals or contractors that can quickly fill in-process production orders during unusual and peak demand periods).

REMEMBER

Good planning won't eliminate all material shortages, but it will reduce risks and consequences.

Shipping your product back home from your foreign location

There are any number of reasons to establish a foreign manufacturing plant: for example, to expand your market base, to improve product availability in a foreign market, to customize your product line to meet specific foreign requirements, and to significantly reduce the total production costs of products that will be returned for sale to your domestic market.

If your reason for establishing a foreign manufacturing line was for the sale and distribution of products in an expanded global environment (that is, either in the country or region of your new manufacturing facility), turn to Part 3 for the logistics of selling what you've made.

If, however, the reason you decided to build your foreign manufacturing plant was to significantly reduce the cost of your domestic products, then you have to determine a method of shipment "home" that allows for movement of your products safely and securely (that is, minimizing damage, theft, and loss), and in a timely manner, while at the same time maintaining or exceeding your domestic quality and quantity standards.

When shipping your finished products from your foreign to domestic location, it's important to choose the appropriate mode or modes of transportation. Sometimes the best shipping solution requires more than one transportation mode. This ensures the products arrive on schedule both efficiently and economically.

The decision to ship by land, sea, or air depends on a careful evaluation of business needs and a comparison of the benefits each method affords. Choosing the best possible means of transportation is critical to the overall success of the global business.

Each transportation mode has its own unique advantages and disadvantages. The optimum method is dependent on the distance to be traveled, the geographic location of your destination, the nature of the items shipped, your shipping budget, and any deadlines or schedules that must be met.

WARNING

Failure to coordinate the optimum mix of transportation modes from your foreign to your domestic operations will erase any savings you had hoped to achieve.

Dealing with your foreign-manufactured product returns: How far back?

Not every product your foreign manufacturing plant distributes will be accepted by its customers. This may be because the product was somehow inferior or defective, requires maintenance or repair, or is no longer needed by the customer (either because of an order error or because the customer can't use or sell the product). When this happens, the product must be returned, if possible.

You will have to determine not only the conditions for return, repair, or replacement, but also where in the corporate line each incident will be handled. Some questions to answer require considerable analysis and corporate involvement, as shown in the following list:

» Will you need to establish an in-country repair operation, will you evacuate the item back to your domestic operations for repair, or will you establish an in-country exchange where the nonworking or damaged item is turned in and a replacement item is issued?

» If you make the decision not to repair or replace, will you take the customer's item back for recycling?

» If your product is highly susceptible to counterfeiting, do you have a process to inspect any item turned in for repair, return, or recycling for counterfeit parts or components?

» Did you build your plant in a country that has mandatory manufacturer recycling or disposition of consumed products?

» Will you want the "bad" item to be returned to the domestic operations to determine the cause of failure or defect?

Policies regarding how much time may elapse between purchase and return will have to be based upon a reasonable amount of time, all warranties in place, the nature of the items, and the reputation of the organization. Tool companies may trade-in specific old and worn tools with no questions asked. Electronic items with a high initial failure expectancy and fast technological turnover rate may have a limited time return policy. But the organization may take these items back as part of a recycling effort.

REMEMBER

Repair, return, replacement, and recycling policies must be comprehensive and written for each country in which you have a manufacturing or sales presence, and they must be written so as to be compliant with all applicable local laws.

Chapter **7**

"Greening" Your Manufacturing Line

E very aspect of manufacturing, stocking, and distributing your products has environmental implications. What are they and how do you go about addressing them? At a minimum, you'll need to comply with your host country's legal requirements. At a maximum, you may need to comply with laws and restrictions at every link in your — and perhaps your suppliers' — supply and distribution chains. The trend in manufacturing, however, is to go beyond compliance. Once considered a good idea that was only embraced by proverbial "tree huggers," green manufacturing increasingly is accepted as a prerequisite for competing successfully in the global marketplace.

Green manufacturing includes both the manufacturing of green products and the "greening" of the manufacturing life cycle. Many companies pursue both through a multi-year greening strategy. Whether you engage in one or both, you will be conserving natural resources, reducing pollutant emissions and discharges, preventing spills of hazardous substances, and minimizing waste generation.

This chapter explores the opportunities in your global logistics chains — from acquisition of raw materials to post-consumer disposal of your products — for environmental stewardship. It addresses challenges you may encounter, tools and approaches to navigate the challenges, and how to integrate environmental performance considerations into the overall planning for your global presence.

Safeguarding the Environment

The Organization for Economic Cooperation and Development (OECD) defines *sustainable manufacturing* as "managing operations in an environmentally and socially responsible manner."

Perhaps your domestic operations are green. If so, you will have a solid starting point for integrating sustainable manufacturing concepts into your new, foreign operation.

Still, how to transfer and adapt your domestic experience to a foreign setting may be challenging. Both the legal landscape as well as community concerns and dynamics are likely to be quite different from those you've learned to navigate domestically.

TIP

Take a deep breath! The lessons other companies inside and outside your industry sector have learned can help you map your own path.

Starting out

Ultimately, you will need to establish the following:

>> Green goals, broadly stated

>> Measurable performance targets

>> Roles and responsibilities

>> Performance assessment schedule and procedures

>> Continuous improvement

Before that, though, you need to build a foundation. Start laying that foundation by formulating an easy-to-understand sustainability vision and communicating it inside your organization. With that vision in hand, you also will have a valuable tool for developing trusted relationships in your new host community. Most importantly, you will need to characterize the potential environmental footprint of your new operation. You can calculate your footprint at different scales: for your entire enterprise; for a specific product, facility, or process; or for a type of impact (for example, "carbon footprint" or "water footprint").

REMEMBER

Your *environmental footprint* refers to the total impact your company has on the environment due to the consumption of energy, water, chemicals, and other materials.

As you build your green foundation, you may be tempted to focus only on the impacts your facilities may have on their immediate environment. Keep in mind, though, that all your decisions — from materials sourcing through manufacturing, distribution, consumer use, and end-of-life repurposing or recycling — shape your ability to limit local environmental impacts.

Demonstrating corporate social responsibility

While exploring the basic concepts and principles of sustainable manufacturing, you've probably heard a lot of talk about *corporate social responsibility* (CSR). Whether or not your company has a domestic CSR policy or program, the business culture where your foreign operation is located may expect you to have one. So, what is CSR, and how does it relate to green or sustainable manufacturing?

Like sustainable manufacturing, CSR means different things to different people. Often, though, you will find the term used as a catchphrase for managing a company to the *triple bottom line* (TBL or 3BL). Also known as "people, planet, and profit," 3BL encompasses economic accountability, environmental sustainability, and social responsibility. Other practices that some include in CSR are corporate philanthropy, ethical business practices, and employee volunteerism.

Your efforts to "go green" at your new foreign operation should clearly demonstrate your company's commitment to the environmental sustainability pillar. "Greening" your manufacturing line will reduce your consumption of natural resources and other materials, reduce the usage of hazardous materials, and limit pollutant loads on the environment, including greenhouse gas emissions.

TIP

Your peers in industry and business have reaped extensive cost savings and even boosted profitability from their green initiatives.

Experience shows that your environmentally friendly practices also may fulfill your goals for economic accountability and social responsibility. Beyond that, adopting sustainable manufacturing boosts your brand, attracts customers who care about the environment, and fosters goodwill in the foreign communities where you operate.

Minimizing local environmental impacts

Corporate social responsibility includes being a good corporate citizen in your new host community. Be prepared for community concerns to bubble up, however, when the people who live or work there hear a new manufacturing facility is on the way. While these concerns may vary according to local circumstances, some common ones include: strange odors, visible air emissions, hazardous spills, and noise. Uncontrolled trash piles, drinking water contamination, and impacts on wildlife habitat or recreational resources are examples of other issues residents may raise. They even may go so far as to protest the location of your operation, a syndrome often called "not in my backyard."

Since you're planning a new operation, you have many opportunities to design a green operation from the ground up that will allay community misgivings. The key to minimizing local environmental impacts lies in assessing the environmental footprint of your product, facility, and processes.

For an existing operation, this footprinting exercise would include at least five basic steps:

1. **Mapping your product's life cycle, your processes, and your supply chain**

2. **Using existing data to calculate your energy, water, and raw materials consumption; leaks and other losses during production; and air emissions, wastewater discharges, and other waste streams**

3. **Looking for opportunities to shrink your environmental footprint**

4. **Prioritizing those opportunities and selecting a manageable number of goals**

5. **Establishing metrics for assessing your actual performance on those goals**

REMEMBER

The more you know what your actual environmental impact is likely to be, the easier it will be to ease the concerns of the community where you're planning to set up operations.

For new operations, you will make a few adjustments, since you're starting with a clean slate and have no operating data. For instance, use the facility blueprints to create the process diagram or life cycle map, and use impact estimates extrapolated from your domestic operating experience or industry-wide data.

So, what are some things you can do that will have significance for the environment and be technically and financially feasible and community-friendly, while at the same time preserve the integrity of your product? Here are a few ideas to think about:

>> Design an energy-efficient, sustainable building to reduce construction and operation impacts.

>> Optimize your manufacturing processes to conserve resources and reduce air and water pollutants.

>> Rethink your raw materials — such as sourcing water-based instead of chemically-based solvents — to reduce pollutants, spills, and employee exposure to toxic substances.

>> Where possible, select green carriers to reduce delivery impacts on local air quality.

>> Use drought-resistant landscaping to reduce water usage.

You may even decide to go for one or more third-party certifications — for example, verifications such as the United States Building Council's LEED (Leadership in Energy and Environmental Design) certifications — of your facilities, processes, or systems to signal your commitment to the environment.

TIP

Not just a US certification, LEED is the most widely used third-party verification for green buildings, with around 1.85 million square feet of global facilities certified daily. For more information about the LEED certification process, go to www.usbc.org/leed.

Creating the initiative of shared prosperity: Everyone wins

Sustainability is good for your business, the host communities for your facilities, your workforce, and the global economy. Reducing energy and water consumption will lower operating costs, potentially contributing to greater profitability. Replacing hazardous materials with less toxic ones will boost worker safety and lower potential risks to the local environment from air emissions, wastewater, and other waste streams. Constructing and operating environmentally friendly buildings will shrink your carbon footprint and contribute to global efforts to mitigate global climate change.

REMEMBER

The cost spent in "greening" your operations does not have to be cost prohibitive, especially when weighed against local acceptance of your operations. Your environmental stewardship efforts will give you a brand advantage and will have a global reach that benefits everyone, everywhere.

Growing a Green Operation

So, how do you cultivate an enduring green operation at your new, foreign location? If you talk to other manufacturing companies that have succeeded in "going green," you will find they have some characteristics in common: a vibrant culture of environmental stewardship; realistic, measurable goals; and green practices embedded into the manufacturing line.

Developing a culture of environmental stewardship

Sustainable manufacturing is an ongoing process of continuous improvement that requires a robust corporate culture of environmental stewardship to succeed. Employees — whether relocating from your domestic operation or new hires drawn from your foreign host community — may resist sustainable approaches because they are unfamiliar. Here are some ways you can deal with that and inspire employee support for "going green" right from the start:

>> **Executive-level commitment:** Creating the culture starts at the top with an executive who has the authority and credibility to lead and commit resources to the sustainability effort.

>> **Environmental strategy, policies, and plans:** Articulating the company's environmental commitment and its link to the business plan will boost employee acceptance.

>> **Clear, feasible, measurable goals:** Starting with a modest number of goals that are financially and technically feasible will help employees get and remain engaged.

>> **Roles and responsibilities for everyone:** Empowering and training managers and employees at all levels to share responsibility for meeting the goals builds an esprit de corps.

>> **Incentives:** Rewarding managers and employees for meeting or exceeding environmental goals inspires them to work hard and look for new ways to improve environmental performance. (Bonuses, spot awards, and commendations are just a few examples.)

REMEMBER

You won't build a culture of environmental stewardship unless all elements of the company are involved.

Establishing goals and priorities for logistics processes

At this point, you're deep into planning your new facilities. You've mapped your environmental footprint, locally and across your entire supply chain; developed a preliminary compliance plan; and started talking about implementing sustainable measures that go beyond compliance.

Now, you have to set specific goals and indicators for measuring them. The process will look something like this:

1. **Set adoption criteria (for example, environmental impact, ease of adoption, importance to all parties affected, feasibility) to help you assess and compare goals.**

2. **Identify possible broad goals that are most consistent with your company's overall business objectives.**

3. **Set priorities to reduce the goals to a manageable number.**

4. **Establish your metrics to assess your performance against your goals.**

5. **Begin embedding your green practices.**

TIP

Don't discard goals that weren't initially adopted. You may elect to develop a multi-year plan for phasing them in later.

Embedding "green" into the manufacturing line

Once you have your short list of priority goals, let your managers and workers identify how to achieve the goals. Some green manufacturing practices in various operations include the following examples:

» **Housekeeping:** Practicing efficient inventory management; robust monitoring and scheduling of the production processes; reducing losses from leaks and spillage; properly maintaining equipment

» **Process optimization:** Modifying your manufacturing processes to conserve raw materials; reducing your use of hazardous materials; minimizing air and water pollutants; reducing solid and hazardous wastes; capturing and reusing byproducts and waste materials

» **Raw material substitution:** Replacing hazardous materials and other chemicals with significant health or environmental impacts with less toxic chemicals and renewable resources, such as using water-based rather than chemical solvents or using sustainably harvested wood

» **New product design:** Addressing environmental impacts from the ground up by redesigning the characteristics of your products and how they are manufactured and ultimately used, leading to using recycled instead of new materials, designing for easy disassembly and end-of-use materials recovery, or simply using less packaging

>> **Technology innovation:** Installing energy-efficient equipment, lighting, and production systems and implementing water conserving technologies

TIP

Implementing these types of changes typically requires capital investment and may be prohibitively expensive for incorporating into existing operations and facilities. However, embedding these practices and technologies into new facilities typically costs less.

Applying Green Logistics Best Practices

A stable, reliable, well-managed supply chain is vital to the success of your operation. Each link in the chain — from the sourcing of raw materials, to the manufacturing of your product, to consumer use of the product, and end-of-life product disposition — is equally important. A failure in any one link may delay production, boost costs unexpectedly, undermine community trust, or put your brand at risk.

MISTAKES CAN HAUNT YOU FOR DECADES

On the night of December 2, 1984, the Union Carbide India Limited (UCIL) chemical plant in Bhopal accidentally released a deadly plume of methyl isocyanate and other toxic gases and chemicals, exposing over 500,000 people living near the plant. While estimates vary on the death toll, we know thousands died almost immediately from either the toxins or the human stampede. Thousands more died later, while others still struggle with a host of health issues; and children born afterwards have a myriad of health defects. UCIL was sued by the government of India and paid an out-of-court settlement of $470 million. After the disaster, Union Carbide Corporation (UCC) — the majority owner of UCIL — had to fight off repeated takeover attempts, eventually selling off many of its popular brands to avoid bankruptcy. In addition, civil and criminal suits resulting in convictions were filed against the senior management of both UCIL and UCC for causing death by corporate negligence. Dow Chemical Company — which bought UCC in 2001 — inherited not only a site that will remain unusable and toxic for decades, but also UCC's public ill will and reputation for environmental devastation.

Why did this happen? The causes were complex and are still unresolved. Underinvestment by UCIL in safety, equipment maintenance, and employee training played a major role. Still, both UCIL and UCC could have avoided what is considered to be the worst industrial disaster in history by adopting a commitment to environmental stewardship.

While you may be under the impression that "greening" the supply chain will be at odds with your financial goals, this is not necessarily the case. Colleagues in your industry and other sectors have discovered that environmentally friendly supply chain practices create resource and process efficiencies that yield cost savings.

REMEMBER

Decisions on how to manage your supply chains need to consider the environmental issues that may arise at all the links in the chains.

Getting all the links in your global logistics chain working together

The environmental footprint exercise you already conducted to identify and minimize local environmental impacts gives you the information you need to "go green" along all the links in the supply chain. An environmental management system (EMS) linked to your other business systems is an important integration tool.

"Greening" acquisition logistics

Manufacturing and subsequent distribution of your product first requires timely delivery of the right quantity and quality of raw materials and other supplies at the right time and price point.

The acquisition link, however, is prone to a number of environmental issues. Suppose you need certain types of metals, for example. Extracting and processing the ore to meet your specifications may create air and water pollutants as well as solid and hazardous waste streams. Further, those processes may be energy- and water-use intensive. Other materials you use at the manufacturing plant, including those for maintenance, also may pose hazards for workers inside the facility as well as the local environment.

TIP

Good environmental practices need to start at the very beginning: in the product design and engineering phases.

Some of the options you have for starting down the road of environmental stewardship during acquisition are as follows:

>> Altering the materials you use in your production, such as substituting water-based solvents for chemically-based ones.

>> Setting a supplier "code of conduct" that specifies the environmental performance you expect. You can base these terms on internationally accepted guidelines (for example, UN Global Compact publications), monitor performance, and assist companies that may not have the technical or financial resources to figure it out on their own.

>> Integrating your enterprise resource planning and your inventory control tools to give you visibility and control over the frequency and quantities of orders and deliveries, thus minimizing unused materials.

>> Agreeing in advance on procedures and terms for returning materials that are inferior or defective.

Promoting green production logistics

Production logistics controls the flow of materials through the manufacturing process, and includes the maintenance and housekeeping necessary to keep the production line running. The specific environmental issues associated with each industry sector are well-documented. Across all industry sectors, manufacturing processes historically have emitted air pollutants, created wastewater, and resulted in solid waste and sometimes hazardous waste streams that must be managed by law. In addition, many manufacturing processes are energy and water hogs.

Some of the best practices you can consider to "green" your production logistics include

>> Establishing a rigorous preventive maintenance program to guard against spills, leaks, and other issues

>> Using process optimization techniques for your industry to conserve raw materials, minimize pollutants, reduce solid and hazardous wastes, and capture and reuse byproducts and waste materials

>> Installing innovative technologies to conserve water and reduce energy consumption and reuse byproducts or waste streams

>> Adopting small product changes — such as reducing packaging — which not only reduces energy consumption and waste generation but also may shorten the supply chain, thus reducing your carbon footprint

"Greening" distribution logistics

Distribution logistics encompasses all activities that support moving your finished goods from the manufacturing facility to a customer. That customer may be a fabricator or assembler who will use your product in another manufacturing line, a wholesale or retail outlet, or an end consumer.

To carry out your distribution logistics functions, you may need one or more warehouses to store your goods and then continue to move them forward to the customer. Transportation to and from the warehouses, as well as operations at the warehouses, impact the environment. In addition to transportation-related energy consumption, other issues include air emissions from both transportation and in-warehouse equipment, warehouse energy consumption, and warehouse generation of solid-waste streams.

TIP

Work with your transportation providers to develop a green strategy that you both can take credit for.

Some of the best practices you can consider to "green" your distribution logistics include

>> Optimizing distribution center locations relative to suppliers, manufacturing locations, and customers through use of network studies

>> Renovating vacant buildings rather than building new ones

>> Adopting environmentally friendly building design and finishing features such as efficient lighting fixtures, occupancy sensors, and daylighting technologies

>> Using electric or hybrid forklifts instead of gas-fueled ones to eliminate tailpipe emissions, improve productivity, and reduce operating costs

>> Installing renewable energy sources, such as solar panels

>> Using certified green cleaning products

Considering consumer use

You may wonder what control you have over consumer use once the product is in the customer's hands. If you think "very little," you're right — but only to a point. What you *can* do is design your products in ways that make them more environmentally friendly. Some general approaches include

>> Using recycled materials instead of new ones

>> Arranging easy-to-use consumer recycling programs for spent products

>> Reducing packaging to minimize consumer-generated solid waste

>> Changing product formulation to reduce consumer energy or water consumption

REMEMBER

The biggest environmental impact of your product may come from consumer use.

Managing disposal logistics

Eliminating all the negative environmental impacts from your supply chain is nearly impossible. Inevitably, you will find yourself having to manage various waste streams. Disposal logistics helps you do that as efficiently and as environmentally responsibly as possible while containing costs. Examples of some best practices that may fit your operations are

>> Using waste exchanges to sell or donate excess wood, metal scraps, solvents, or other materials

>> Complying with legal requirements for proper disposal or treatment at licensed facilities and for recovery and recycling of materials

>> Selecting disposal service vendors with green reputations

Adopting an environmental management system will help keep all your environmental stewardship efforts organized, on track, and integrated with other business systems. The best known EMS is ISO 14001:2015, the International Standard Organization (ISO) standard that is suitable for use by organizations across industry sectors.

So, you've heard of ISO 14001:2015 and think it's costly to adopt, and even more expensive to get certification? That's true! But, you can create an EMS that is faithful to the general principles of ISO 14001:2015, yet is right-sized for your company.

Just be sure your EMS has the following elements, at a minimum:

>> Management commitment

>> Environmental policy

>> Aspects, impacts, goals, and objectives

>> Implementation and operation

>> Metrics and measurement

>> Checking and corrective action

>> Management review

>> Continual process improvement

You'll supplement the corporate EMS with operating guides for specific activities or facilities.

Minimizing your carbon footprint

Carbon footprint management increasingly is of concern to governments around the world. Hundreds of countries have ratified treaties and protocols designed to limit emissions of pollutants that contribute to global warming. No matter where you choose to locate your foreign operations, you most likely will be required to do your part by minimizing your carbon footprint.

So, what is a carbon footprint and how is it calculated? Simply put, the term *carbon footprint* is a shorthand way of describing the climate change impact of an organization, a facility, or an activity.

You'll find many methods and tools for calculating a carbon footprint for activities inside your operation and across your supply chain. All have the common goal of measuring and aggregating emissions of CO_2 and other greenhouse gases (for example, methane and nitrous oxide) into a single number known as carbon dioxide equivalent (CO_2e). You can incorporate measurement of these pollutants into your exercise to characterize your overall environmental footprint. Because the use of fossil fuels is at the root of your carbon footprint's size, many of the best practices you adopt to "green" your acquisition, production, distribution, and disposal logistics also will help curb your carbon footprint.

Reducing, reusing, and recycling from within

Maybe you have a preconceived notion that reducing and recycling from within simply applies to office paper, aluminum beverage cans, plastic bottles, and printer cartridges. Not so! Reducing, recycling, and reusing (R3) from within does, indeed, include all those items. However, R3 has become very sophisticated, reaching far beyond your office operations and into your manufacturing and warehouse activities. Obviously, managing your consumption of and reusing office supplies whenever possible will go a long way toward "reducing." Just a few examples of items and materials recovered and reused inside the manufacturing or warehouse facility are

» Solvents, scrap metals, glass off-cuts, and tires

» Packing materials

» Pallets

Beyond that, you can follow in the footsteps of other companies and enter into partnerships to extract these and other materials from the host country's waste stream and incorporate recycled materials into your products and manufacturing processes.

Perhaps the most visible positive measure of corporate social responsibility is how successful your company is in managing operations in an environmentally and socially responsible manner.

Chapter **8**

Keeping Everything Running Smoothly

You've made the decision to open another manufacturing plant, this time in a foreign country. And you're confident of success there, based on the success you have experienced at your domestic location. But, is that really the case? While you may have replicated your domestic manufacturing processes, your foreign operation has a number of differences that can't be overlooked or discounted. Are you using the exact same machinery? Is your supply chain for incoming materials as robust? Is your foreign workforce as well trained?

In this chapter we address many of the challenges you need to consider to ensure you keep everything running smoothly. Once you have adequately addressed those challenges, you need to develop plans and schedules to help you predict and respond to production stoppages in your manufacturing processes — including preparing for major production disasters.

Maintaining the Line

To keep the foreign manufacturing line running smoothly, you must determine your desired operational tempo (that is, how much product you want in what period of time). Is it to be the same level of production as at your domestic locations?

If not, what situations need to be considered or factored in for either a decreased or increased level of production?

Once you've established your desired levels of production, you need to know what to monitor and measure and when to do so in order to prevent unwanted interruptions. Having plans that allow you to respond quickly to unexpected delays or temporary stoppages can preclude total production shutdowns. You can avoid failures by establishing prevention measures and creating preventive maintenance schedules. Both approaches serve to ensure efficiency and cost effectiveness.

Establishing your level of foreign operational readiness

Operational readiness assesses the maturity of a given technology, component, or system from a manufacturing perspective. While your global operation should be able to produce most of its product components, there also may be a need to get components or parts from a local (that is, within the foreign area of operation) supplier to fill customer orders. The foreign manufacturing capabilities may not be as robust or advanced as those supporting your domestic operations. Conversely, they may be more so.

When operating in a foreign market, determining operational readiness must include a comprehensive and realistic assessment of foreign technology and manufacturing methods. Such an assessment provides decision makers with an understanding of the relative technology and manufacturing maturity and attendant risks associated with manufacturing in your foreign location.

To determine the probable level of operational readiness at your foreign location, your assessment should include the following:

>> Defining the foreign level of technology and manufacturing maturity levels, and comparing them to your desired operational tempo

>> Identifying technology and manufacturing maturity shortfalls

>> Determining the level of risk management — including associated costs — necessary to overcome technology and manufacturing maturity shortfalls

>> Adjusting for foreign technology and manufacturing capability shortfalls during production planning and design

>> Accommodating technology and manufacturing maturity shortfalls in the establishment and management of local supply chains

>> Verifying local workforce knowledge, skills, and certifications

>> Verifying the availability of foreign production materials and components

MEASURING TO DETERMINE SUCCESS

William Thomson, 1st Baron Kelvin (1824–1907) — the famous Irish mathematical physicist and engineer — once said, "I often say that when you can measure what you are speaking about and express it in numbers, you know something about it; but when you cannot measure it, when you cannot express it in numbers, your knowledge is of a meager and unsatisfactory kind. It may be the beginning of knowledge, but you have scarcely, in your thoughts, advanced to the stage of science, whatever the matter may be."

TIP

Assessing your level of technology and manufacturing maturity *before* you establish your foreign production operations will prevent many errors and reduce avoidable manufacturing failures.

Knowing what and when to measure

There are two types of measurements that should be used when determining your operational level of success: those that are *quantitative* (that is, measurements that are reducible to numerical values) and those that are *qualitative* (that is, factors or conditions that you can observe but cannot measure numerically). By employing both types of measurements, the health of foreign manufacturing capabilities can be determined and compared to other foreign and domestic efforts.

Based on those comparisons, you then establish your operational baseline and develop your unique and specific metrics for logistics operational performance. Then, by addressing any deviations from the baseline before out-of-tolerance conditions occur, you can significantly maintain your global operations at their desired levels.

Monitoring both quantitative and qualitative measurements allows you to achieve the following:

>> Identification of problems in foreign manufacturing lines

>> Evaluation of the performance of the foreign workforce

>> Determination of the corrective measures required

>> Understanding of when to increase or decrease foreign supply resources

>> Effective computation of reorder levels

>> Provision of timely information to operators and managers

>> Objective evaluation of foreign performance, services, and activities

Developing preventive maintenance schedules

Preventive maintenance (or scheduled maintenance) is maintenance that is regularly performed on equipment to reduce the risk of failure. It is performed while the equipment is still in working condition, so as to prevent the equipment from breaking down at unexpected or inopportune times. Planning and timing the maintenance minimizes the impact to the overall manufacturing schedules. It also ensures that any required tools or repair items are on hand and available.

The performance of preventive maintenance can be based on equipment operating time or triggered by usage rates (for example, the number of products produced or miles driven). Determining when preventive maintenance should be performed can be based on a calculation of equipment reliability when operational risks (such as unusually high usage) are high, or that of previous failure history when risks are low (as in periods of diminished usage). Local operating environmental conditions like weather, humidity, and dust, as well as the skill level of the production and maintenance workforce, should also dictate maintenance scheduling at each location.

Studies have shown that performing routine preventive maintenance on working equipment can sometimes have the opposite effect. Equipment may fail sooner because of maintenance-induced issues, either because of improper maintenance or the parts wearing out or breaking in the maintenance process. Skill levels of foreign maintenance workers may be significantly different from those of domestic repair personnel. Statistics in each location will show whether it is more cost effective to perform periodic maintenance or to let the equipment operate until it fails. If any manufacturer recommendations or warranties are involved, addressing them first is advisable.

REMEMBER

The best time to do periodic maintenance is during normal work stoppages. Additionally, intentionally stopping work for short periods can prevent longer, unplanned, or unscheduled work stoppages.

Adjusting for unscheduled failures and equipment downtime

Your foreign manufacturing line needs to have a plan to continue operations when items fail or experience unusually long periods of unavailability. If a redundant capability has been built into the line, then the entire manufacturing process may not have to be shut down. However, if it does need to be shut down, then the downtime may be used to make planned improvements and perform preventive maintenance on other components in the line. The amount of redundancy needed in each foreign location can be determined through careful analysis of manufacturing capabilities and customer demands.

Not every unexpected failure can be anticipated and addressed in plans. However, by prioritizing the importance of each major item or component as well as understanding the impact of the failure of those items, individual plans can be put in place to mitigate the most common, most expensive, or most detrimental of those failure events.

REMEMBER

Failure reporting systems should include whom to contact, how to report a problem or deficiency, and what emergency procedures to take in the event of failure of a critical item or component.

Every failure event must be understood so that it can be corrected. First, the fault requires the identification of the root cause of the failure. Then, restorative action is performed to return the item or system to an operating condition. Finally, functional testing may be required to ensure that the equipment or process is ready to be returned to operation.

Keep good records on individual foreign manufacturing line failures and unscheduled maintenance events. They are used to understand the events in relation to their respective locations and markets, in order to eliminate future occurrences.

TIP

Monitor each site's failure history to ensure that the cost of maintenance doesn't exceed the cost of failures.

Implementing Tools and Metrics

In order to maintain, monitor, and continuously improve your foreign operations, you must identify what logistics indicators you need to measure — that is, what measurements to take and metrics to use — and then employ integrated formulas to evaluate the complete foreign logistics effort. This is not to say that you need to be a mathematical genius to calculate results: Simple formulas can be most effective.

Deciding what logistics indicators to measure

To show improvement in foreign operations, implement manufacturing and supply chain performance indicators and metrics. Focus not only on those areas that are underperforming but also those that are aligned with overall global supply chain and domestic best–practice corporate strategies:

>> **Quality indicators** show how well you are performing a specific activity. Accuracy is a common logistics indicator (for example, ordering accuracy, inventory accuracy, picking accuracy, and so forth). Variations within each of your foreign operations and between your domestic and foreign operations are to be expected.

>> **Time indicators** focus on the time it takes to complete specific activities. They indicate where saving time during specific activities can improve overall logistics performance. For example, the time it takes to fill orders and receive inventory are as important a set of measurements as are customer wait time and time in transit. Reducing delivery time is often a major reason to establish foreign manufacturing and distribution operations.

>> **Financial indicators** help managers identify logistics cost drivers (for example, cost per unit of packaging) as well as help establish an efficiently managed supply chain. Comparing cost with schedule helps to determine the strength of decision-making. Further, exchange rates and local taxes should automatically be considered, in addition to all specialized and unique costs.

>> **Productivity indicators** (such as the number of items produced in a specified period of time) examine how well foreign resources are utilized. (Resources include materials, equipment, and labor.)

TIP

View indicators holistically to make sure they identify the trade–offs required to strategically improve overall global performance.

Stocking your logistics toolbox with metrics

To help with making decisions, every logistics manager should have a collection of mathematical tools available to use. Many papers and books have been published that provide insight into commonly used quantitative measurements for logistics.

The best logistics metrics should be

>> **Multidimensional:** Metrics that balance utilization, production, and performance as trade-offs

>> **Quantitative:** Metrics that are expressed as an objective, numerical value

>> **Transparent:** Measurements whose effects are apparent to everyone involved

>> **Understandable:** Metrics that clearly identify what is being measured and how the measurement was derived

To be effective, logistics metrics should also address the following:

>> **Mutual definition and acceptance:** All elements of the logistics operations involved help to develop and define the metric; all individuals involved in the process agree to accept them as the level of measurement.

>> **Integration of all inputs and outputs:** Factors from all aspects of the process have been integrated into the metric.

>> **Reward of productive behavior:** The measurement of the logistics element or process encourages productive behaviors and discourages destructive ones.

>> **Encouragement of trust:** The participation by all users in the measurement process builds an environment of trust in both the process and the end product.

>> **Measurement of what is really important:** Collection of only critical data allows for the focus on key performance indicators, rather than collecting data for the sake of data collection.

>> **Effectiveness of measurement:** The benefits of data collection and measurement outweigh the costs to do so.

There are hundreds of metrics you can choose to analyze, assuming you have the data available and depending on the breadth and depth of the operation that you choose to review. One way to refine what you may want to address is to look at what others are measuring — specifically, what other firms with similar products and global operations are measuring.

Other good sources for production and logistics metrics include not-for-profit professional associations or alliances. Look for associations of manufacturers similar to you: for example, the Institute of Electrical and Electronics Engineers (www.ieee.org), SAE International (www.sae.org), or MESA International (www.mesa.org). Many of the groups are global communities of manufacturing companies, system integrators, or designers whose members' goal is to improve business results and production operations through best management practices.

TIP

Collecting data for the measurement of production and process elements shouldn't get in the way of work performance. It should be a normal and routine part of the overall business and production process.

Developing integrated logistics formulas and strategies for success

The reason logistics managers develop and use mathematical formulas, algorithms, and models is to turn the measurement data that's been collected into usable and useful information for global decision-making. Complicated formulas that use many variables, while impressive, are not necessarily better than those that are fundamental.

Some people assume that because logisticians deal with statistics, performance analysis, and quantitative performance metrics, their job requires an advanced knowledge of mathematics. This is not the case. However, the more one uses statistical analysis and formulas to measure logistics performance, the easier and more effective decision-making becomes.

For example: Statistical analysis is used to measure the quality of collected data, modeling helps to understand complex tasks, and the mathematical identification of probable outcomes helps manage risk and uncertainty.

REMEMBER

Logistics models and measurements must be easy to understand by everyone using them, as well as standardized so as to apply to each global operation.

Managing Risks and Crisis

Not everything within the production line and its logistics and supply chains runs smoothly. There is always a certain amount of risk and uncertainty that, if not monitored and contained, inevitably leads to crisis and the need for intervention and management.

Always work toward reducing the risk of manufacturing failures and the possibility of production stoppage. Progress toward restoring the manufacturing line must be measured against production or process metrics with the goal of preventing reoccurrence.

Reducing the risk of failures and stoppages

Ensuring that the production lines run according to plan and schedule is critical to the company's bottom line. Managers can reduce risk by designing manufacturing and support processes so that risk is contained or eliminated. Communication systems (that is, progress reports, line performance measurement, anomaly reporting, and so forth) must be designed such that they don't accidentally contribute to work stoppage or failure, but do enable speedy restoration should failure occur.

Recurring risks — that is, those caused by production or demand fluctuation — require that a company focus on efficiency in determining supply and demand requirements. *Nonrecurring risks* — that is, those risks that are inherently unpredictable — require that a company builds in resiliency capability without regard to the cost of the capability. Planning for both types of risks is critical to the ability to recover from failure or disruption.

TIP

Having the right levels of inventory at the appropriate location is more efficient and less costly than having too much inventory at all locations "just in case."

Any risk that is nonrecurring can cause a chain reaction, not only in your foreign production lines but also throughout your entire foreign and domestic operations. By contrast, recurring risks, such as demand fluctuations or supply delays, are often localized and independent. Establishing separate foreign operations helps reduce risk by providing the ability to shift work to other unaffected locations.

Reporting progress against logistics metrics and goals

Companies with global operations must consider the level of technology available in the foreign area of operations when developing a range of performance measurements and metrics. Metrics often must differ in their inherent focus and the type of measurement system used. While they may be different, performance measures for foreign operations must be compatible with and aligned to the company's domestic operations and overall manufacturing objectives.

Performance management reports compare actual performance at each foreign site with predetermined standards and goals in each area of the logistics operation, and they play an important role in the company-wide budgeting, planning, and control activities. These reports provide manufacturing visibility using well-defined metrics and business rules. Each foreign operation may have different performance goals based upon what is necessary to achieve capacity at that specific location.

Adjusting the processes to restore the line

There must be built-in flexibility within the foreign operation production process in order to recover from and restart a stopped manufacturing line. The ultimate solution may not be readily apparent, so several different approaches may need to be assessed to find the best course of action to implement. It may also require adjusting other policy or process failures that may have caused or contributed to the stoppage.

It can't be emphasized enough that one can't implement a successful course of production restoration that excludes sound safety and security strategies. Successful safety and security strategies require a comprehensive understanding of what to protect and how to do so. Policies need to focus on manufacturing needs and provide a strategy for applying effective safety and security technologies and best practices. While safeguards should not inhibit the manufacturing operation, the proper level of safety and security should not be compromised by an ill-advised desire to control costs.

Policies should ensure that a company maintains an acceptable level of safety and security. Physical and electronic procedure policies should define and contain the behavior of both personnel and the process components of your manufacturing operations. Define what your supply chain and manufacturing safety and security needs are, and identify, evaluate, and prioritize all potential risks. Perform risk assessments to identify vulnerabilities. Then determine mitigation techniques.

REMEMBER

Whatever course of action you decide on, safety and security must be as important as speed in the restoration of the manufacturing line.

Once the full cause of the stoppage has been identified, and any safety and security policy or process adjustments have been made, some of the logistics process adjustments may involve the following:

>> Adjusting course of action plans

>> Altering inventory delivery strategies

>> Reallocating logistics resources (such as inventory, personnel, and equipment)

>> Reducing production lead times of manufactured items

>> Revising output objectives

>> Writing contracts to allow for unexpected production delays

Closing the circle: Precluding future failures

In order to prevent failures, management must continuously monitor and assess how closely each foreign location implements the various safety, security, and performance plans. While monitoring focuses on the activities and outputs of each foreign operation, evaluation focuses on the desired performance goals and outcomes. The company's senior management then communicates what actions need to take place at each specific location.

To minimize the impact on foreign operations of any future manufacturing or supply chain disruption and improve resiliency, increase flexibility by making changes to product design or manufacturing methods at the earliest stages possible. Take into account the foreign markets, supply chains, and local infrastructures. Standardize manufacturing processes, use generic interchangeable components wherever possible on the production line, and reduce dependency on particular components or suppliers.

Establishing a Production Continuity of Operations Plan (Production COOP)

Continuity planning is accomplished through the development of a production continuity of operations plan, also known as a production COOP. This practice ensures the continued execution of essential functions. It is the responsibility of a company both to itself and its stakeholders to keep the production lines up and running in the event of the unexpected. It is vitally important to ensure that primary essential functions continue during unusual and emergency situations. These include acts of nature, accidents, intentional or unintentional disruptions, international political incidents, and technological emergencies.

In most companies only a few people are made aware of all the information that is critical to the overall processes. As a result, many times critical continuity information is not shared with all those who need the information to ensure foreign operations continue without significant interruption.

Identifying critical logistics functions and personnel

Every company contains critical operations that can only be performed by qualified personnel. Therefore, it is important to identify which process components, suppliers, and personnel are critical at each foreign manufacturing location. Compare and group the common ones (that is, those that are critical at all locations), and identify those that are unique to each location. When conducting your analysis, address at least the following elements:

>> **Essential functions:** Identify the critical activities that must be performed by each manufacturing location immediately following a significant disruption of normal activities.

>> **Delegations of authority:** Identify the authorities for each management position, specifically focusing on the authority to make policy determinations and decisions at each foreign operating location. Delegations of authority should take effect as soon as possible after a significant disruption.

>> **Human capital:** During a continuity event, activate emergency employees and other special categories of employees, as defined by the emergency delegations of authority.

>> **Orders of succession:** Identify who will assume the duties of any senior management officials who are unavailable to execute their legal duties. Make sure to specify both the scope of duties authorized and the period of time the authorization will be in effect.

>> **Continuity of communications:** Specify what backup methods of communication will provide the capability to conduct essential internal foreign-location operations, as well as ensure liaison with domestic functions and other agencies.

>> **Vital records management:** Develop a plan for the identification, protection, and provision of access to electronic and hard copy documents, references, records, information systems, data management software, and equipment needed to support the essential functions during a crisis. Additional post-event plans must be in place for the restoration of all records that haven't been lost or the reconstruction of those that have been lost.

>> **Continuity of facilities:** Designate and put in place the mechanisms (such as emergency facility leasing arrangements or policies for telecommuting) to provide for relocation of essential functions to alternate locations both during the crisis event and into the period of recovery.

WARNING

Even the smallest disruption at your foreign operation can snowball so as to cause harm to corporate operations. Something as seemingly insignificant as not being able to find the employee holding the password, key, or lock combination, or not being able to get in contact with a key employee usually does not shut down domestic operations. Unless your foreign operation plans allow for personnel redundancy, be prepared for the insignificant to quickly become a potential operational crisis.

Developing corporate policies and plans to respond to production disasters

Any event that could negatively affect global operations must be included in your production continuity of operations plan. This includes foreign supply chain interruption, or loss or damage to critical local facilities, such as major machinery and computing or communications network resources. Accordingly, risk management practices must be embedded in the company's plans, policies, and culture.

Management's capability to transfer authority and responsibility of essential functions from a company's primary operating staff and facilities to other employees and facilities is probably the most effective of risk-management practices.

Control is given to individuals at alternate sites that are unaffected by the disaster event. Policies have to ensure that those individuals temporarily in charge understand that they will have to give back control when recovery has been affected.

Tests, training, and exercises of the risk-management plans must be conducted routinely to ensure that a company's production COOP is capable of supporting continuation of essential functions throughout the duration of a production disaster at every foreign manufacturing location.

TIP

Tabletop exercises can be performed without interrupting domestic or foreign manufacturing lines. Exercise participants explain how they would react to various "what-if" scenarios. Using historical event scenarios brings a sense of reality to the hypothetical situations.

Implementing your production COOP

The production COOP needs to be implemented immediately upon the occurrence of disaster events. Communication is vital to COOP implementation. While this may be difficult during natural disasters, the COOP should have defined the protocol for the establishment of emergency communications. Compromised computer systems need to be brought back online as soon as possible to get your foreign sites back in operation. The plan may have both manual and automatic processes that will be implemented online as soon as the need arises.

The following are the phases of response to any disastrous event:

>> **Phase I (Readiness and preparedness):** Development and rehearsal of the plans.

>> **Phase II (Activation and relocation):** Plans, procedures, and schedules initiated for the transfer of activities, personnel, records, and equipment to alternate operating locations.

>> **Phase III (Continuity operations):** Full execution of essential operations at alternate operating locations.

>> **Phase IV (Reconstitution):** Operations at alternate facility are ended and normal operations resume.

TIP

Post printed "In Case of Emergency" lists of key and strategic personnel and their contact information. Include a short checklist of what to do in the event of a production crisis, especially so that disruptions of computer and communication equipment will not stop the continuity process. Update it *every* time any piece of the information changes. Failure to keep phone numbers and key duties updated may well stop your ability to react and respond to the disaster.

Chapter **9**

Protecting Your Designs and Data

Though it is a cliché, every company is different — or at least tries to be. You may have your own unique processes, materials, marketing, or pricing strategies to gain a competitive advantage. And although you may feel confident in your ability to keep others from copying your unique capabilities in your domestic market, you may be surprised to learn how hard it is when you venture into the global marketplace and establish supply chains that carry with them increased fragility and vulnerability.

In addition to exploring the management of global supply chain risk, this chapter discusses some of the ways to help you protect your unique intellectual property and sensitive trade data in an expanded foreign environment. You'll also learn what to do if you've become a victim of industrial espionage, and you'll find suggestions for the prevention of and recovery from either accidental or malicious attacks on your logistics systems and data.

Developing Your Supply Chain Risk Management Plan

The more you manufacture and distribute your products globally, the more fragile your manufacturing supply chain becomes. Developing a plan for *supply chain risk management* (SCRM) allows your company to better establish its foreign supply chains, identify what and where your risks are, and prioritize when and how you mitigate those risks. Because minimizing risks always comes with a price, a SCRM plan allows a company to expend resources effectively to achieve an acceptable measure of risk management. This is especially true if your products are a part of a larger or multi-company manufacturing or supplier obligation.

When developing your SCRM plan, include everyone in your company who has a management responsibility for your manufacturing success. Your lead engineer, production and quality control supervisors, your contracts manager or lead buyer, your security manager, and even your human resource manager are all key players in the plan's development; to exclude any one of them increases the chance of plan failure.

Identifying risk throughout the supply chain

Delays in material flow often occur when suppliers can't respond quickly enough to changes in supply and demand. Disruptions can occur anywhere in the supply chain, are unpredictable, and are often very damaging to operations. Natural or man-made disasters, prolonged internal or external labor strikes, fires, sabotage, and terrorism all are potential risks to the supply chains. For example, the 2011 earthquake and tsunami in Japan stopped the manufacture and outbound delivery of Toyota automotive repair parts worldwide, and the 2004 strike shutdown of the Port of Long Beach, California, halted the shipment of $1 billion a day in goods and put 2.8 million jobs at risk across the globe.

Equally damaging can be a shutdown or compromise of your (or any of your suppliers') information technology systems or infrastructure severe enough to disrupt the flow of critical information across your manufacturing lines and their supporting supply chains.

REMEMBER

The more dependent a company's supply chain is on its automated information systems, the greater the risk that a failure at any point will cause failures at all points.

In addition to the more frequently occurring examples of the supply chain risks we've just discussed, your SCRM plan also should address recovery from the following additional risks:

>> Unreliable delivery of raw materials or your finished products

>> Introduction of counterfeit parts or finished components into your manufacturing line

>> Shutdown of the production line due to breakage, sabotage, or political upheaval

>> Errors or gross over/under-estimations in production or demand forecasts

>> Theft of material in storage or in transit

>> Compromise or theft of data and intellectual property (for example, design and production drawings, trademarks, formulas, or marketing plans)

Prioritizing internal and external supply chain risk

Supply chain management involves a number of inherent risks and opportunities. The risks apply both to activities within your company (that is, *internal risk*) and your outside suppliers, the suppliers' suppliers, and the organization's customers and their customers (your *external risk*). Risks and opportunities affect the entire supply chain and must be prioritized according to specific classifications that coincide with business goals and objectives. Classification categories may include economics, business growth, brand recognition, customer service, and so forth.

TIP

Rank the risk items that affect your supply chains the most and then create plans that reduce the risk each item has on your overall operations.

As you develop your SCRM plan, remember that many sources of help are available. There are some excellent websites that list best business practices for the development of a SCRM. Additionally, there are organizations (like professional associations with international chapters) that specialize in the development of SCRM practices and plans. Because you may be manufacturing in multiple locations, it is a good idea to check with each area's local business organizations, such as the chambers of commerce or economic development councils, to determine whether unique SCRM challenges are associated with your manufacturing region.

REMEMBER

A wide variety of websites — from simple to complex — can help you develop your supply chain risk management plan. Choose the one that is best for your particular operation.

Mitigating the effects of supply chain risk on operations

Creating a company-wide understanding of supply chain risk helps minimize the damage when risk becomes reality. Determine how to adapt individual risk mitigation approaches to the specific circumstances. Managers can employ virtual stress testing of the supply chain to further refine solutions.

Stress testing is a group exercise that helps managers and their companies understand and prioritize supply chain risk. "What if" scenarios help managers focus on the supply chain one link at a time. This strategy offers an effective way to gain endorsement of the SCRM plan by shared-ownership project teams. Through stress testing, managers can identify risk mitigation priorities for the near, medium, and long term. This helps identify not only products at risk but also the associated manufacturing plants, shipping lanes, suppliers, or customers that are at risk. Upon completion of the virtual stress test, a company gains a clearer idea of what risks might have an impact on sales, procurement costs, revenues, prices, market share, or even brand recognition and reputation.

One risk management strategy involves adjusting raw materials and finished product inventory to production capacity, according to the end value of the products. Another strategy adjusts the amount of inventory held based on different modes of transport or shipment. Companies can counter disruptions in material flow by building in safety levels of inventory or by having multiple suppliers.

REMEMBER

Supply chain risk management only succeeds when everyone inside the company is aware of and participates in the minimization and recovery processes.

Safeguarding Your Intellectual Property

You have to know what your company's intellectual property (IP) is to be able to protect it. Then you have to decide if the items need to be safeguarded by registering or trademarking designs and processes, copyrighting documents, or patenting products. Creating and maintaining a comprehensive intellectual property protection plan can be expensive. Ultimately, though, the cost invested is minimal compared to the losses incurred if your intellectual property is compromised.

Your company already may have a number of design and manufacturing patents, registered marks, trademarks, or copyrights issued for your domestic operations and products. Before you take your manufacturing operations to a location outside of the country that issued the intellectual property protection(s), you must know not only what protection and rights you have in a foreign location but also what recourse you have should those rights be violated. Because patents and trademarks are territorial, it is almost a certainty that any rights you acquired for IP protection in your home country will have no effect in another country unless the original right was multinational or global in nature (such as an international design patent or a regional trademark).

Almost every country has its own laws and requirements for filing, acquiring, and enforcing IP protection. Further, many of those countries also have complicated systems of additional regional or local requirements for the issue and enforcement of IP protection.

The discussion that follows is not intended to provide the detailed steps of acquiring IP protection for each and every element of your foreign manufacturing operations. Rather, it is meant to serve as a frame of reference and general guideline for what must be considered when you take your IP away from your area of domestic protection.

WARNING

The information and discussion presented here by no means constitutes expert or legal advice, and should not be a substitute for the advice of counsel.

Protecting designs and processes

Protecting your designs and manufacturing processes overseas is difficult, at best, for a large company and may seem overwhelming for a small company just beginning to expand into the global arena. While very few companies, large or small, have international IP experts on staff, a few low-cost steps to consider are as follows:

>> Work with legal counsel with a demonstrated record of international IP protection to develop an overall foreign IP protection strategy and plan.

>> Develop detailed, region- or country-specific IP protection language for licensing and subcontracting agreements and contracts.

>> Conduct comprehensive due diligence of potential foreign partners' record of IP protection or abuses.

>> Record all your domestic-based IP protections (that is, patents, registered trademarks, and copyrights) with the appropriate agency responsible for cross-border protection. (For example, work with your country's agency responsible for customs and border protection or with your country's ministry of commerce.)

>> Make sure that all domestic-issued IP protections (especially design patents, trademarks, and copyrights) are secured and registered in key foreign markets (that is, where you intend to set up your foreign manufacturing operation) well in advance of the start of any discussions with your intended foreign hosts. This especially includes establishing protections in countries where you know IP violations are the rule, rather than the exception.

REMEMBER

Obtaining IP protection in foreign markets requires a considerable investment of specialized expertise, cost, and — most of all — time. Don't even think about foreign manufacturing without having the appropriate IP protections in place well in advance.

Determining how to acquire foreign intellectual property protections and rights

Once you've determined what IP protection is needed for your foreign expansion, contact the intellectual property office in each country of your prospective new manufacturing operations. A list of the contact information of most intellectual property offices worldwide, as well as country profiles, can be found on the World Intellectual Property Organization website at www.wipo.int. (Information on that site can be found in English, French, and Spanish.)

In addition, the Patent Cooperation Treaty (PCT) of 1970, the Hague Agreement Concerning the International Registration of Industrial Designs, and other international cooperative patent projects and agreements may afford your company the opportunity to streamline the process of filing your IP protection applications. For example, filing one patent application with the US Patent and Trademark Office (USPTO) allows US applicants to concurrently seek protection in up to 143 countries. The Madrid Protocol allows applicants to file an international trademark registration application that can concurrently afford protection in up to 92 countries.

Most countries do not require copyright registration in order to have the right to copyright protection. Many countries have reciprocal copyright agreements that allow for the honoring of each other's copyrights.

TIP

Take advantage of the multinational IP protections that treaties, conventions, and protocols offer when seeking IP protections in your new foreign location. The more protections you can acquire at the beginning, the easier it will be if and when you decide to move into another global location.

Protecting other trade secrets

Your company may value its know-how as trade secrets and not want competitors to learn about it. (For example, you may not want your competitors to know who your suppliers or customers are.) Make sure that only a limited number of people have access to the information and that they understand that the information is company proprietary and confidential.

When dealing with third parties or licensing, enter into legally-binding, mutual confidentiality agreements to ensure that all parties know what information is to be protected as well as the penalties for violation.

A company must continuously and affirmatively behave in a way that proves not only its ability to keep its IP protected, but also its partners' and suppliers' IP. Always take reasonable precautions to protect your and others' trade secrets. Extraordinary protection measures aren't always necessary. Reasonable precautions include marking documents with an appropriate security classification, safeguarding materials after hours, maintaining computer security, or providing access only to people with a need to know. The use of nondisclosure agreements is an effective way for a company to protect proprietary and confidential information.

REMEMBER

Protection of trade secrets, company proprietary information, and information deemed to be confidential is a reciprocal responsibility. You cannot expect your foreign partners or suppliers to protect your information if you don't also respect their protection requirements.

Fighting Industrial Espionage

You have to be able to identify your company's IP vulnerabilities and potential security threats to be able to protect against loss of your IP through industrial espionage. Firewalls are not just for computers. They are the means by which a company can protect its sensitive information, regardless of the type of information (for example, marketing, personnel, IP, and financial). Your company's safeguards must be robust enough to protect not only against the risk of the information accidentally getting out but also to protect against the deliberate acts of those intent on stealing that information, either by human or electronic means.

After the safeguards supporting your IP protection strategy and plan are in place, they should be tested regularly to ensure that they are executed and enforced, and are doing the job for which they were designed.

Information about your company can be gathered both illegally and legally. Any activity that is a matter of pubic record can easily be acquired, especially in this age of social media. Information contained, reported, or released in newspapers or magazines, at trade shows, in company press releases and brochures, and even through the casual conversations of employees with their friends and family can cause a leak of sensitive information. The unauthorized public release of a company's data and sensitive information must be monitored, and contained before the loss has a chance to cause harm.

TIP

If you want to know whether you have a problem with what the public knows about your company's operations, search the web and social media networks thoroughly and frequently.

Recognizing industrial espionage

You've gone on the Internet and been surprised about how much information is there about your company. Some of the information on other websites is the same information as that on your company's own website or in its publications. But what about the information that isn't? What might be some indications that you have been the victim of industrial espionage? Ask yourself the following questions:

>> Is any of the information sensitive personnel information (such as salaries, home addresses, or private telephone numbers) that is only obtainable from your company's internal human resources files or data bases?

>> Is any of the financial information confidential and only published internally? (For example, your overhead rates, your profit margins, your confidential profit and loss statements, or your strategic plan)

>> Are there design drawings or plant blueprints?

>> Is someone marketing a product that looks almost identical to yours?

>> Are there reports of counterfeit parts in your products?

>> Have reports of sensitive negotiations, proposals, or investigations been made public?

REMEMBER

Your competitors can use any opportunity to gain a competitive advantage over you — including gaining access to company proprietary and sensitive information. Once your private information becomes public, you will have to assume that it will remain public and respond accordingly.

It's important to understand that the vulnerabilities you may have identified to your domestic operations may be substantively different from those that may threaten your foreign facility and operations. The risk of IP breach at your new location is high, particularly during the start-up process.

Don't become complacent: Remember that the protection of your trade information must be continuous. Your competitors are likely to continue to find and attempt new ways to obtain any and all secrets they can.

Building your manufacturing and data firewalls

Firewalls are meant to prevent individuals and other computers from stealing, disrupting, or corrupting your computer systems and computer-controlled devices. An effective firewall provides separation between networks and controls the types of communication that are allowed between networks and various devices.

While you won't be able to achieve 100 percent protection when selecting a hardware-based firewall system, the following steps help you get the most for your investment:

1. **Assess your network and computer system requirements and determine what firewall features you need.**

2. **Consider adding additional IP security protection capabilities, such as the installation of intrusion protection, antivirus, and malware detection software.**

3. **Talk with multiple firewall vendors for recommendations based on their experience.**

4. **Prior to installation, select multiple vendors for an off-line production environment lab test.**

TIP

Talk to other companies that have done or are doing business in your new location. Ask them what firewall systems worked best for them, as well as which ones didn't and — more importantly — *why* they did or didn't work.

Embedding safeguards into your production and support lines

Successful security strategies require a comprehensive understanding of what to protect and how to do so. Security policies need to focus on manufacturing needs and provide a strategy for applying effective security technologies and best practices. While safeguards should not inhibit the manufacturing operation, the proper level of security should not be compromised by an ill-advised desire to control costs. Many of the same safeguarding policies used by your information technology operations can be applied to manufacturing and logistics functions.

Security policies should ensure that a company maintains an acceptable level of security. Physical and electronic procedure policies should define and constrain the behavior of both personnel and the process components of your manufacturing operations. Define what your supply chain and manufacturing security needs are and identify, evaluate, and prioritize all potential risks. Perform risk assessments to identify vulnerabilities. Then, determine mitigation techniques.

WARNING

Be as vigilant against internal breaches as you are against external threats. Remember that internal leaks, personnel compromise, and disgruntled employees are a major source of industrial espionage.

Testing your safeguards: Performing and responding to IP security audits

There are many advantages to performing security audits. The company can control the pace and schedule of an internal audit by determining the best time and resources to apply. It can schedule audits when they have the least impact on production schedules.

However, internal audits often are undertaken with a prejudice or slant toward a desired outcome. They can lead to a false sense of security, in that there is a tendency to use the same audit framework and objectives repeatedly. When that happens significant shortfalls in your security may go undetected, unreported, and, ultimately, uncorrected. Accordingly, it is good practice to contract for an external security audit on a scheduled basis to ensure maximum protection.

Performing an IP security audit

It is important to properly prepare for any audit, whether conducted by either an internal or external audit team. Start by defining your IP security objectives. What are your security priorities: your information, your equipment, your supplies, or your people?

Next, baseline your IP security posture by using the results of previous audits as a guide. By using previous results, you may be able to more quickly identify and respond to new security risks.

Finally, select your audit team. If you use an internal audit team, make sure they are not simply performing the audit to validate previously determined objectives. If you use an external audit team, ensure both that they have the right credentials to conduct an audit on your particular type of company or operations and that they will formally report their findings in such a way that you can take the appropriate corrective actions.

Responding to an IP security audit

Depending on the severity of the findings, corrective actions may be immediately necessary or can be phased in. For example, if the audit determines that your facility is subject to frequent theft by company personnel you will want to take immediate corrective action.

Perhaps the audit reveals that some of your processes have critical weaknesses or vulnerabilities that could enable the theft of your proprietary information or supplies. In that case you should immediately require the owner of the process in question to respond to the audit findings with a plan to adjust the process within a specific timeline.

Often, an audit finds that while the processes are sufficient, the training of the workforce on those processes is not adequate. As a result, you might initiate a retraining program as a preventative measure.

Regardless of the audit findings, each finding should be addressed expeditiously to reestablish a highly-secured position.

REMEMBER

Intellectual property security audits can achieve your desired results only if your objectives are clearly defined, the audits are objectively conducted and reported, and audit findings are acted upon in a time frame so as to improve your security position. An audit with no subsequent action required is an audit that likely overlooked a weakness.

All audits should become part of an iterative and ongoing process designed to provide management an understanding of the company's security position, such that risk can be managed to a predetermined level of acceptance. Based on that level, management then accepts the known risks and approves an appropriate security system for implementation. Additionally, and when applicable, security audits can be used for certification and accreditation of the company's security system where that is required by government agencies or insurance carriers.

Preventing and Recovering from Logistics Data Disasters

Logistics data plays a critical role in the composition of both your company's IP and what your company considers its trade secrets. Logistics data can be as simple as a list of suppliers or as complex as the components of your manufacturing processes. It can be contained in any number of formats, from paper to formal software systems (both proprietary and commercial off-the-shelf applications) to embedded software in your manufactured products.

With good plans in place, identifying, preparing for, and recovering from logistics data losses and breaches should be almost second nature. All the critical automated systems and data should be identified, documented, maintained, and backed up routinely. Recovery can then be swift with minimized interruption or impact to daily operations or, at the most, with interruptions minimized.

Identifying critical logistics automated systems and data

All automated inventory systems are completely dependent on the availability of accurate and timely data from suppliers and service providers. Most inventory cataloging systems include specific information about the item's physical and financial components (such as height, weight, unit of packaging, unit price, and so on). Inventory management systems record demand rates (both historical and current), inventory levels and condition, storage locations, and new or replenishment order status. Automated logistics information systems that are critical to supplying the company with timely data should be safeguarded through contingency plans and procedures.

Preparing your critical logistics data systems in a global environment

You need to give special consideration to your critical automated logistics requirements and systems when moving to a new foreign location. Assuming that your systems will operate as smoothly in a foreign environment as they do domestically is an invitation to disaster. The following are some things to consider:

>> What are your power requirements, and how will you meet them? Do you need to have consistent, uninterrupted power in your new location?

>> What kind of back-up power is going to be available? Do you need to reevaluate your emergency power requirements based on the likelihood for going for

longer periods without primary power? If using emergency generators, is your new workforce trained to operate and maintain them?

>> Are you using a commercial off-the-shelf software product (that is, commercially manufactured software that you install and use "as is") to manage your logistics data, or have you developed a sophisticated, proprietary data system? In either case, can software maintenance at your foreign location be delivered within your defined timelines? If you are depending on local sources for software support, can you guarantee that there will be no accidental or intentional introduction of malware (that is, worms, viruses, tracking cookies, and other hidden coding designed to steal your data or attack your hardware or software)?

>> Are you using the same hardware (that is, computers, network servers, printers, and other peripheral equipment) in your new location? Is local support available for both routine and emergency hardware maintenance? How safe is that support with respect to the availability and reliability of parts? Can all local suppliers guarantee that counterfeit parts will not be introduced to your hardware through their inventory?

>> What is the communications infrastructure at your new location? Are communication networks available 24 hours a day/7 days a week, or do those networks have a history of being either unavailable or unreliable? Do you now have to consider storing data during outages or periods of network or signal instability until a time when the connectivity becomes more reliable?

>> When bandwidth is available, is it secure, or does your data need to be encrypted prior to transmission or storage?

Exporting your critical logistics data to a global environment

While it may be safe to assume that the logistics data you have identified as critical to your domestic operations will be just as critical in your new foreign location, there are still some obvious questions you need to ask. Does your product or packaging have to conform to a different system of measurement (for example, will you have to convert everything to the metric system)? What spoken and written language will you be using in your production line, marketing, and back office systems (that is, if your operational language is currently English, will you have to also use your host country's language)? Are there new operational metrics and data sources (for example, demographic information, usage demands) you need to collect and monitor either on a permanent basis or only during your initial transitional period?

REMEMBER

Your logistics data is the critical lifeblood of your company's operations. It is imperative that you thoroughly understand how your data systems need to operate and be safeguarded in an expanded global environment.

Preparing for logistics data disasters

Having now established a global operation with its supporting global supply chains, you need to ensure that the data systems you have been using domestically can be used and supported in your foreign operations.

Be aware of and sensitive to the increased need to manage your critical foreign logistics systems and data. Identify what logistics data you manage in your foreign operation that is also an integral part of the overall health and success of domestic operations. Separately, identify what data is essential only to your foreign operations. Understand that both types of data may require separate levels of management and protection.

Assume that data disasters in your new foreign location are inevitable and plan accordingly. Identify both the local and company-wide impacts of logistics systems and data loss, and develop specific local or company-integrated continuity of operations plans (COOP) as well as the supporting disaster recovery plans for each of your foreign operations long before a loss event occurs.

Before you develop your COOP and recovery plans, first imagine the loss of all your data. Then, identify what data you need to recover first, how fast you need to recover it, and how you plan to retrieve it. This allows for the identification of the most important systems and data needed to avoid stoppage of operations due to delays in system or data recovery. It also helps in the selection of the types of storage and recovery options that best fit the operational needs.

It goes without saying that system redundancy and alternate data storage locations can help ensure continuity of operations. Having at least two back-up systems containing copies of all essential information may require significant storage capacity. Keeping data back-ups on site is generally effective only in instances of individual equipment failure or human error. Offsite storage at a secure third-party server — one geographically removed from your primary site — is the option most effective if your primary site is prone to natural disaster or local disturbances.

REMEMBER

Foreign operation COOP and logistics systems and data disaster recovery plans need to presume that the domestic operation will need to serve as the primary backup.

Establishing a response and recovery plan for logistics data breaches and compromises

Once you've developed your COOP and logistics systems and data recovery plans, your foreign operation is well prepared and ready to react should disaster strike. The COOP plan should be able to guide you through the first few hours of most disaster events. Once you've ensured continuity of operations, the first step to recovering what you've lost should be to get the communication infrastructure back up online. At the start, you will likely need to rely on work–arounds that provide temporary measures to keep the information flowing to first responders.

The following suggestions may be useful in the development of your COOP, response, and recovery planning:

>> Identify your most sensitive local and company-wide data and protect that data based on risk and severity of impact.

>> Perform a high-level risk assessment of your logistics data systems infrastructure and environment.

>> Identify vulnerable areas and processes where logistics data breaches could occur.

>> Identify those processes and areas that are prone to breach by human error and adjust accordingly.

>> Educate all employees on data protection and malware infection protection practices.

>> Where required, ensure all passwords and data keys are robust and updated on both a regularly scheduled and randomly announced basis.

>> Continuously review and improve all operational processes to maximize data and systems security.

>> Be aware of and comply with all national, regional, and local data-breach reporting requirements and laws.

>> Develop proactive relationships with national, regional, and local law-enforcement agencies.

>> Give data-breach response teams the authority and autonomy to immediately respond and react.

>> Continuously provide and refresh training for the data-breach response teams, and underwrite all necessary licenses and certifications.

>> On both a scheduled and unscheduled basis, frequently test the logistics systems and data disaster response and recovery plans, and expeditiously correct any and all deficiencies and weaknesses.

>> Develop internal and external company-wide and local public information strategies and policies to advise and inform of potential or actual logistics system or data breaches.

TIP

Test, test, and test again to ensure all logistics systems and data COOP, response, and recovery plans are up to date, adequate, and effective.

Identifying the breach: When, what, and how bad?

Most automated logistics systems and data operations will suffer an attempted or actual attack. Ideally, few of those attempts or attacks will result in a breach. Realistically, however, you need to prepare for a major security breach.

Unfortunately, minor breaches occur frequently. While they initially may have less of an operational impact, they can open the door for larger and more disastrous damage long-term.

So, how do you recognize a successful attack or breach? The easiest way to know that a logistics system or data breach has occurred is to understand or recognize when the system's operation or data displays do not match a specific documented baseline of correct operation or data display. Logistics systems and data analysts (including users) may then be better able to spot attacks as they are happening, thus preventing or minimizing catastrophic systems damage or logistics data loss from occurring.

Some symptoms of system attacks could be unusually slow computer processing times, visual indications that a computer appears to have been tampered with, or no longer being able to access routine files.

TIP

By knowing what normal logistics systems operations and data displays should be, quickly responding to incidents that aren't the norm may prevent catastrophic systems damage and data loss. If you suspect that your logistics systems or data have been attacked or compromised, immediately ask the following questions:

>> What systems or data were affected, and to what extent?

>> What is the short-, mid-, and long-term impact of the compromise or damage?

>> Whom do we report the attack to?

>> Who needs to know about the attack?

>> Can we identify who the attacker was, and how he or she did it?

>> Is the event really over, or is it likely to happen again?

>> What do we need to resume normal operations?

>> How do we prevent a similar attack in the future?

Perhaps the hardest question to answer on your own is "How were we attacked (or compromised)?" To answer that, the following steps may help in determining where a breach occurred and how attackers may have entered the network:

>> Review all systems, applications, network devices, and access control systems data logs and transaction registers.

>> Check the system security protocols and active network connections.

>> Identify all network traffic, to include all incoming and outgoing transmission of data, files, packets, and metadata.

>> Examine security event data from antivirus programs, intrusion detection systems, firewall events, and other data security applications.

Establishing continuity of operations and effecting recovery as quickly as possible

Based on your analysis of the scope of the logistics system and data attack or compromise, you should have put the applicable portions of your continuity of operation and recovery plans into effect. You will certainly have notified corporate headquarters of the situation. Your headquarters will, in turn, have analyzed whether the foreign logistics systems breach or data compromise will have had any impact on domestic operations. If necessary, your headquarters may not only activate corporate firewalls and protections, but also involve the domestic data security and teams.

Both domestic and foreign operations data recovery teams must thoroughly and effectively monitor the data flow to spot unusual and potentially malicious breaches, hacks, and events. These information security groups investigate and understand ongoing known events when there are clear indicators of compromises, either through automated reporting systems or by human detection.

REMEMBER

Know and understand the normal attributes and operation of your logistics systems and data environments. When a breach or event occurs in your foreign operation, find the root cause of the event, implement COOP and data recovery plans, and take all necessary measures at all locations to preclude the recurrence of similar disasters. Bottom line — what happens in your foreign operation affects the entire company's operations.

3

Selling What You've Already Made

IN THIS PART . . .

Understand how to select the transportation system and modes in each segment of the distribution chain that best supports your company's global operations.

Discover methods to protect your products and cargo against loss or damage, as well as how to investigate and respond to threats in your distribution chain should that protection fail.

Explore how to establish foreign points of sales; adjust domestic product configuration and packaging to enhance product acceptance by foreign customers; and create a profitable global sales strategy.

Enhance your understanding of how to deal with losses, theft, counterfeit products, damages, and returns as they relate to operating and distributing on a global level.

Chapter **10**

Moving It from "Here" to "There"

You've probably come to realize that a lot of planning must take place before you enter a new foreign market. Whereas Part 2 discusses transportation's role in foreign manufacturing operations, this chapter focuses on the movement of product that has been made domestically and is to be shipped to foreign markets for sale and distribution.

It is a common sight in many countries to see trucks, containers on trains, and even aircraft incorporate the term "logistics" in the company's name. While transportation is certainly a critical element of global sales and marketing, it is only a part of the larger whole. Given that, it is an extremely important part, as its cost and effectiveness often drive other decisions concerning your domestic inventory and production rates.

Choosing Your Transportation Modes

Most people view logistics as moving things in trucks on roads. While it's true that the trucking industry carries a large share of the traffic, there are other modes of transportation to consider as well — especially in foreign markets. It is important to choose the right mode or modes to move everything from inventory, to finished goods, to the return or disposal of used items.

Shipping by land, sea, and air — the pieces and parts

Transportation is the movement of goods from one location to another. Table 10-1 covers the major types of transportation within the supply chain network.

TABLE 10-1   **Transportation Types within the Supply Chain Network**

Mode	Carrier	Purpose or Use
Individual	Walking, bicycles, or animal conveyance	Messenger service
Airlift	Fixed wing or helicopter	Cargo or passenger movement, and emergency medical services
Sealift	Barge, container ship, or tanker	Heavy or hazardous cargo shipment
Ground	Truck or motor transport (for example, semi-trailer, armored car, light van, bus, taxi)	Time-specific cargo or personnel movement, secure delivery (such as currency or weapons)
Rail	Train, subway, or rapid transit	Long-distance, specialized or intermodal bulk freight, and passenger movement (for example, cars, refrigerated goods, and chemicals)
Pipeline	Commodity-specific line	Natural gas, water, or petroleum delivery
Other	Special conveyances (such as conveyor belts, cable cars, mining cars)	Industrial production and distribution operations

Following are some important points to keep in mind about each of these transportation types:

» **Airlift:** Air cargo services should be used when time and speed are the most important factors. It is generally the most expensive transportation mode.

» **Sealift:** Ships move the most tons of freight per mile, but they are the slowest transportation mode. However, they are very economical.

» **Ground:** Shipping by land includes trucks and specialized motor conveyances. These transport the most goods and are generally the most versatile. They are often combined with other modes of transportation to move just about everything.

» **Rail:** Freight rail service is most often used for the shipment of agricultural products, construction materials, hazardous chemicals, and large items that can't be shipped over highway. It is generally economical, and is most frequently connected with port operations (freight) and movement in and around metropolitan areas (passengers).

>> **Pipeline:** Pipelines can carry gasses, liquids, and solids in liquids (slurries). Pipelines are mostly permanent structures that transport unique products over long distances and unusual terrain, including under water.

TIP

When all factors are considered use the mode of transportation that is not just the least expensive but the one that gets product to the final destination on time, provides the appropriate protection and security, and that does so with little or no damage.

Table 10-2 provides a general comparison of the characteristics of transportation modes. Quite often the quality of transportation depends on the funding for each mode at the national or regional level. Accordingly, it's not uncommon to find highways (as an example) that differ greatly in a country, due to regional funding priorities. Further, standardization of mode characteristics — such as rail gauges and container sizes — is not universal, and disconnects between modes and between countries is often a challenge. Additionally, the more susceptible a mode is to weather conditions, the more likely it is to be unreliable at certain times of the year.

TABLE 10-2   ## Attribute Comparison of Transportation Modes

	Airlift	Sealift	Ground	Rail	Pipeline
Dependability	High	Average	High	Average	High
Availability	Average	Limited	Extensive	Low	Very Limited
Frequency	Average	Very Low	High	Low	High
Flexibility	Low	Very High	Average	High	Very Low
Speed	Very Fast	Very Slow	Fast	Average	Low

The different types of carriers include the following:

>> **Common:** Carriers transporting goods for anyone in the public market

>> **Contract:** Carriers transporting goods only for select customers based on agreements

>> **Private:** Companies transporting their own products

>> **Exempt:** Farm and commodity shippers operating under special rules

Transportation modes can be used in any combination. *Intermodal* shipping involves the transportation of freight in an intermodal container or vehicle, using multiple modes of transportation, without any handling of the freight itself when changing modes. Because intermodal shipping reduces cargo handling, it improves security, reduces damage and loss, and allows freight to be transported faster. Intermodal shipments are usually packaged in standard-sized shipping containers that are picked up and delivered by truck chassis. The loads are transferred to or from railroads or ports for movement between major shipping facilities.

Multimodal shipping entails using multiple modes and involves the physical handling of the product to fit a different container or carrier unique to the next specific mode — as in the shipment and transfer of natural gas or petroleum from pipeline to rail car to tanker. Because of the frequency of handling, it is more expensive than intermodal shipping. However, when dealing with shipments to foreign markets, it is generally the only viable option as the shipping mode is limited by the transportation infrastructure of the country to which the load is being shipped.

The less developed your foreign market's transportation infrastructure is, the more likely your transportation network will be multimodal.

When you are contracting for the delivery of goods under sales contracts for both domestic and international trade, you need to ensure that you (as the buyer of delivery services) and the seller of the delivery services have the same understanding of the terms of the delivery. The International Chamber of Commerce first published International Commercial Terms (Incoterms) in 1936 to provide internationally accepted definitions and rules of interpretation for most common commercial terms.

As of this edition, Incoterms 2010 is the most recent version and went into effect on January 1, 2011. Incoterms' rules apportion transportation costs and responsibilities between the buyer and seller of the delivery service, thereby reducing the misunderstanding among traders and minimizing trade disputes and litigation.

TIP

To obtain a copy of Incoterms 2010, go to the International Chamber of Commerce website at `www.iccwbo.org/products-and-services/trade-facilitation/incoterms-2010`.

FOB (free on board) is a term specifying at what point the seller transfers ownership of the goods to the buyer. The owner of the goods is responsible for damage or loss during transportation, so the point at which ownership is transferred becomes very important. Table 10-3 provides a general framework for FOB costs and responsibilities.

TABLE 10-3   ## FOB Costs and Responsibilities

Sales Term (Free on Board Pricing)		Who Pays for Cost of Freight	Who Is Responsible for the Cost of Freight Movement	Who Owns the Freight While in Movement	Who Files the Loss or Damage Claims
FOB	**Freight Charge Type**				
Origin	Collect	Buyer	Buyer	Buyer	Buyer
Origin	Prepaid	Seller	Seller	Buyer	Buyer
Origin	Prepaid and Charged Back	Seller	Buyer	Buyer	Buyer
Destination	Collect	Buyer	Buyer	Seller	Seller
Destination	Prepaid (Delivered)	Seller	Seller	Seller	Seller
Destination	Collect and Allowed	Buyer	Buyer	Seller	Seller

Deciding which mode is right for which product

When determining which transportation mode to use, cost is often the most important factor in your decision-making. However, the final decision will include a number of other considerations. How critical to the shipment is the need for speed? Are the items perishable, or do they have a shelf life or expiration date? What are the risks if the shipment arrives at a later time or date? Some modes and routes are more suitable for hazardous cargo than others, while other routes may restrict shipments by weight or size. This can be a major consideration with local laws, especially when crossing geographical or political borders. Valuable cargo may require a shipping mode with robust security and tracking systems that, while available domestically, may or may not be available in your foreign market. If, after analysis, the same level of shipment security and tracking is not available in the foreign market as it is domestically, corporate headquarters must ultimately make the decision to either accept the risk or develop operational alternatives.

REMEMBER

Consider the size, weight, shape, fragility, perishability, and hazards of the items to be shipped; then consider the velocity at which it can and should be moved. Efficiency helps drive down costs and creates a more environmentally friendly transportation network.

When moving your products by ground, consider the following:

>> **Pros:** Both individual and ground transportation are relatively inexpensive, very convenient, and normally the most available and flexible modes. These

modes of shipment are generally fast, reliable, and semi-secure. Often, courier services can operate more efficiently in cities where traffic can slow other delivery methods.

>> **Cons:** The use of special couriers for individual transportation is costly and restrictive, in that only smaller and lighter items are delivered over shorter distances or limited routes. Additionally, ground transportation is generally the most environmentally unfriendly mode. In addition to size and weight restrictions to contend with, traffic and construction delays are inevitable.

When moving your products by rail, consider the following:

>> **Pros:** Rail transportation is fast, efficient, more environmentally friendly, and less subject to congestion or delays. Railroads become economically viable with large ton shipments or hazardous cargo sent many miles between rail terminals.

>> **Cons:** Rail is inflexible and can be expensive. Ground transportation is usually still required on either end.

Types of railroad vehicles include

>> **Traction vehicles or self-propelled cars:** Hand trolleys or motorized track maintenance trucks.

>> **Passenger-use vehicles:** Passenger, baggage, and mail cars.

>> **Freight-use vehicles:** Box or flat cars, refrigerator containers, fuel and chemical tankers, and vehicle carriers.

>> **Container vehicles:** International standard sizes are either 10, 20, 40, or 45 feet long by 8 feet wide, with the height, depending on type of container, between 8½ and 9½ inches.

>> **Bulk freight vehicles:** Coal and grain cars and gondolas.

>> **Specialty use vehicles:** Aircraft parts, livestock cars, and circus cars.

>> **Intermodal vehicles:** Roadrailers (trucks configured to operate on both rail tracks and highways) or well cars for handling multiple containers.

When moving your products by airlift, consider the following:

>> **Pros:** Airlift is the fastest way to transport products over long distances. Cargo can be carried on both passenger and freight-only aircraft.

>> **Cons:** Airlift is expensive and not at all environmentally friendly. Size and weight matter, in terms of both price and schedule. Additional fees that can be levied

include special handling, fuel and risk surcharges, international customs, screening, and security fees. Hazardous material is often excluded from air transport. Ground transportation is usually still required on either end.

Types of aircraft include:

>> **Commercial passenger aircraft (fixed wing) and helicopters (rotary wing):** Limited cargo capacity

>> **Freight-specific aircraft:** For heavy cargo

>> **Super-freight aircraft:** Special-purpose, converted military cargo planes, generally used for air courier service

>> **Commuter aircraft:** For short hops; or for routes servicing airports with limited capability or with runway length and weight limitations

>> **General aviation aircraft:** Primarily for lightweight cargo

>> **Private or charter aircraft:** Includes unmanned drones

When moving your products by sealift, consider the following:

>> **Pros:** Compared to airlift, shipping by water is relatively inexpensive, especially in large or bulk volume. There are two methods of transporting by vessel: Liner vessels take cargo from multiple clients and adhere to standard routes and timelines, while charter vessels are contracted for specific charter, and go where and when as directed by the client.

>> **Cons:** Shipment by sealift is slow and fairly inflexible. Few inland ports are available, except on riverways, and the latest generations of supertankers require deep-water ports. Depending on the competition for berthing at the sending or receiving port, ships can be delayed for days. Ground or rail transportation is usually still required on either end.

Types of vessels include

>> **Container ships:** Carry standard-sized shipping containers

>> **Cargo ships:** Carry loose and palletized cargo

>> **Bulk carriers:** Carry unpackaged goods, like farm commodities

>> **Tankers:** Carry liquids (such as chemicals and petroleum products)

>> **Roll-on/roll-off vessels (RO/RO):** Carry rolling cargo and vehicles

Whichever method of shipment you choose, pay close attention to your carrier's restrictions, as well as its insurance requirements and coverage. You may have to obtain additional insurance to fully cover the value of your products in the event they are stolen, lost, damaged, or destroyed in shipment.

Achieving efficiency through speed and flexibility

Rapid transportation can often reduce overall business costs. Manufacturers want to reduce the time it takes to get products to customers as much as possible. An easy way to shorten the time is to locate the shipping point closer to the delivery points.

But when you are moving your products in a global market you often must rely on a network of transportation options that will vary, depending on the location of your production facility and the final destination. For example, if you are moving your domestically-manufactured products to customers located near foreign seaports or airports, your transportation requirements are more easily defined. If, however, your final destination is deep in the interior of another country or continent, you are likely going to have a much more complex distribution requirement that may depend on multiple transportation modes as well as on rapid intermodal capabilities.

Global distribution may or may not be able to rely on regionalization. Regional distribution centers are more compatible with quick-response or on-demand delivery requirements. These distribution centers may be located in outlying areas of large markets where real estate, construction, labor, and other costs are lower. Locating in areas that have access to all the transportation modes is preferred, and regional distribution centers excel at providing the rapid intermodal capability that keeps your products moving.

The speed with which your product gets to your customer is dependent on both the type of transportation mode you use as well as the time it takes to move your product between transportation modes.

Establishing, Managing, and Maintaining Your Own Fleet

Owning or leasing your own transportation fleet, versus contracting out your transportation requirements to a third party, has both advantages and disadvantages. Should you choose to own your own transportation assets, you have to be prepared to incur the expense and manage the logistics of ownership. This ownership includes having the right number of assets — both vehicles and product movers (such as forklifts, dollies, and conveyers) — in your possession and maintaining them so that they are available when needed. Alternatively, you may choose to lease your equipment and contract out its maintenance.

Deciding whether to own or lease

The choice of owning or leasing your fleet of vehicles and support equipment can come down to simple economics; however, there are many factors to consider before making the decision. For example:

>> Will the warranties on owned assets be recognized or honored in the country of your foreign operations?

>> Do the foreign leasing companies have sufficient maintenance support?

>> What are the foreign tax implications of asset ownership?

>> Are the assets that are available through foreign leasing companies compatible with your product lines' current packaging, or will you have to redesign your packaging to fit the leased equipment?

Sometimes, the best decision is a combination of both owning and leasing, depending on the types of assets required and fluctuations in supply and demand for your product.

REMEMBER

Before making any own-or-lease decisions in your new foreign location, be sure to fully investigate how those operations may differ from those in your domestic location.

When making the own-or-lease decision, you usually can consider the same factors that you may have used in making a similar decision for your domestic operations. At a minimum, these include the following:

>> **Financial benefits:** When you purchase a fleet of vehicles, you pay for the entire operation and maintenance of the vehicle over the time you own it. When you lease vehicles, you only pay for a portion of the usage of the vehicles. Purchasing can provide your business with valuable assets. But unless your company has the cash to buy vehicles without financing (which may or may not be available in your foreign location), the monthly payment is probably higher than leasing. Leasing vehicles frees up operating capital for other purposes. In addition, there may be tax benefits to leasing, yet depreciation benefits to owning. Insurance rates can also be a deciding factor: You

may have to domestically underwrite your foreign coverage. (If you can even get coverage, the premium will be significantly higher.)

>> **Incentives and discounts:** By buying or leasing in volume from a specific dealer or manufacturer, you may be able to leverage a better business deal for obtaining multiple assets. You may further save by negotiating maintenance and support services from the dealer. Consider negotiating to have your assets replaced regularly: Not only will you likely obtain a lower initial upfront cost, you will ensure the availability of future assets.

>> **Corporate image:** When you own your own assets, the company's image is reflected as vehicles get older and start to look less than pristine. With a leased fleet, employees are normally using the latest model vehicles. Additionally, operators may benefit from the latest vehicle operating, safety, navigation, and communication technologies — plus higher fuel efficiency technologies. When owning your fleet, you can more freely display your company's brand on them so they become moving advertising billboards.

>> **Administration:** When owning your assets, you must manage maintenance and support data, control your equipment inventory, consolidate invoices and costs, source insurance, and find other services that keep the assets available and operational. When leasing your assets — particularly vehicular — fleet management specialists may provide additional services such as roadside assistance, operator or driver training, and insurance coverage.

>> **Maintenance and support:** By owning the assets, you are responsible for routine servicing, maintenance, and all associated costs. When leasing, these responsibilities are left up to the fleet management partner, and the costs are often lower with predictable fixed costs. Further, because leased assets are generally newer, you should have fewer maintenance issues and less downtime to contend with.

WARNING

Much like the latest-technology generation of private sedans, newer cargo vehicles are increasingly difficult to maintain without the proper test and diagnostic equipment.

Managing fleet maintenance to avoid delays

Companies must have a well-maintained array of transportation and distribution assets so as to maintain focus on core business functions. A dedicated fleet maintenance and repair shop — whether internal to your foreign operations or as part of a leasing agreement — can keep your vehicles on the road. These shops should provide trained personnel, shop tools and equipment, and a robust repair parts inventory; allow for flexible scheduling; and provide quick turnaround times.

They need to be capable of performing both preventive and corrective maintenance, providing emergency and on-site repairs, and improving overall equipment operating reliability.

Whether you own your shop or use a leased-asset repair shop, it should track each asset's service history and parts usage, warranty information, preventive maintenance, and unscheduled maintenance or emergency repairs.

Specialized software can help manage parts inventories to ensure the parts needed for repairs are sufficiently available, thereby minimizing maintenance downtime.

Be proactive in determining your preventive maintenance practices and schedules so as to minimize downtime and reduce overall maintenance costs. Preventive maintenance schedules should be set up for each type of vehicle or support equipment so that downtime — that is, time out of service — occurs during opportune times, and not unexpectedly, when equipment is most needed or vehicles become stranded in remote locations. Scheduled services are less expensive, more convenient, and more expedient. Repair parts can be ordered so that they are available at the time maintenance is performed. If a problem is found during a preventive maintenance inspection, corrective maintenance can be performed immediately, preventing smaller problems from becoming larger ones and minimizing equipment downtime.

Establishing the optimum transportation footprint

Companies with foreign operations that transport most of the various components of the product life cycle — including raw materials, manufacturing, packaging, and customer delivery — should develop strategies to determine the optimum transportation footprint.

The size of your foreign operation's transportation network must provide for moving materials to and from the manufacturing facilities to fully meet demands and schedules. It must also allow for a certain percentage of the equipment being unavailable for a variety of reasons, ranging from requiring maintenance to awaiting parts, unavailability of fuel, equipment already in use, or perhaps a shortage of operators or drivers.

A robust record-keeping program that analyzes historical trends and statistical events allows forecasters to anticipate the proper size of the fleet at any given time in the supply and demand cycles. Other variables such as weather, road and infrastructure construction, and local holiday traffic can all have an impact on short-term fleet availability.

The equipment — whether owned or leased — may not need to reside at the company's facilities all the time. In fact, the optimum solution is to have most of the equipment out transporting goods or performing services. The local transportation footprint only needs to be sized to allow for the loading and unloading of goods, with a small amount of area designated to allow for fluctuations in delivery times. Maintenance areas must allow for vehicles or equipment that may not be able to move for extended periods.

Transportation metrics measure performance and focus on time, quality, availability, cost, profit, and reliability. They help reduce operating costs, drive revenue growth, and — ultimately — enhance shareholder value. Transportation metrics should measure the performance of internal components within the overall foreign logistics enterprise (manufacturing plant, warehouses, and distribution equipment). These metrics are used to assist managers in correctly sizing their transportation and distribution assets.

Transportation and distribution metrics may include:

>> Cost savings from consolidation (for example, storage locations)

>> Shipping and receiving performance

>> Productive miles driven

>> Order and shipment counts (that is, numbers and quantities)

>> Volume by transportation mode

>> Mode of product returns (that is, type of transportation used)

>> Frequency and cost of on-time versus delayed deliveries

>> Freight claims (for example, number and dollar value of, shipping mode)

>> Freight billing costs

Modernizing the fleet: Both hardware and software

Business strategies should include the provision of sufficient funds to allow for the modernization of new vehicles and support equipment, as well as the upgrading or refitting of existing equipment with new technology. A typical high-volume business model has a company's transportation fleet renewed about every three to five years. This is especially true of high-technology vehicles and equipment such as that used in the aviation and aerospace industries, where hardware and software upgrades are constantly released.

The reasons for modernization include providing better fuel efficiency, increasing environmental stewardship, achieving higher safety ratings, and, in the end, and expending lower costs so as to raise the company's profits. Part of this strategy can be the initial purchase of warranties that provide for the full-value replacement of failed items with newly manufactured or remanufactured items that meet the latest specifications.

TIP

Replacing equipment on a recurring and scheduled basis ensures both that the risk of failure of older assets or components is significantly diminished and that newer technology and capabilities are introduced.

At some point, you may be faced with such a drastic change in vehicle hardware and fleet support software technology that it requires an almost complete turnover of the vehicles and equipment or their computerized systems. Operator or driver training may have to be part of the new acquisition strategy, and time must be allowed for reduced productivity while employees learn to use the new items. The long-term results should be more productive asset management, equipment that is more fuel efficient and economically friendly, items that are less expensive and safer to operate, and higher levels of availability.

Using Freight Forwarders

Freight forwarders are in business to help your company ship your products on a global basis. They help with the legalities of customs, taxes, and tariffs. They can also provide transportation for both unusual shipments and shipments to remote or geographically hostile environments. They can also assist in avoiding transportation events that don't go as smoothly as you planned.

Using experts to ship internationally

Until such time as a company has developed sufficient experience with international shipping, it can be advantageous to hire experts who understand the complexity of international shipping, including the specifics of customs rules and regulations. Shipping items to foreign countries can be a labor-intensive and time-consuming process, involving paperwork, tariffs, and countless regulations. International shipping experts can make international shipping efforts go smoothly.

International shipping experts can also provide packing and shipping guarantees that can reimburse the cost of loss or repair to damaged items. And because this is their primary business, they have unmatched flexibility to allow for guaranteed and timely delivery in most of their markets.

Dealing with customs, taxes, and tariffs

International customs processes and procedures can be extremely complex, and if not handled correctly can result in significant delays. Marketing products for global distribution requires an in-depth knowledge of how customs-levied charges are calculated, especially if a product's final sale price includes all transportation costs.

Tariffs (or duties) are taxes levied by governments on the value — including freight and insurance costs — of imported products. Countries set tariffs based on the specific product being imported. Additional national and local sales taxes, and sometimes customs fees, can also be charged. The tariff and other assessments are collected when clearing customs in foreign ports. These tariffs and taxes increase the end cost of products to foreign buyers. This can have a huge impact on market competition. Knowing the buyer's post-assessment cost is necessary to price products in each market.

The cost of these duties and taxes can range from very high to very low, depending on each country, and the country's political relationship with your own country on any given day. Your country may qualify for duty-free entry into countries with free-trade agreements. Most countries are members of one or more multilateral and bilateral agreements. And while "free trade" is a misnomer (*free trade* often means the tariffs are not to exceed the lowest tariff levied on any one of the member nations), the net price of goods is much less in countries with agreements.

Once in country and when storing products in a customs-bonded warehouse, you may only have to pay the associated customs fees after a sales order has been shipped from that warehouse. As such, this type of warehouse can provide a significant cost advantage in that it puts less strain on your initial import cash requirements.

REMEMBER

Customs, tariffs (duties), and taxes can significantly add to an item's final sale price.

Accommodating and managing the exceptional shipment

Shippers use standard-size and -weight shipping boxes, pallets, and containers both to estimate shipping costs and to use standardized transportation equipment. However, items to be shipped occasionally fall into the category of "other."

Examples of "other" items are live animals, hazardous materials, military weapons, and hazardous agents. Extremely large items or those that do not fit within normal shipping packaging boundaries are called *out of gauge.* These include pre-assembled items such as agricultural machinery, wind turbine blades, and large outdoor works of art.

Knowing the location of the cargo's center of gravity is critical to prevent it from shifting off the flat rack during transit, resulting in damage and/or injuries. The weight of the cargo should be centered on the flat rack. If possible, mark the center of gravity on the exterior of crates for handling and securing reference purposes. The weight must be properly distributed and the cargo properly lashed in place to prevent movement during shipping.

Cargo that is over height, over length, or over width or has dimensions that protrude outside of the normal shipping envelope areas should be marked in red or yellow in order both to clearly identify the product shape and to help prevent possible handling damage. Depending upon the type, size, and nature of the cargo, the shipper may require special deck loading or even on-deck stowage.

The shipment of hazardous goods is of significant concern. The United Nations (UN) Committee and Subcommittee of Experts on the Transport of Dangerous Goods is composed of representatives from many countries around the world. The UN Model Regulations were developed as a tool to promote consistency in international hazardous materials regulations worldwide. While they are not legally binding, they are used as a basis for the international as well as the national regulations of many countries. Most countries have developed their own set of regulations for the shipment of hazardous goods by air, sea, and ground.

Unusual shipments may require special handling and handling equipment to ensure the health of all those involved in the shipment, even to possibly include the cargo.

WARNING

If you are shipping human or animal food products, understand that there have been recent rule changes in several countries. These rules require the transporters to follow best practices for sanitary transportation, such as properly refrigerating food, adequately cleaning vehicles between loads, and properly protecting the food products during transportation.

There are shippers that specialize in all types of cargos. They have procedures for palletizing and crating that meet international safety rules and regulations for these types of shipments. When a situation falls outside of everything that has been shipped so far, consult the regulatory agencies within the country of origin, the destination country, and all countries that the items must travel through.

Handling the exceptions, hiccoughs, and delays

Shipments don't always arrive as expected, for any number of reasons. The items may have been incorrectly entered into databases, barcodes incompletely or incorrectly read, items sorted and sent on the wrong truck to the wrong destination, and many other possibilities. When an error is caught and corrected soon enough, the impact can be minimal. Otherwise, significant delays can occur that may have far-reaching impact on the shipment's financials.

Shipment delay is one of the major risks to any company. Delay insurance can be purchased, and special geo-tracking devices can be placed on containers or individual items to help ensure timely arrival. If the items are eventually delayed — or more critically, lost — then the monetary investment in insurance or tracking devices is justified. Obviously, minimizing financial loss is of no consolation if the shipment is critical to a time-sensitive mission or process.

TIP

Continuous and detailed communication must occur between shippers and receivers to identify and locate potential problems so as to minimize and prevent shipping delays during all phases of the global shipment.

Package shipments that once were stamped "allow 6 to 8 weeks for international delivery" are now being received in two to three days even if you didn't pay extra for one-day delivery. You can now track packages on many sellers' and shippers' online websites. You have all the shipping tracking numbers at your fingertips, along with the contact information of whom to call if the items are delayed. So, while packages still get lost, at least the transparency within the shipping process lowers risk by allowing the shipper and receiver to make plans to mitigate the risk in a timely manner.

Planning for what could — and does — go wrong

Any time a shipment leaves one destination for another, there is always the risk that it will not reach the intended destination. Plans need to be in place to minimize risk. If the risk is great enough, use multiple carriers, ship on multiple routes, and, if need be, ship redundant items to be sure that at least one of the shipments arrives at the right place, on time, and in the proper condition.

Common shipping mistakes include the following:

>> Selection of the wrong shipping service

>> Inexperience with shipping to specific locations

>> Lack of proper documentation (such as waybills, bills-of-lading, freight bills, and other necessary paperwork)

>> Incomplete shipper and consignee (that is, receiver) information

>> Needless address corrections or constant redirection to different destinations

>> Improper packaging or damage prevention (usually the result of a failure to consider or adapt to the shipment environments)

>> Improper handling techniques and equipment

>> Lack of description for customs documentation and inspections

>> Failure to get the proper help with international shipping services

Embedding agility and flexibility to keep moving

To ensure shipments are made when needed, flexibility in the date or time when items are shipped must be maintained. On-call pickup can provide that flexibility, as long as the items won't sit in the distribution warehouse for an extended period of time (for example, waiting for the next scheduled truck, rail, or ship departure). Current shipping technology must be flexible enough to accommodate different fuels, speeds, weather, and operating conditions, while still optimizing shipping agility and efficiency.

REMEMBER

Your company's foreign operation distribution plans should allow for the inevitable transportation delays.

Shipments are "flexible" if they can be allocated and adjusted in response to consumer demand while still in transit. At that point the shipment becomes a mobile warehouse, and its cargo becomes inventory to be managed while still in transit. During times of unusually high demand or a natural disaster, shipments may be directed from areas that can better absorb delay to areas where the safe and timely arrival of the cargo is of a much more critical nature.

It is essential to know both what and where shipments are in the pipeline and to have almost instantaneous access to shipment tracking information. Being in direct communication with the shipping dispatchers is necessary to redirect cargo. All the regulatory permissions and accounting paperwork must be in place to allow shipments to seamlessly proceed to the next destination. You should be able to instantly access, analyze, and react to any changes in supply and demand.

Getting it to the right place
for the right cost

Companies must maintain cost-effective and high-performance distribution and transportation networks. To deal with increasing demand, shipping managers should collaborate and share shipping forecasts with their carriers so as to allow them time to offer the best routing options. Developing partnership relationships with carriers ensures free-flowing information and rapid decision-making capabilities.

Take advantage of supply-chain volatility. The best route may not necessarily be the fastest given the other considerations of efficiency and economy, but may offer the least risk. Shipping managers can employ modeling techniques to measure the true cost of all routing options. Total costs include actual shipping costs as well as the potential costs to your company if there are problems.

TIP

Analyze the variables that affect your current global transportation and distribution network, and create plans to take advantage of models that allow for adjustments based on routing, infrastructure, technology, or capacity improvements.

Shipping managers should also plan for the future by engaging with carriers early to determine the impact of shipping technology and infrastructure expansion on their existing distribution networks. Review how effective existing transportation and distribution chains are to determine their likelihood of meeting both current and projected demands. Review the current level of internal and external influences on the processes and predict what that level may look like in the next year, five years, and beyond.

By incorporating these techniques into your transportation and distribution strategies, your company becomes better positioned to adjust to changing dynamics. The result is more efficient and cost-effective strategies to get the right products to the right place to meet your overall global goals and objectives.

Chapter **11**

Keeping Everything Secure

You've decided to distribute your domestically manufactured products globally and have invested heavily in their production and distribution. But how safe are your investments? When you're operating in a global environment, there are many concerns.

Even domestic distribution chains can experience delays caused by natural or man-made incidents. Your goods will inevitably experience damage or loss. This chapter discusses some of the reasons for interruptions in your distribution chain and how to account for them.

Identifying Potential Distribution Chain Threats

A host of things can go wrong with your global distribution chain, either through natural or man-made events. Because your global distribution chain is a continuous chain made up of various entities called "links," the weakest links need to be identified to prevent unnecessary failures that would negatively impact your company and its foreign operations.

Planning for natural and man-made breaks in the distribution chain

Distribution chain disruptions can have negative long-term effects on a company's profitability and its reputation. Small companies are particularly vulnerable to failure within the distribution chain because they typically have fewer shipping options. However, by identifying the most common failures and planning accordingly, breaks in the chain do not have to be major or catastrophic events.

Identify and evaluate all possible risks facing your company. Begin with the natural hazards that are prevalent in the customer's regions (for example: hurricanes, floods, inclement weather, or earthquakes), along with other disruptions that might occur in the local community, such as chemical leaks or power outages. Then look for possible human risks such as labor shortages or strikes, sabotage, and terrorism.

As an example, if a despondent person threatens to jump off a railroad overpass onto the tracks below, the ensuing standoff with authorities inadvertently holds up railroad traffic on the major mainlines. Stopped trains straddling grade crossings prevent truck traffic from reaching highways. Local businesses are disrupted as local traffic that normally flows over the bridge has to be rerouted onto secondary and tertiary roads. The smallest inconvenient act can cause major impacts to several transportation modes at once.

TIP

There are many other reasons for breaks in your global distribution chain. They range from vandalism or theft, black-market and counterfeit sales competition, and smuggling of inferior goods to piracy and terrorism, or even sabotage.

The following may help your company prepare for most distribution-chain disasters:

>> **All distribution chains have an element of risk.** While the risks cannot be eliminated, they can be managed. The best solution is to make the chain more agile. If possible, have multiple shippers and backup shipping and distribution plans.

>> **Ask shippers to do their own risk assessment.** Find out whether they're prepared to handle the same types of interruptions as your own company is prepared to handle.

- » **Assess your vulnerability by reviewing the services or products each supplier or vendor supports.** Where are they located? Are they the sole source for this product?

- » **Communication is imperative before, during, and after any disruption.** Identify all stakeholders — including carriers, distribution centers, and customers — and make sure you have their primary and alternate contacts' information. Ensure they all understand their associated responsibilities during events that "break" the distribution process.

- » **Complex global distribution chains require close monitoring to catch issues early and mitigate problems as they occur.** Having historical data from similar events can assist in quick resolutions.

- » **Develop recovery plans, test them often, and update the plans on a regular schedule.** These plans can also be part of your customer's disaster recovery plans, since your company is a part of your customer's community.

- » **Know where your goods are at all times to proactively react to disaster situations.** Shipments may need to be diverted or rerouted away from the disaster area to minimize or mitigate disruptions.

- » **Use multiple suppliers or carriers in diverse regions and geographic locations that can supply vital components following a localized disaster.** Have relationships with alternate carriers in case the primary shippers also suffered the same interruption or natural disaster.

Identifying the weakest links in the chain

A weak or broken link in any part of your distribution chain can have a domino effect. Most distribution chains consist of more than just a few shippers and carriers. They often involve third parties, product distributors, service providers, manufacturers, contractors, and logistics partners. All are dependent on electric and utility companies, Internet providers, communication services, and the transportation infrastructure. And, they are likely to have their own interdependent distribution networks.

Analyze the strength of your distribution chain by identifying the critical providers, and then prioritize their importance to your operations. Identify the risks based on any disruption caused by any problem they may encounter. To conduct this analysis, you need to ask:

- » Which products or services do you most depend on for profitability, reputation, and competitive advantage?

>> What time-sensitive activities, services, or systems are those whose disruption or failure would severely interrupt your company's operations?

>> Which of your suppliers' products or services are so critical that an interruption would seriously affect your company's ability to deliver its products?

>> What alternatives do you have if sole source providers can no longer deliver to your company or if they go out of business?

Safeguarding the bottom line from distribution chain failures

Select suppliers who take a "best practices" approach to risk management and business continuity planning. Strengthen your links by choosing shippers and carriers that offer to help you stay in business following natural and man-made disasters. Planning for distribution chain disruptions reduces your company's financial vulnerability and provides a competitive edge in the global economy.

WARNING

Watch for early warning signs of provider trouble, such as lengthening or consistently delayed cycle and delivery times, or changes regarding the provider's management structure or ownership.

Select the best and most reliable shippers and carriers for your company. The least-expensive providers aren't always the most reliable. Develop close relationships with your providers and understand their issues and challenges — and make sure that they understand yours. While single-source shippers may reduce complexity, multiple suppliers reduce distribution chain vulnerability.

Monitor geographical regions where natural and man-made disasters are common. Determine which of your distribution providers are located in those areas and how they would be affected. Then, involve your providers in your business continuity plans and exercises so that they understand their role in the overall success of the partnership.

Combating Piracy: On and Off the Seas

Piracy isn't just about swashbucklers. It's an increasingly serious threat to companies that operate in the global marketplace. Piracy happens just as easily on land or in the air as it does on the seas. Like any risk, the causes for piracy need to be fully understood to plan for them and mitigate the risk of loss of life or goods, as well as recover from the act.

Understanding the cause and avoiding the risks

Piracy is a major problem on some highly-traveled global trade routes along the Indian Ocean, Gulf of Aden, and South China Seas (among other routes). It makes international trade both risky and expensive. Pirates attack civilian ships and capture their crew members; then they resell the high-value cargo goods while holding the hostages for ransom. According to one international trade association, losses due to piracy in the Horn of Africa, alone, are in the billions of dollars each year.

Acts of piracy include the following aspects:

>> The loss of cargo delays product deliveries and results in significant financial loss.

>> Rerouting vessels around high-risk areas increases shipping times and transportation expenses while unnecessarily lengthening the distribution chain.

>> Because of higher risks of attack, shipping companies pay higher insurance premiums. The costs are passed down and ultimately increase the end price of the product.

>> Piracy is a threat to labor. Crew members for high-risk routes are harder to recruit. Those who do sign on command higher salaries. This also increases shipping and product costs.

Piracy aggravates the economics of distribution-chain operations by decreasing the availability of goods and reducing the number of available cargo vessels. Shipping companies pay large ransoms to free captured ships and crews, often leading to bankruptcy, and thus threatening the entire shipping industry operating in those high-risk routes.

REMEMBER

Piracy isn't restricted to just the high seas. It occurs on land and in the air.

Truck semi-trailers and containers on trailer chassis are relatively easy to steal. Cargo theft continues to grow by clever and organized cargo thieves. Cargo theft is a lucrative criminal enterprise, yielding easy and lucrative returns. Almost all are proficient in the logistics of piracy.

Most thefts occur when trucks are left unattended in unsecured parking lots. Consumable goods are the most frequently stolen cargo, followed by consumer electronics, and then home and garden products.

Railroad thefts have occurred since the building of the rail systems, especially when cars are left unattended on side rails. With the cars, trailers, and containers often stretching for miles or more in remote locations, thieves have an excellent chance of finding something valuable and desirable while not getting caught in the process.

Thieves usually don't know what is in many of the cars or containers without some knowledge provided by someone "inside." Without prior knowledge, there is an equal chance of finding less useful raw materials as there is of finding high-end electronic consumer products. Equipment is being redesigned to physically prevent doors from being opened while the train's manifest is being assembled. The good news is that it has become relatively easy for law-enforcement officials in many countries to track down and catch rail cargo thieves.

Air piracy, by definition, only involves the extremely rare hijacking of aircraft. Hijacking aside, thefts often occur during the handling of cargo at or near the airport. These thefts are smaller in size, but the goods taken are usually many times more valuable.

Protecting everyone's investment

Shippers are encouraged to avoid pirates by sailing in corridors that are relatively and routinely protected by a coalition of naval vessels with the specific mission of preventing piracy. However, pirates are extremely resourceful, nimble, and usually violent, and almost always rely on larger companion vessels for their logistical support. The lure of a quick, multimillion-dollar payday is often too great to resist.

REMEMBER

With electronic tracking and satellite global-positioning technology becoming more sophisticated, it is getting harder, but not impossible, for thieves to succeed in high-seas piracy.

Crimes of theft result from highly specific opportunities. They are usually concentrated in time and place and dependent on movements scheduled on a consistent basis. One crime often produces the opportunity for another. Some products offer more tempting crime opportunities than others. Changes in technology constantly offer new opportunities to commit crimes. While the opportunities for crime can be reduced, reducing the opportunities doesn't usually displace the crime. But reductions can be accomplished by focused efforts on reducing the opportunities to commit most crimes.

Planning for and recovering from acts of piracy

Incidents of piracy and theft increase shipping costs and transit times. They jeopardize the tight schedules that many distribution chains rely on. Rising insurance premiums in high-risk areas affect everyone. Buyers and carriers must decide to reroute freight to longer, safer, and more expensive routes. Smaller shipping companies may continue to gamble on the risk of being attacked and having their cargo stolen on the shorter and faster routes.

Suppliers in less-stable financial positions are more likely to take risks to minimize cost. But, even if the cargo arrives safely, that gamble might not save money after paying the insurance premiums. Just the threat of piracy or theft could be enough to put a carrier out of business. By continuing to operate in pirate-prone areas, carriers continue to enable the occurrence of piracy.

REMEMBER

Identify which of your company's transportation providers are vulnerable to piracy and theft, based on security practices and historical events. Designate alternate carriers for high-risk cargo. Determine how critical each shipment is to your company's bottom line. The goal is to try to run nearly perfect distribution chains in an imperfect world.

Screening Cargo: Both Coming and Going

Cargo is screened for compliance with shipping laws and regulations, and also to stop the flow of contraband between countries. The shipments may be screened on both ends of the distribution chain to curb the flow of illegal items, look for stolen goods, provide for public and environmental safety, and prevent the export of national treasures. In addition to mandatory government screening, shippers can help by performing voluntary screenings to help prevent unnecessary delays from illegal items sneaking into cargo.

Sharing the load: Your role in screening

It is not just the government's responsibility to ensure that your shipments meet all national and regional regulatory requirements. While their main focus is to catch contraband goods before they leave or enter the country, it is the shipper's responsibility to ensure they are not present in the first place.

Companies need to balance cargo screening requirements with demands for swift delivery of goods. Many governments are pushing for 100 percent screening.

Screening has the effect of slowing down the distribution chain. Sharing the burden between government agencies and the transportation industry helps expedite the process and release shipments sooner.

Some regulatory agencies allow shippers, freight forwarders, logistics services providers, and air carriers to screen cargo at their own facilities before moving it by a secure chain of custody to the port, where it can go directly onto the aircraft or vessel without undergoing additional screening. This is creating an industry of independent cargo-screening firms.

Third-party security companies can help with screening and security issues by offering the following services:

>> Screening (X-ray, explosive, physical, botanical, food service)

>> Chain-of-custody escort for shipments and cargo

>> Controlled access to aircraft, ship, and warehouse shipments and cargo

>> Trace (swiping for material) and bulk (visual tunnel) screening services

TIP

The screening process creates a distributed, shared network that allows screening to be performed at the most cost-effective point in the distribution chain. This helps mitigate the impact of screening on costs and expedites the shipment of cargo to your global market destinations.

Building and costing delay in the distribution schedule

Because it's *not* a perfect world where global shipments get to their end destination without delay to the customer, as promised, your domestic production-line output must be adjusted to accommodate those delays and their costs.

Delay occurs when actual delivery dates differ from contracted delivery dates. The duration of a delay is an essential piece of information required both to help in determining the reason for each delay and adjusting domestic production schedules.

On-demand production and "just in time" deliveries are becoming attractive operational practices not only to minimize distribution delay but also to reduce the amount of warehouse space and inventory footprint, and streamline the flow of production. However, the tighter delivery schedules get, the more delays become inevitable. Managers must be able to determine the potential of cost of delay and determine whether it is manageable or detrimental to the overall business goals and objectives.

Delay can sometimes be predicted based on historical data from within your company, using data provided by similar companies or from those of governmental watchdogs. Delay may be random, systemic in nature, or seasonal. It may be brought about by political unrest, unpredictable weather, or change within the transportation infrastructure.

REMEMBER

While delay is not completely preventable, domestic production schedules should factor in delay to better manage disruption of the distribution chain.

Whatever the root causes of delay, there is both acceptable and unacceptable variability. Statistics should be kept to understand the reason for delay, the length of delay, and any action to be taken to decrease or prevent delay in the future.

Dealing with quarantines or impoundment

Shipments and cargo may be seized by a governmental or law-enforcement agency if they have reasonable cause. The reasons can be many, but usually stem from either an infraction of the law, a hazard to public safety, incomplete paperwork, or when temporary seizure is just a standard practice upon entering a certain country.

Cargo may be quarantined either temporarily or permanently to prevent the spread of infected or infested items. The regulated items might be treated, returned to the shipper or to a quarantined area, or destroyed in a manner so as to prevent further infestation.

Fees are often associated with the quarantine or impoundment and must be paid when and if the shipment or items are released back in the owner's custody. Cash bonds paid can include the total charges against the cargo, interest, administrative costs, and attorney's fees.

Usually, all costs of quarantine are ultimately borne by the shipper: While the carrier may initially pay the costs, they are either directly passed on to the shipper as reimbursable expenses or included in the upfront shipping cost.

In most countries, highway or rail accidents that involve cargo of edible products may be immediately impounded for reasons of public health. If the shipment involves potentially hazardous foods, proper temperature must be maintained at all times. In order to salvage these types of shipments, arrangements must be made by the firm shipping the product to keep the cargo properly refrigerated. The quality and temperature of the food products being held must be evaluated and verified by health department authorities prior to being released back to the carrier.

WARNING

Quarantined and impounded cargos are disruptions to the distribution chain that must be planned for and managed to reduce the overall cost and distribution impact.

When cargo is impounded for any reason, a receipt should be given to the carrier that identifies the cargo or items impounded, the date impounded, where it is being taken and stored, the names of the impounding authorities, and other pertinent legal information. The carrier or freight-forwarding agent normally has the right to an administrative hearing to try to get the cargo back within a specified amount of time. It is important to note both that this entire process can significantly differ from country to country, depending on what point in the distribution chain the cargo is impounded, and that the same cargo could be impounded at multiple points.

Dealing with Dunnage, Demurrage, and Damage

It goes without saying that it's extremely important to protect cargo during shipment. Just as dry goods packages often state "some settling of the contents may occur during shipping and handling," unexpected things can happen to cargo — or even to the shipping vessels, vehicles, or the transportation infrastructure itself. Losses due to avoidable damage should be minimized at least and eliminated at best.

Further costs can be incurred if demurrage charges are levied for the late return of shipping containers, truck trailers, or rail cars, or if ships are not released on time. Sometimes delays are caused by problems in loading and unloading cargo, or if the cargo itself causes damage requiring immediate repair to the carrier.

Controlling loss and damage in shipment

Losses and damage can easily result during transport due to the movement or shifting of cargo. To prevent such loss or damage, cargo is stabilized for shipment. This stabilization is called *dunnage* and is typically made up of loose materials used to support, brace, and protect cargo while in transit.

The use of separators to distinguish one customer's load from another can sometimes be designed so as to also serve as dunnage. Dunnage items are usually the property of the carrier, although sometimes the shipper may partner with the carrier to provide permanent, recyclable solutions to protect cargo.

Inflatable air bags are gaining popularity, as they conform easily to the space between the items shipped. Another degree of protection incorporates lashing cargo to vessels and vehicles. Lashing can consist of ropes, cables, wires, chains, rods, tensioners, turnbuckles, and other mechanical devices. To be effective, they should be of a suitable size and capacity for the weight of the cargo to be secured and approved by a regulatory agency. Excessive wear and subsequent failure of the lashings, along with damage caused by cargo rubbing, can be reduced or prevented by using chafing protection.

WARNING

Cargo must be adequately secured and protected from all predicted hazards while in transit.

Wooden packaging and dunnage coming into many countries has to meet strict guidelines, including being heat-treated, fumigated, and de-barked; and labeled or marked accordingly. Wood that is too green is never suitable for stabilizing cargo. In areas of high humidity, dunnage must also allow for air circulation and moisture drainage to protect cargo from weather or sea spray.

Minimizing the impact of shipment loss and damage

Most cargo losses should be preventable. For the small percentage that is not, many factors are involved when calculating the true financial cost of lost or damaged shipments. At a minimum these include interruptions to the distribution chain, higher insurance premium and claim costs, expedited freight assessments, and lost revenues and opportunities from cancelled deliveries.

Properly prepared, packed, and marked shipments have the greatest chance of being delivered without damage or loss. Applying the basic principles and techniques of packing for long-haul distribution helps reduce loss of cargo from theft, improper handling and transport, and unforeseen natural disasters.

Damage can result from improper cargo handling equipment and techniques used by unskilled labor. The transit environment (for example, rough seas, turbulent air, or substandard roads) can subject cargo to extreme motion and impact. Efforts to reduce the amount of time and expenses in tracing, locating, and making adjustments for lost, damaged, or stolen goods contribute to a healthier company financial status.

REMEMBER

While loss of and damage to global shipments is never totally avoidable, taking proactive measures to reduce known risk significantly minimizes its impact on both the entire distribution chain and domestic operations.

Chapter **12**

Making the Sale

There's an old saying in business: "Give the customers what they want." If you're considering expanding your business to a foreign market, you have most likely been successful in providing your domestic customers what they want. But have you fully considered what the customers want in your new foreign marketplace? Even if you're convinced that they want the products you manufacture, have you given sufficient thought to how your foreign customers expect the product to be packaged, delivered, and supported?

In this chapter, we will discuss some of the ways logistics can support the delivery and sale of your product to your foreign customer, in a manner that provides customer satisfaction at a competitive price.

Identifying and Establishing Your Points of Sale

A common practice when expanding one's marketplace to a foreign location is to start by completing a test distribution of your product that is then followed by a survey of your potential customers. This test distribution can be done independently if you are confident you have sufficiently identified your foreign customers *and* have a means of getting your product to them. But often the test distribution is accomplished by partnering with a complementary company that already has an established customer base and distribution network in the country you're targeting. For example, if you're manufacturing sports clothing, conduct your test distribution in partnership with a company that is already selling sports shoes in your potential market.

When conducting your test distribution, you need to ensure that you receive the necessary feedback to identify what modifications may be needed to your domestic product to better ensure customer acceptance. There are several ways the survey can be conducted, but a survey that includes both on-site personnel asking about the acceptance of your product as well as providing the ability for the customer to submit the completed survey electronically seems to work the best.

Logistics is important in enhancing overall market strategies. There have been numerous studies concerning what customers want: Value at a competitive price, quality and reliability, good customer service, and ease of doing business are all at the top of most lists. Sales are increased when products are readily available at the time and place desired.

Leveraging logistics to enhance your marketing strategy

Logistics can provide a competitive advantage by leveraging excellent supply-chain distribution linked to your overall marketing strategies. When all else is equal, superior logistics performance may be the best marketing tool because it provides unparalleled recognized value for customers. Logistics capabilities are often very difficult to imitate by competitors.

Managers striving to achieve competitive advantages by leveraging their logistics must understand the role that logistics plays in a company's overall marketing strategy. Logisticians are trained to focus on reducing costs and improving efficiencies. They have to become experts in unusual problem solving. They develop relationships with diverse partners to provide continuous support throughout the entire business process. Logistics is often the last point of contact between the manufacturer and the customer. Making a positive impact on customer satisfaction will ultimately improve corporate profitability and shareholder value.

TIP

Customers have to be convinced that your company will do everything it can to produce and deliver your product to them in a timeline that meets their expectations.

When part of the overall marketing strategy, logistics can result in more efficient operations, more satisfied customers, increased market share, and higher profitability. Your customers must know that the overall performance of the supply chain is very important to *both* the company and its customers.

Market research identifies what customers need and expect in the way of logistics and supply chain activities. These customer needs and expectations should be promoted along with those of the usual product-placement marketing attributes. Customers have to be convinced that the company has their best interests in mind when it comes to providing competitive logistics elements, such as optimum packaging and delivery times.

Adapting your product and packaging to satisfy customer needs

Consumers are concerned not only with the product's design and operation but also with such additional features as warranties and user guides or instructions. You may find that minor modifications to your product — for example, product color or the way cautions are displayed — will enhance your product in your new foreign market. But, you must then weigh the costs associated with making those changes, to ensure you can still retain your cost competitiveness.

Product packaging is important for many reasons. In addition to protecting the merchandise, it can also become a factor in how the items are shipped, marketed, stored, and displayed. Often (in Japan, for example), the packaging is as important or valuable to the customer as the product it contains. Products must also be packaged to create efficiency and economy within your foreign distribution chain. When possible, your packaging should be sized and shaped to maximize the number of units that can be shipped within a given amount of space.

"Green" logistics is driving toward reusable and recyclable consumer packaging, boxing, palletizing, and shipping containers. But in some countries with limited natural resources, the wooden pallets and shipping crates themselves provide a much-needed and highly sought-after resource for raw material and construction needs, so little gets returned for reuse.

Each foreign market country may have its own set of packaging and labeling rules and regulations. These are designed to protect the public from any hazards from either the packaging or the contents within. Effective markings and labeling will further protect both the contents and anything that comes in contact with the products.

TIP

Packaging must be designed so as to meet regulatory requirements, yet still be attractive to the consumer.

Branding and labeling products in global markets must be carefully considered. International brand names are used to globally identify products, while local brands and private labels must be able to create and sustain local interest. Colors used on labels and packages must be attractive to foreign buyers while not being culturally offensive. Specific colors or color combinations may produce negative messages in your foreign marketplace.

Labeling and instructions must be produced in official or customary languages when required by law, and easily understood within the market. Translations must be correct for the dialects. Detailed information regarding the product's content may need to be included, along with the content's country of origin. Weights and measures must be stated using local and international units. Further, it is very important for the product's packaging to provide an accurate description of both its volume and weight in the country-specific units of measurement (for example, kilograms or liters versus ounces or pounds).

Working with national and regional agencies to establish your territories

To gain penetration into global markets, national and regional agencies can assist companies with both establishing international territories and marketing requirements. Agencies such as local trade associations can help determine the customer demographics, point out primary and secondary markets, and identify the potential market share within the total geographical areas to be served. They work closely with organizations to help create timely and cost-effective distribution chains.

Agency assistance may include the following:

>> Identification of regional carriers and logistics intermediaries

>> Evaluation of potential regional partners

>> Promotion of regional import and export law compliance

>> Assistance with the development of logistics strategies and processes for entering specific territories

Building a Winning Strategy

Companies almost always want to grow larger and become more profitable. Their goal is to find and attract more and more customers to purchase and use their products. Having said that, be aware that increased sales result in the requirement for increased management of the local distributors. Part of that management will involve setting realistic goals and metrics within the company's strategic plans and objectives.

Growing a customer base for your product

Successful companies understand their market's needs and desires. New customers are gained by communicating the benefits of the company's products and services to the individuals who want them. Many entrepreneurs fail to define their potential customers or lack the skills, resources, and strategies necessary to establish business relationships with them. An effective logistics marketing plan that focuses on promoting the supply chain is essential.

Create customer loyalty. Providing customers with exceptional service will turn them into loyal, word-of-mouth champions for your business. Their recommendations cost nothing and are the most effective form of advertising. Design a referral program that rewards customers for bringing others into the customer base.

Contact potential customers by direct communication — either by mail, telephone, or email. Do your homework to identify your potential customers' basic needs. What types of products do they currently own? How long have they used them? What are their future needs?

Assuming that 80 percent of a company's business will come from 20 percent of its customer base, concentrate on growing the business from that 20 percent by identifying which of those 20 percent can provide the greatest amount of return (that is, new business) for the least amount of costs (that is, new product development).

Consider partnering with companies that are important to the customer base but that are not in competition with your business. Partners can leverage off of each other's customer base.

REMEMBER

The effort required to find, identify, and attract a new customer is greater than that needed to retain an existing one.

Turn single-product customers into multiple-product customers by introducing them to other products in your line. Also, remember that once you've lost a customer it's extremely hard to get that customer's business back. Increase loyalty by informing and educating customers about alternate choices that benefit their bottom line, as well as yours.

Using local distributors to manage your sales

Local and regional distributors, such as sales agents and wholesalers, can be very helpful in selling your company's products. Sales agents and distributors are usually well established in your primary targeted markets. There is little need to build your own markets from the ground up.

Using a sales agent and wholesaler is very advantageous when operating within new foreign markets where your organization lacks experience and expertise. When selling to agents or distributors, you must convince them that they will also benefit by representing your company.

Manage distributors by keeping them up-to-date with your product and marketing information. Communication must be two-way, so that you also stay informed of how well the distributors are performing. Develop working relationships with distributors to provide as much support as they require. This may require your providing product training, participating in sales planning, and providing joint promotions.

Distributors are entitled to the same logistics support and customer service as direct customers. They can easily become disenchanted with companies that let them and their customers down. Here are some suggestions for selecting and working with local distributors:

>> Select distributors based on previous successes.

>> Maintain control over the marketing strategy — after all, it's *your* product that they're selling.

>> Confirm that distributors are capable of developing new markets.

>> Use local distributors for long-term partners, not just to gain entry into markets.

>> Commit financial resources, management, and proven marketing strategies to support market entry.

>> Require distributors to provide detailed market and financial performance data and statistics.

Setting realistic distribution metrics

Distribution metrics must track your company's actual performance. Focus on a limited number of measurements that are of value to decision-making. Overanalyzing performance data can cause confusion and lead to conflicting goals. Limit the number of key performance indicators to only those that can be readily measured and controlled.

These metrics are used with planned goals and objectives to track distributor performance to see whether they are meeting your company's expectations. Include company goals when setting supply-chain targets, since supply-chain objectives must not conflict with basic company objectives.

Know and understand exactly what it is being measured. Find out what drives and causes changes within the metrics, as well as how the metrics identify failure. Measure the data that you have direct control over. Metrics need to be able to identify areas of improvement. Benchmark or baseline the current data, and set goals based on how and in what areas the company plans to improve upon the metrics. Set a time limit as to when the goals should be reached before new goal-setting measures are initiated.

REMEMBER

You will know where to focus your efforts by using the right metrics with the proper goals.

Identifying the right distribution metrics can be challenging. One methodology we recommend is the use of "SMART" goals. "SMART" criteria are commonly attributed to Peter Drucker's concept of "Management by Objectives" in the mid-1950s. The first known use of the acronym SMART occurred in the November 1981 issue of *Management Review* by George T. Doran:

Specific: State exactly what is being measured so that there is complete understanding between the company and distributors about how each metric is calculated.

Measurable: Distribution metrics must be reliable and repeatable so that they accurately measure supplier performance.

Attainable: Distribution targets must provide a reasonable stretch to be reached, but not so lofty as to be unattainable or unrealistic.

Realistic: Plan only a few things that can be successful rather than many things (thus being unsuccessful in the effort). Distribution goals should be challenging, but realistic.

Timely: There must be a schedule as to when goal percentages must be obtained by, and a final date when 100 percent of the goal effort is complete or reevaluated.

REMEMBER

Distribution optimization is not difficult to achieve. But the right metrics must be in place when setting goals so as to be able to focus resources on those things that can be changed.

"Capturing" the Sale

After successfully marketing and gaining customers, a global point-of-sale strategy must be implemented, and customer loyalty must be gained and retained to continue those sales.

Designing and managing a global "point-of-sale" strategy

Global point-of-sale strategies should ease the management of recording sales and provide an improved return on investment. Point-of-sale applications should include receiving payments, printing bills, managing inventory, and carrying out loyalty programs. Global point-of-sale systems must increase the reliability and security of collected data in comparison to traditional sales systems. The higher reliability leads to a significant reduction in risk of incorrectly recorded sales, thereby reducing the total cost of ownership.

REMEMBER

Global point-of-sale systems include both the hardware to capture the sales information and the software systems to process and share the information.

Global point-of-sale systems can help make financial decisions that will provide for significantly improved customer service. Global managers can use point-of-sale systems to track inventory, receive payment, advertise sales, and boost customer service. They can also help a company improve its general bookkeeping and tracking of purchasing trends.

Point-of-sale systems allow a company to maintain consistency in product pricing by basing prices on the number of units sold. They can generate sales reports, display inventory levels, and project shipment due dates. Systems can serve all point-of-sale locations while maintaining data backup and security functions. They also can allow independent use when individual point-of-sale locations become disconnected from the main system.

Any smartphone can now be a global point-of-sale device. Credit card information can be swiped into a phone, with the bank transaction taking place within seconds of the product or service exchanging hands. But, as sales recording and financial transactions become easier, more sophisticated means of capturing that data for illegal purposes emerge. This isn't to say that these types of point-of-sale systems shouldn't be used. Reasonable care must be afforded to ensure that the risks are worth the rewards.

Many companies are having great success selling their products on the Internet instead of from a more traditional "brick-and-mortar" store. In that case, the Internet becomes a company's foreign point-of-sale. When you are selling over the Internet, all the aspects of finding and retaining new customers that we have discussed previously are still relevant. But now the "personal" connection between the customer and your company is far removed from any foreign manufacturing or distribution site.

Companies operating in the global marketplace have had to make adjustments to their domestic websites to accommodate their foreign customers. Some companies have established links on their home page, with country-specific pages posted in the customer's foreign language. Customer service and technical support contact information should be accessible by your customers through a no-cost-to-the-customer telephone number that uses either using a traditional land line or a voice over Internet provider (VOIP) number. Remember that your employees working in those customer-service call centers need to be able to communicate rather fluently in the language of your customer.

REMEMBER

Customers usually will withdraw their loyalty to your company and its products if there is no easy way to interact with a "real live" person who can be understood and, in turn, understands them.

Getting and keeping customer loyalty through logistics

The growing complexity of supply and distribution chains in the global economy has created challenges for companies when it comes to achieving and maintaining a quality customer experience. The most important service any logistics organization can perform is to provide cost-effective and timely delivery in a dynamic and changing global economy. The ability to track and interact with shipments in route is vital.

Customers measure and evaluate how their customer experience is being provided. They are very aware of how your supply-chain operation works out any kinks or troubles, especially when those troubles are beyond anyone's control.

Empowering employees can help build relationships with customers that will retain their loyalty. Promised shipping and receiving dates must be kept, and any delays must be transparent, with accurate forecasts as to when the items will eventually be delivered. Missing one delivery date might be forgiven — missing two in a row usually leads to lost customers and sales.

TIP

Customer loyalty begins with employee loyalty. When employees are committed to the company's objectives, loyal customers will soon follow.

Employees must understand the importance of deadlines to ensure that high levels of productivity are maintained and orders are fulfilled both accurately and on time. Improving efficiency allows companies to control their logistics costs, further improving customer experiences. Addressing supply chain issues quickly will always improve customer satisfaction.

You should create a culture of excellent customer service at all levels within the company. Incentive-based initiatives will generate a customer-first environment, leading to higher productivity and overall customer satisfaction.

Supporting and Educating Your Customers

Although the "customer is always right," an educated customer is a better-informed customer who will make better decisions about the product that is eventually purchased. Supporting customers and helping them make good choices will keep them coming back. Having a good logistics support network will give them confidence that you will be there to support them over the length of the partnership.

Creating a logistics support network

Healthy companies maintain a logistics strategy that provides the highest service levels, no matter what changes may be happening in other areas of the company. This is a big challenge for complex organizations, those in dynamically fluid or fluctuating supply chains, and those having multiple product lines in multiple countries with multiple customers.

To create a competitive logistics network, various alternative networks must be developed, analyzed, and compared. This involves a variety of quantitative and qualitative criteria to consider with potential partners having different functional backgrounds and disciplines. A logistics network design framework should be created by decision makers so as to both reduce the complexity of the task and increase the quality of the final network.

REMEMBER

An effective logistics network provides good communication between every link in the supply and distribution chain, regardless of where in the world that link occurs.

The framework should begin with an analysis of external and internal developments and uncertainties. Choices are then made based on the company's business plans and objectives, technological issues, organizational needs, and human resource availability. These are combined into individual scenarios, creating alternative logistics networks. The last step in framework development is the final selection of the optimum logistics network. This is accomplished through a decision-support process that reviews, authorizes, and implements the selected network.

Leveraging logistics to keep customers informed

Companies must keep up with the dynamics of changing markets and technologies, along with ever-changing customer dynamics. Customers expect more in the way of service communication and want to utilize innovative new ways to transact business. Companies have to keep up with these changes to retain customers and attract new business. The challenge is often to find new ways to deliver increased customer service with reduced profit margins.

Supply chain companies must provide a local bridge between retailers and customers. They have to provide seamless customer service across multiple international borders. Companies need to establish their presence on the customer's preferred means of communication, to include the Internet (World Wide Web), mobile device applications, email, and even social media. Self-serve customer service tools — like menu-driven information requests and frequently asked questions — are handling more and more of the routine inquiries.

Customers now want the flexibility and freedom to change their orders to adjust for their own dynamic situations. They also want visible and transparent disclosure throughout the order placement and delivery processes in real time. They have a need to scale up their deliveries during peak seasons such as holidays, and return them to normal levels during slack times in the economy or market.

Customers are often eagerly and impatiently waiting for their deliveries. If customers cannot locate their shipment quickly online, a "live chat," toll-free customer service number, or website should quickly get them in touch with someone who has the ability and authority to find the shipment and update them on the delivery status. Calls should be routed quickly to the representative who can best answer each question or concern, or escalate them to managers when necessary.

TIP

Excellent, personal one-on-one customer service is still the best way to interact with customers.

All relevant customer information and case histories should be easily shared with business partners to make the supply chain function seamlessly. Customer service agents should have this information readily available while keeping it secure from competitors. Such information should include order tracking, billing queries, service requests, account history, and special request preferences.

Logistics — to include sales and distribution — is a client-driven business. Customers will judge your company by how well it handles day-to-day interactions. This is regardless of any sophisticated tools, advanced technology, or engineered processes you employ.

25

Chapter **13**

Dealing with Losses, Theft, Damages, and Returns

Product loss, theft, damage, and return are inevitable, especially when operating in the global marketplace. When selling your product to a new customer base, especially one in a foreign market, there is a strong likelihood that such incidents will increase. Your foreign sales and distribution networks are far removed from your domestic operations and networks: That added distance to market will almost assuredly add to your losses from theft and in-transit damage.

How you market your product will also have a major impact on theft, damages, and returns. If your product is sold through conventional retail stores, losses from theft will be higher. If your product is sold primarily via the Internet, expect damages in shipment to be greater.

Depending on what you are selling, returns of items purchased on the Internet can be significant. A number of recent trade studies have shown that 20 percent of many types of items purchased over the Internet are returned, and that 30–35 percent of online purchased clothing and accessories are returned annually.

Both proactive and reactive measures need to be developed to reduce the impact of losses, damaged products, and returns. That includes taking preventative steps from the start, as well as having a framework firmly in place to expeditiously respond to incidents as they occur.

You may well find that your foreign return experiences will bear little resemblance to those of your domestic operations, thus requiring you to develop completely different policies as well as a country-by-country unique return model. Further, when selling in a foreign market, you face additional issues associated with local laws governing returns in the countries of your foreign operations. Finally, domestically unfamiliar cultural issues and buying patterns (such as purchase for the sole intent of creating a knockoff) play a large role in your operation's vulnerability to loss from returns.

Minimizing the Risk at the Point of Sale

Many things can go wrong at the point of sale, whether it occurs at a commercial storefront or over the Internet. For some customers, this is the only time and place they may interact with your company.

Policies must be in place to ensure safe and secure warehousing, handling, packing, and shipping. This is normally the last time that your company is going to have possession of the product. But when customers try to return unwanted or defective products, processes must be in place to deal with the returns. If the items were damaged as a result of the distribution chain, then appropriate action must be taken to prevent reoccurrence.

Identifying what can go wrong and where

While many point-of-sale problems result from inexperienced, dishonest, or improperly trained personnel, a number of them occur because of security vulnerabilities throughout the sales and distribution process. Companies should have security controls in place at all the points in the foreign sales and distribution network that they either control or can influence. While the controls can't eliminate all vulnerabilities, they should address the most critical ones.

Precautionary measures should include:

>> Ensuring all point-of-sale computer systems are up-to-date with security patches and anti-virus signature files

» Installing file integrity monitoring and network-based intrusion detection software that can detect abnormal behavior

» Separating point-of-sale networks from other nonrelated networks so as to prevent cross-network intrusion

» Ensuring you have conducted sufficient background security checks on your personnel, and verifying that your distribution partners and stores that sell your products have done the same with their employees

» Validating employee training programs

» Monitoring, recording, and analyzing all abnormal activity (both human and data system)

» Performing regular penetration testing of your sales computer systems, as well as those of your distribution chain partners or vendors

Point-of-sale equipment includes cash registers, scanners, and weighing scales. These items need to be kept in good repair and properly calibrated according to governmental guidelines. Routinely scheduled preventative maintenance minimizes the risk of problems occurring during business hours. But, unless you own the foreign store, your product is likely one of many offered at that location. In that instance, it would be prudent to check on how well the store is maintaining its point-of-sale equipment.

REMEMBER

The more diverse and expansive your foreign sales and distribution network is and the less of it that is under your direct control, the higher your risk of loss is as a result of security vulnerability.

Since the use of credit cards has become not only the exclusive payment method for online sales but also the primary instrument of monetary exchange in most countries, you also need to ensure that the equipment associated with the use and acceptance of credit or debit card transactions is functioning not only properly but also securely. If you notice a spike occurring in fraudulent transactions you need to immediately contact the financial institutions associated with the issue and control of those cards. This can often be difficult to effect in time to prevent loss of not only revenue but also product.

It's wise to go slowly and extremely cautiously when it comes to accepting foreign credit and debit cards for payment. You may find that your foreign sales payment policies will need to be thoroughly researched and tested before you even agree to accept forms of payment other than cash.

When malicious activity is detected, companies should take all point-of-sale systems offline immediately to prevent further damage throughout the network. The information security department, systems security department, or those partner vendors charged with the protection of your customer information should be notified immediately of the attack.

WARNING

Unless you know exactly whom to report suspected fraudulent foreign credit card sales to and what recourse you have to either freeze (that is, stop product shipment before successful validation of payment authenticity and receipt of funds) or reverse fraudulent transactions, stick to foreign wire transfers or cash-only payments to avoid loss.

Developing secure storage, shipping, and handling policies

Companies must implement policies to ensure the safe and secure handling, storing, packaging, and delivery of their products. This results in the reduction of damaged or lost goods, as well as the time and costs (both direct and indirect) wasted in replacing those goods. The receipt of the expected product in good condition results in customer satisfaction.

Policies must provide methods and means of product handling that prevent damage or deterioration. Storage and stocking policies must prevent damage and loss of products in inventory, especially if your product can deteriorate while in storage. Packing and preservation policies must ensure conformance to the specified requirements of your product or packaging. Delivery policies must ensure that products arrive not only when and where stated but also in good condition. Further, these policies must ensure the integrity of products from the point of sale or time of receipt until such time as the supplier's responsibility ceases.

REMEMBER

All storage, shipping, and handling policies must be in agreement with your company's goals and objectives. Goals to attain a specified level of security must be understood and enforced throughout the distribution and sales networks.

Audits and unannounced inspections are a good way to ensure that security policies and processes are effective and are being followed at every point in the distribution and sales network. Acceptable ratings are awarded when policies meet or exceed expectations. Nonconformance issues are acted on when the audit reveals that full expectations were not met. Major nonconformance results when major deficiencies are observed. Critical nonconformance results in unsafe conditions, regulatory requirements not being met, and violation of company policies. Critical nonconformance always results in a failed audit or inspection.

Both physical and electronic security measures must be established to safeguard products from damage and theft. Levels of acceptable pilferage and damage must be established, and losses then identified within your inventory tracking systems so that both the level of loss and its impact on revenue are fully understood.

Recovering from the Damage or Loss

Determine how much profit you would have had if the inventory had not been lost or damaged. Subtract the original cost, advertising expenses, shipping and handling, and any other expenses. This is the *net realizable value,* that is, the value of what the inventory was worth to you.

Then, determine the replacement cost. The cost of inventory between the time the sale was made and the date the loss or damage occurred probably increased. At a minimum, a new shipping and handling charge has probably been passed down the distribution chain. Determine the true cost to you to replace the lost or damage inventory. This is your *replacement value.*

Choose an advantageous costing method when writing off loss and damage expenses, especially if such a method has been established by your country of manufacturing.

TIP

Accepting financial losses resulting from lost or damaged goods is never easy. However, knowing the risks of and planning for a certain amount of loss or damage in your foreign inventory management and distribution schedules can provide some level of stockage cushioning within your sales and distribution networks.

Getting a replacement in the customer's hands

Minor faults to purchased items sometimes can be dealt with at the point of sale or by service representatives. But if the merchandise has major faults or defects that make it unusable, in most countries customers have some legal degree of right to exchange the defective product for a defect-free one. As in your domestic operations, such a replacement can be challenging if the item was a gift or the customer can't produce a receipt of sale. Further, depending on the language used to convey the message, in many cultures selling items under notice of "no refund or exchange" may imply that the goods are known to be defective, and that by purchasing such items, the buyer accepts any hidden defects. However, this is not always the case if the merchandise does not perform as advertised. Make sure you understand the rules in all countries where your product is sold or distributed.

It is always in your company's best interest to accommodate customers as much as possible. Happy customers are generally repeat customers. Studies have shown that customers who have to return products as a result of an item not being what was expected tend not to become repeat customers.

If one of your sales network merchants is currently out of stock for the particular item or model to be replaced or exchanged, replacing the faulty item with the next available upgrade is prudent. If the cost is significant and the customer is not willing or able to wait until a replacement can be located and shipped, then the merchant may be able to obtain it quickly from a competitor at wholesale prices by reciprocal agreement. Both companies win because they both record a sale, and customer satisfaction will likely be maintained.

Replacement, repair, and return policies must be made known to the customer and specific as to what can be replaced, repaired, or returned; the condition the product must be in; the documentation required for exchange; the time frame during which a claim will be honored; and what, if any, additional restocking fees the customer may be expected to pay. These restocking fees are generally set high enough to discourage customers from making impulse purchases that can be exchanged easily. Policies must also state the conditions under which special-ordered or custom-made items can be replaced or returned. In these cases, if replacement or return is allowable, the costs generally will be shared by both the seller and the buyer.

Items that are delivered directly to a customer's home or place of business are often more difficult for the customer to return because of the size, weight, or some other physical attribute that caused the original requirement for direct delivery. Arrangements must be made for quick on-site inspection prior to authorization of replacement or return.

REMEMBER

Goods that are defective or damaged through no fault of the customer must be promptly replaced whenever possible. Your replacement, repair, and return policies must be specific enough to avoid any preventable customer dissatisfaction.

Modifying the process to prevent future occurrences

Solutions to problems at the point of sale should be planned for ahead of time, not just implemented on the spot or after the fact. While it is impossible to predict all problems you may encounter, most risks associated with returns are predictable and should already be addressed in standing company policies and procedures.

Prior to selling your product in a new foreign marketplace, make sure to investigate if there are country-specific reasons for loss or damage of items that you may not have encountered in your domestic market. Is there a documented high incidence of theft in your new distribution and sales network? Does the climate impact your product or packaging? Talk to other companies selling similar products as well as to your distribution partners and vendors for area-unique conditions.

As new or location-unique damage or loss incidents are encountered, regular policy reviews and updates must address and outline the policies and procedures for delays arising from physical or regulatory shipping restrictions; storage, preservation, and shelf life deficiencies; in-transit losses; damaged products or packaging due to mishandling and misrouting; and even faulty software and technical information.

REMEMBER

Companies must ensure that *all* new damage and loss incidents are analyzed and addressed in updated policies and procedures.

Accepting Damages and Returns: Taking It All Back

There are many reasons why customers may want to return purchased items. There may be some defect in the item purchased (damaged, missing, or incorrect parts), or perhaps the customer has had a change of mind and wants a red one instead of a blue one. We live in a dynamic and changing global marketplace where a sale may not always be final. Allowing customers to return or exchange items often provides a degree of customer service that is worth the cost and effort.

The process of returning products and goods from what is typically considered to be their final destination for proper disposal or recovery of what would be lost revenue is called *reverse logistics.* This process includes not only the return of products back through the sales and distribution network to the manufacturing company for return to inventory, but also the return of products to remanufacturing and refurbishing (that is, for repair or upgrade) activities.

WARNING

Be sure to inspect all returned items before returning them to inventory. Returns often are used to embed counterfeit parts into electronics and malicious code into software. Clothing and accessories are frequently purchased and then returned so as to provide an opportunity for copying and the subsequent manufacturing of knockoffs.

Reversing the logistics chain

Products for sale normally arrive at distributors in economic quantities, for further issue to retailers for placement on shelves in smaller quantities. When products are returned by customers for whatever reason, they usually come back in single-unit quantities known as stock-keeping units. In order to efficiently return the items back through the distribution network, they must be bundled into economic quantities as well.

Sometimes the manufacturer or distributor does not want the items brought back into inventory. This is especially true where the cost of shipping, inspecting, and returning the item back into inventory exceeds the net realizable value of the item. The manufacturer and retailer must then work together to ensure the secure disposal of the item so that it can't be resold or scavenged in operating or usable condition, particularly if the item is to be disposed of in a foreign market.

Other times your company may direct that the item be returned to a specific point within the foreign distribution network for redistribution to other wholesalers or retailers in other markets, specialized outlets, or secondhand merchants; or for repair or remanufacturing, recycling, or disposal. Because your foreign point of sale is far removed from your domestic distribution chain, you will need to weigh the costs and the risks associated with the intermediate location you are considering.

TIP

Products with the highest risk of being returned should be designed specifically to be repackaged, restocked, resold, reused, or recycled.

Each reverse logistics network must be designed to the product involved and the economics of the recovery and reuse of the product. Bulk products require different handling than small, fragile, or electronic products. Companies should consider the costs for shipping and storing, the speed at which the returned products decline in value, and the need to have total distribution control over the products.

Reverse logistics efforts should consider the following aspects:

>> All reverse logistics activities are distribution chain activities requiring at least as much attention as getting your products to market.

>> Reverse logistics can be complex, and may require outsourcing if the process exceeds the capabilities of your established distribution network.

>> Returns should be processed in a specially designed returns center.

>> Product recalls must be planned for in the reverse logistics process.

>> Data on returns must be collected to help ensure future customer satisfaction.

If the product your company makes is in high demand to be used as gifts during your foreign market's gift-giving season, you likely accelerated (that is, "surged") your production to meet the anticipated demand. Once the season is over, you may find your production schedule slowing down at the same time the volume of returns increases. You may then want to consider designating some of your sales employees as return specialists, in order to ensure you do not get overwhelmed with the volume of the returns.

The impact of counterfeit goods on your company and the global economy

The International Chamber of Commerce estimates that the value of counterfeit goods now exceeds $600 billion annually (5–7 percent of all world trade), an amount that is rapidly increasing. This affects product lines as varied as food and beverage, farm machinery, clothing and accessories, pharmaceuticals, and technology-based equipment.

As companies have moved their manufacturing to countries with cheaper labor costs and provided the equipment and manufacturing technology to make their products, they have frequently enabled the manufacturers in the foreign countries to realize that a greater profit could be made by copying (or slightly modifying) the original products and selling them through their own global or national markets.

In many cases the countries where the counterfeit items are being made or sold only passively attempt to control the counterfeiting, simply ignore the activity, or openly encourage it as a significant part of that country's economic base. While most studies (including those conducted by governments) view China as the principle country of counterfeit production, Russia, Taiwan, North Korea, Paraguay, and India also have a significant counterfeit base. China and Russia also top most lists of the countries that consume the largest amount of counterfeit goods.

Even skilled craftsmen in many poor countries can make realistic, name-brand handbags or clothing items with relatively little capital equipment and proprietary knowledge. If these counterfeit goods are sold for even a fraction of the original good's price, the counterfeiters still make a good profit.

In addition to impact on the profit of the original manufacturers, as well as the estimated 2 to 3 million jobs that have been replaced by counterfeit production, much of the counterfeit merchandise is unsafe. Investigators have seized power strips, extension cords, and smoke alarms, with phony Underwriters Laboratories (UL) marks, that frequently melt when plugged into an electric outlet; brake pads made of kitty litter, sawdust, and dried grass; toothpaste made with a chemical found in antifreeze; medical test kits that give faulty readings; and cellphone batteries that could explode. Counterfeit pharmaceuticals are particularly troubling, especially in poorer markets, where studies estimate that up to 25 percent of all drugs are counterfeit, do not provide the necessary protection, or do more harm than good.

The counterfeit production and sale of your product can drastically affect your profit and adversely affect your company's reputation.

When manufacturing or selling in a foreign country, make sure that you have sufficient patents and copyrights in place to avoid the loss of your intellectual property and that those patents and copyrights are honored in the country you are targeting for sales. If not, understand that you will have little or no recourse for recovery of lost capital and even less chance of restoring your company's good name and branding.

If you suspect that your goods are being counterfeited, report it immediately to your local and national law-enforcement agencies. Additionally, the International Chamber of Commerce's Counterfeiting Intelligence Bureau can be a source of excellent advice and assistance.

While the effort to prevent product counterfeiting can sometimes feel like bailing out a sinking boat, your company can explore some steps that at least make it harder to successfully copy your products. Some rely on incorporating design elements or identifying marks unique to your company — such as lasering holograms onto critical or hidden components. Others include development of country-unique designs that are not distributed outside of a specific geographic market, as well as limited-quantity production runs.

Unfortunately, as long as there are products being sold, there will always be products being counterfeited.

4

Providing Logistics Services to Global Customers

Develop an awareness of and sensitivity to the critical cultural issues that affect not only your foreign operations and workforce but also your foreign customers.

Explore some of the unique types of insurance that may be necessary when providing foreign logistics support services, to include the critical elements to cover in developing your company's intellectual property rights protection plan.

Find out about the various options you have in staffing foreign logistics support service operations, including the differences between expatriates, third-country nationals, and local nationals.

Examine not only the labor laws that you may have to comply with, but also the resulting impact on the cost of workforce scheduling, accommodating restrictions, and your company's ability to successfully fulfill its logistics support services contract.

Chapter **14**

Understanding and Accommodating Cultural Differences

You have been successful in your domestic market and have decided that now is a good time to take your firm's capabilities and expand them into the global marketplace. Your company has significant expertise in the logistics of retail operations, logistics consulting, and distribution, as well as logistics management for the public and private sectors. You've either been approached by someone in the global marketplace to provide logistics services or are thinking about responding to a request for proposal for foreign logistics support. Before you throw your hat in the global logistics services ring, how sure are you that your services will be successful in a foreign market?

In this chapter, we will discuss dealing with language or cultural barriers that are frequently encountered by even the most successful firms while working in an environment where the goal and objectives of your domestic company (and its domestic owners or stakeholders) may differ from the objectives found in your new foreign environment. Finally, once you have successfully adapted your domestic expertise to a foreign environment, how will you anticipate and prepare for social or political upheaval in your new area of operation?

Confronting Cultural and Language Barriers

When choosing where to expand, potential language barriers are fairly easy to recognize. You may have already encountered those issues to some extent in your domestic operations. But some countries have a significant number of regional languages, such as the 22 official languages in India (not to mention over 2,000 dialects, with money printed in 12 languages), 9 regional languages in China, and 5 regional languages in the Democratic Republic of the Congo. If your new area of operation is truly global, bear in mind that over 6,900 known languages are spoken in the world today. Remember, the more technical the logistics service you're providing is, the more likely it is that there will not be a word-for-word or sufficiently technical translation in your new support area.

While language barriers are more obvious, cultural barriers can be much harder to identify, understand, and overcome. A famous example is the U.S. retailer Walmart, which opened 85 stores in Germany in the late 1990s only to pull out of that market in 2005 (at an estimated loss of $1 billion). The Walmart model of low prices and high-volume sales did not fit into the culture of Germany, where stores do not operate 24 hours a day and the people are often skeptical about discount pricing.

Anticipating and adjusting to language issues

As part of your decision-making prior to venturing into a new foreign market, you undoubtedly conducted your own (or hired others to conduct) comprehensive market research for the service you will be providing. If you are confident you have identified all the languages and dialects in your potential market area, based on your anticipated customers, you are ready to make the necessary adjustments to your services and marketing — assuming that you have completed a cost analysis of the required changes and still want to proceed.

Remember, too, that with your foreign area of operation comes interaction with and reliance on local companies such as suppliers, banks, and real estate firms. Here is where the language issue can become much more complex. Be sure that all contracts for goods or services are translated properly! While good translation software tools are now available, none are 100 percent effective, and all have weaknesses in the translation of complex business arrangements.

REMEMBER

Get a second translation — in all the languages in your foreign area of operation — of your most critical documents from an established translation company that routinely handles those types of business documents.

LANGUAGE OBSTACLES IN MARKETING

There is an old saying that "a picture is worth a thousand words." That can be true if there are language or cultural misunderstandings as well. An example of just how true that is has been used in business classes for decades: the story of the U.S. baby food manufacturer Gerber and its initial attempt in the 1960s to market its products in Africa. The first obstacle Gerber faced was the translation of the company name: In Africa "gerber" can be translated in French as "to vomit" — not a positive start in the former French colonies of Africa! Worse, at that time in Africa many consumers were used to seeing the product being sold depicted on the label. Gerber's jars of baby food had the picture of a cute baby's face on its jars. The consumers were horrified, thinking Gerber was selling jars of babies instead of jars of baby food.

Undoubtedly, the most critical potential problem area is communicating with your foreign client and its workforce, as well as any foreign nationals you may employ to provide your logistics services. In the services business, your workforce is your point-of-sale to your clients: It is obvious that those you employ need to effectively speak the language and dialect of the local market. But, it is also important that your foreign workforce understands and learns the processes that have made you successful domestically. The best solution is to ensure that all internal workplace instructions appear not only in your own language but also all the languages of those you employ, and to insist that at least one level of supervisory management is multilingual. Having a workforce that speaks a language your management is not conversant in creates a significant barrier between management and the labor force that can lead to misunderstanding and resentment.

REMEMBER

The Gerber story in the nearby sidebar is one of many instances where the name of a company, product, or service sold in the language of one country can be interpreted negatively to mean something entirely different in other languages.

Building respect and relationships

While language differences can be an obstacle in developing respect and good relationships with your workforce, clients, customers, and local business partners, understanding cultural differences is equally important. You may have already encountered situations with cultural differences in your domestic workplace as a result of different generations, social status, or religious beliefs. But those differences are multiplied when providing logistics services in multiple foreign areas of operation, and the cultural differences become much more complicated.

It is important to study the countries and their cultures before initiating any marketing campaigns or entering into a foreign logistics services agreement and hiring the workforce at your client's location. Some examples of cultural differences that must be respected in order to be successful in foreign areas of operation can be fatal to success if not accommodated:

» In many Middle Eastern countries, society recognizes only children and adults: teenagers (that is, individuals having gone through puberty) are treated and operate as adults, regardless of their age.

» Many residents of the Middle East shake hands only with someone of the same gender, unless related. Marketing and media that depicts unrelated men and women in non-family settings, or that uses sexually suggestive language or actions would be highly offensive and cause a negative reaction to the company using it.

» Weak handshakes (or a simple bow at the waist) are preferred in many countries in the Orient and in South America, compared to the preference for firm handshakes in North America and Europe.

» Success in many non-Western cultures is measured collectively (versus individually in Western cultures), and the measure of individual success is that of conquering one's self (spiritual), as opposed to the Western value of conquering one's goals (material).

REMEMBER

Researching, understanding, and honoring the local customs and traditions of any country or region in which you plan to establish a physical presence and market your logistics services is vital. Do your research *before* you "go global."

Adjusting to the role of religion in business

Just as you must identify and adjust to the languages, social traditions, and customs in your new foreign location, you need to be aware of the religious climate of the area. Many times it is hard to recognize the difference between customs and religious practices. Incorrectly identifying one from the other can have significant repercussions.

All regions of the world are affected by the religions that are prevalent in those areas. Religious practice may be manifested in dietary restrictions, such as the Hindu prohibition of the consumption of beef and the Islamic and Jewish prohibitions of eating pork. It also may affect the timing of work hours and communication with your domestic headquarters. For example, in Muslim countries, Fridays and Saturdays constitute weekends. Some countries still do not allow work for profit on Sundays. Many countries' official holidays accommodate the prevalent religions and, in some cases, change annually based on the religious calendars.

The clothing that people wear (such as turbans or burkas) or how they look (for example, beards and hairstyles) may also be dictated by their religion. As a company operating in those countries, you have to understand, respect, and accommodate each individual's personal religious practices.

Finally, you must recognize that the Islamic religion requires followers to pray toward Mecca five times a day. In many Middle Eastern countries, all Muslims have the right to attend the Hajj at least once in their lifetime, a pilgrimage for which you must grant paid leave (in addition to the normal vacation time). That said, many Christian-based denominations require their members to attend religious services on days that may not be considered official local holidays.

REMEMBER

Nearly every country has a mix of religions and cultures, whether a result of immigration or an influx of other nationalities carrying out business. Don't accommodate the majority at the expense of the minority. Not all people in your new foreign logistics support area — whether customers or employees — are the same.

Understanding the Corporate Climate

In addition to accommodating the traditions, customs, and religions in your new foreign logistics service market, it is important to recognize that the way business is conducted may also be different from that at your domestic location. As such, a reevaluation of your corporate goals and objectives as they relate to your foreign location is imperative.

Identifying the impact of your goals and objectives

In many regions business is conducted differently than you are used to in your domestic operations. For example, while the hiring of family members is frequently discouraged in the Western world, it is a common practice in many other regions. Still other regions gauge the growth of a business by the number of employees rather than by its profit margin. This can cause friction between your domestic stakeholders and your foreign management team.

Business relationships in many foreign markets are based on having first established a prior personal relationship. For this reason, it is often good to have a local liaison to help plan, coordinate, and execute your plans to enter the new foreign market. Establishing relationships and contracts with foreign companies is often a slow process; if you have to coordinate with the regional or national government, expect significant delays. The same can be said for business disagreements. In many Middle Eastern and Asian countries, officials and businessmen are reluctant to say "no." They will simply delay reaching an agreement until you give up or go away.

There is also a different perception of the risk of failure in many parts of the world. In many Asian countries, failure of a business is viewed harshly and blame is assessed personally, not corporately. Conversely, in many European and Western Hemisphere countries, failure is viewed as a means of gaining experience, and risky endeavors are often more accepted.

WARNING

In some countries graft and corruption are prevalent, especially when trying to establish a new business. These practices are probably contrary to the ethical standards you have established for yourself or your company headquarters. Many countries have strict laws with severe penalties that forbid such practices; other countries turn a blind eye. Be aware that more often than not there may be a disconnect between the laws and either the enforcement of the laws or your ability to seek protection should the laws be ignored or violated.

Dealing with global versus local company perceptions

Your foreign logistics service workforce likely will be made up of personnel from both your domestic operations (at least initially) and local nationals. Despite the fact that all of them work for the same parent company, each may have a much different perception of your type of business, as well as of the parameters for the logistics services you are providing.

Resentment can often arise with respect to the generation of profits. Your domestic stakeholders may not understand the foreign operating environment and thus question your foreign operation profit margin. At the same time, your foreign client and workforce may feel that too much of the revenue they are generating is going to subsidize your domestic operations.

There may also be a perception that your company is not paying sufficient attention to the traditions and culture of your foreign operations, despite what you perceive to be successful accommodation efforts. This includes such areas as the establishment of work hours and work breaks, vacations and paid leave, overtime pay, or simply the percentage of local workers in relation to the overall workforce.

Further, while your workforce may be happy, there may be resentment in the local community, especially if the introduction of your logistics services business can be perceived as the reason other local businesses are failing.

TIP

In many countries, there is an expectation (sometimes a law) that a certain percentage of local business profits is donated to local charities or to support specific government projects like the building of new schools. Do not underestimate the significant goodwill of supporting your host community.

Regardless of the reason for a difference in perception between your local foreign operations and your domestic operations, it is imperative that you monitor the situation and address grievances quickly. Good companies often fail simply because of perceptions. As the old adage goes, "Perception is reality."

Adjusting and Responding to Social and Political Uncertainty

For some companies the opportunity to make significant profit is too hard to pass up. As a result, profit wins out over risk. Other companies are much more risk adverse. Which is your company — and more importantly — its investors?

Major social or political upheaval such as the Arab Spring of 2011; the continuous internal and external military conflicts in Iraq, Syria, Afghanistan, and elsewhere in the Middle East and parts of Africa; and the 2016 attempted coup in Turkey have had both an immediate and long-term negative effect on both foreign business initiatives and investment in those areas.

Investors are usually quick to pull their money out of politically turbulent areas but cautiously return when the situation calms. The impact on foreign businesses operating in those countries can be more dramatic and long-term, especially if their business infrastructure is adversely affected or they find their insurance rates so high as to prevent continued operation. The chaos resulting from political upheaval in either local, regional, or national governments can further delay the establishment of new companies.

But political uncertainty can also affect your business in countries that do not routinely experience such upheaval. Countries that are not able to pay their debts or have significant inflation often experience a decline in the value of their currency that subsequently adversely affects all businesses operating there.

Accepting the impact of political uncertainty in developed countries

Even in developed countries — those with a fairly stable economy and government — there can be social or political uncertainty. The recent attempt in Scotland to leave the British Commonwealth, the impact of Syrian refugees on many of the countries in the European Union (EU), and even the 2016 vote of the British to leave the EU are examples.

While the impact of upheaval on local business in relatively stable areas is much less than it is in those countries where there is major upheaval, there are still precautions that can be taken to minimize the impact of uncertainty. The greatest threat to business financials occurs when the value of the local currency suddenly drops. Larger corporations that deal in the global economy often have a team whose job it is to buy the currencies of their foreign markets when the exchange rate is favorable just to reduce the impact on their profit during any subsequent currency devaluation.

A rise in national inflation may also cause a significant increase in the cost of your materials or salaries. The decision to offset these rising costs by passing them on to the client or customer must be considered carefully. Commensurately raising your fees or rates to absorb such an increase may well lose you your client or, worse yet, price you out of competition.

Countries may also experience periods of higher-than-average national unemployment. While this may increase the size of your national labor pool, it generally negatively impacts the financial posture of your client by reducing their customers' buying power.

TIP

Normally, the best recourse is not to panic and do something drastic but to simply wait out the situation. Having said that, in the event that the situation becomes longer term or more volatile, safer financial strategies should be explored in conjunction with your domestic headquarters and alternative plans set in place as expeditiously as possible.

Dealing with social or political upheaval

If you decide to provide logistics support services in countries that are currently experiencing significant social or political upheaval, or have a history of such crises, you must be fully aware of the risks and rewards prior to agreeing to provide your support. The risk is not merely to your profit-and-loss posture, but also to your foreign facilities and to your workforce.

When negotiating a contract to provide logistics services, one way you can protect yourself is to insist on including a *force majeure* clause in all your contracts. Force majeure is a legal term defining any unforeseen condition or situation that would prevent either party from fulfilling its contractual obligation, and it may be used as a legal defense for not carrying out any or all of the terms of the contract. Such a clause must be fully understood and agreed to by both parties at the beginning of any contract negotiations. That said, expect to get push-back from the other contracting party (your clients or suppliers), as most contracts are written to the benefit of the supplier or your client. You may well encounter reluctance to release you from any level of risk that transfers the cost burden away from you.

The following is an example of a standard comprehensive force majeure clause:

> "Neither party shall be liable for any failure to perform its obligations where such failure is a result of Acts of Nature (including fire, flood, earthquake, storm, hurricane, or other natural disaster), war, invasion, acts of foreign enemies, hostilities (whether war is declared or not), civil war, rebellion, revolution, insurrection, military or usurped power or confiscation, terrorist activities, nationalization, government sanction, blockage, embargo, labor dispute, strike, lockout, or interruption or failure of power sources."

REMEMBER

The defense of force majeure — assuming such a clause is included in your contract *and* recognized under the laws governing the contract's compliance — may not apply if there are other clauses in your contract that require contingency plans.

While insurance is often available for both foreign operation facilities and workforces, expect the coverage to be limited and any premiums expensive. Again, this must be addressed before you even agree to enter into a logistics services contract and set up operations in your client's country. Although the insurance policies may cover your financial and property losses, they normally do not cover or underwrite the loss of your intellectual property from violation (as in the case of trademarks and registrations) or theft by known or unknown parties (for example, patent infringement or data theft or compromise). While some larger corporations with robust in-house legal staff may choose to self-insure, the potential for loss of a foreign facility or personnel is simply too great for most companies to accept.

WARNING

If you are seeking to insure your foreign operations and workforce while operating in a hostile environment, be sure to select a policy that does not have any exclusions for "acts of man" or "acts of war" — and be willing to pay significantly higher premiums.

But simply having insurance is not enough. Your clients, stakeholders, workforce, and their families justifiably want to know that you have planned for and have mechanisms in place to protect both your operations and them from as many negative situations as possible (predicted or unpredicted). For example:

>> What are your security plans? Have you considered hiring your own security force?

>> Do you have evacuation plans to get your workforce and critical operating documents to a safe location? Does your workforce know the plans and have they exercised them? Have you designated sufficient personnel as "critical" to ensure evacuation and continuity of operations?

>> What are your medical contingency plans? Is your medical coverage adequate? Do you have sufficient medical supplies on hand to cover the delta between first need and evacuation to a medical treatment facility? Do you have mechanisms in place to guarantee the evacuation of injured personnel to a higher level of medical care?

>> Do you have backup emergency power in the event your local power is interrupted or terminated?

>> Do you have reliable lines of communication to local authorities, your embassy, and your domestic operations? Do you have a way of contacting your workforce in the event that they need to either stay home or go to a rendezvous site?

>> Do you have sufficient food and water on hand, in the event that your workforce can't leave the facility for both limited (not to exceed 72 hours) and extended periods of time? If you do not maintain stocks for extended periods of time, do you have guaranteed contracts in place to meet your needs?

>> Will your vehicles — either owned or leased — be immediately available in sufficient quantities should they need to be used to recover or relocate your workforce? If not, what mechanisms have you put in place to ensure the movement of your personnel to safety?

>> If the most unfortunate situation arises, do you have a plan for the recovery and evacuation of deceased employees or their family members?

>> What are your plans for the protection of your computers and data? Do you send backup data to your domestic operations more frequently if the situation is getting worse? In the event that you have to evacuate your facilities, what gets taken and what gets destroyed — in what priority and by whom?

If these questions cause you alarm, they should. Not being sufficiently prepared to deal with the realities of the chaos caused by social or political upheaval could destroy your operations both abroad and at home.

TIP

Planning for all contingencies to deal with social or political unrest must be deliberately undertaken by both you, in your foreign location, *and* your corporate headquarters. Take advantage of as many "expert" sources as possible — such as a reliable security company in your foreign area of operations or other domestic companies with a similar foreign presence — to assist you in your planning.

Probably the most important aspect to be aware of is that your company may be asked to "take sides" or "make a statement" in times of social or political unrest. Your workforce will certainly reflect and may even actively support *both* sides of an issue or conflict. Make sure employees know to keep their preferences to themselves while in the workplace. As for your company's preference, a nonpolitical stance is normally the best. But, if the local situation escalates to the point that you — and not your corporate headquarters — are forced to issue a statement, do so with the full support of and agreement by corporate headquarters and an understanding of the potential outcome.

Anticipating the near future

The number of companies that will rush into a new foreign market unaware of the potential for social or political upheaval is amazing. These possibilities must be considered and included as part of your investment strategy. Talk to the local trade associations, as well as other companies doing business in your potential new area of logistics services support.

The Internet is a powerful tool. With the exception of terrorist activity, rarely does an event occur that has not already been discussed in local chat rooms or other social media venues. Subscribe to local news outlets as well.

After you are established in your new foreign location, getting a feel for the social and political climate becomes easier. While you may first hear of issues from your workforce, continue to talk to other companies in-country as well as local business authorities to gain the broadest understanding.

Regardless of the level of severity of the social or political unrest, be prepared to see changes in that country's laws — either through legislation (such as increasing the percentage of local workers) or through decree (for example, a local dictate to increase wage rates) — that could impact your ability to provide quality logistics services or support.

Chapter **15**

Identifying Insurance and License Requirements

As you make the decision to export your logistics services capabilities to a foreign location, your business plan must consider the associated insurance, permits, and licensing requirements you will face — both in terms of the expense and the time it takes to become fully operational. Where you choose to operate will obviously make a significant difference in coverage and could result in insurance, licensing, and other legal requirements that are vastly different from what is required for your domestic operations.

Identifying the Ground Rules

Insurance, licensing, and permitting requirements vary by country, and even location within a country, and are subject to frequent change. Before starting to support your foreign clients in a new foreign location, it is vital to check with the regulatory agencies in the country to ensure you have the proper licenses for your company, your employees, and perhaps even your subcontractors. You also need to ensure you have both the amount and type of insurance coverage to be able to maintain your operations.

Additionally, your contractual business relationships will affect the type of licenses and insurance you may need. If you are subcontracting to another company, that company may have the responsibility for insurance and licensing, depending on the laws that govern the operations. If you are leasing equipment or vehicles for your foreign operations, some of the insurance may be included as part of the leasing agreement.

Determining the types of insurance required

When investigating insurance requirements for your foreign location, there are two basic types to consider. Compulsory insurance is that which is required by law, while noncompulsory insurance is not required but often a smart practice depending on the type of logistics services you are providing. You may also see the term *admitted insurance*, which refers to insurance policies issued by a country's specified and licensed insurance carrier.

WARNING

Most countries have laws against the use of nonadmitted insurance carriers, which — more often than not — require local (in other words, national) underwriting.

While compulsory insurance coverage varies by country, several types of compulsory insurance are usually required. Examples include:

» **Group life insurance:** Covers all employees providing services in the foreign country.

» **Third-party vehicle liability insurance:** Note that while companies leasing vehicles may provide minimum coverage for the vehicle itself, few automatically provide third-party insurance underwriting for loss of life and disability, or property damage or loss (such as the theft of personal property or company assets).

» **Loss of income insurance:** Covers your employees in the event of lost wages due to illness or accident.

» **Public liability insurance:** Protects against claims by third parties against negligence, death, loss, injury, damage of property, or damages and loss caused by errors or omissions.

» **Healthcare professional indemnity insurance:** Applies if you employ healthcare workers. Be specific when identifying your employees as "healthcare professionals," as the definition of a "healthcare professional" is not standard. As such, the designation could include both licensed and unlicensed workers and caregivers.

>> **Builders liability insurance:** Applies if you are part of a construction project or are providing building maintenance services.

>> **Hazardous waste and pollution insurance:** Applies if your client works in those environments.

If you intend to build or occupy an office, other types of insurance may be required, depending on the geographic area of and whether you own or lease the facility. If you're providing logistics support services in high-risk geographic areas, you may well need to obtain coverage against earthquake, fire, flood, hurricane, or typhoon, not only for your facility but also for the contents of your buildings. Don't be surprised, however, if no local carrier is willing to underwrite such a policy, or, if available, the premiums for such a policy are prohibitive.

Further, many different types of noncompulsory insurance are available. Determining which policies are best for your operations should be part of your business plan. These types of policies can cover everything from business interruption (compensating you for lost revenue in the event that you're temporarily unable to provide your contracted services) to terrorism and sabotage, to professional errors and omissions. It is extremely important to make sure that the language in your policy is specific enough to enable you to make a claim with some likelihood of success.

Many times, both compulsory and noncompulsory insurance options may already be available to you through the international provisions of your domestic insurance policies. If your domestic underwriter can provide coverage by issuing riders to your existing coverage, that is usually more cost effective than having to get a totally new policy. Just make sure that your domestic insurance policies are issued by companies that are authorized to underwrite in the foreign country where you will be providing your logistics support services.

Your client (or the laws of the country in which you're providing your logistics support services) may require that both your company and its employees are bonded. Because bonding is normally not sold as insurance, if you are providing security or dealing with more than normal amounts of foreign currency as part of your logistics support services, you will definitely need to obtain this critical additional coverage.

A *surety bond* is a formal and legally enforceable contract between your company and a third party (such as a bank, a bonding company, or an insurance company) that agrees to guarantee payment or compensation to your foreign client in the event that either you fail to deliver your contracted services or something that your company does causes your client loss or damage. Such a bond can be useful to protect your foreign client from domestic operational failures, such as corporate bankruptcy, death of the principal owner, lawsuits, or dissolution resulting from merger or takeover. While you will still have to pay on claims, bonding has a side benefit of making your services more desirable to potential clients.

Additionally, if you are able to conduct as complete a background personnel investigation as you would domestically, taking out either a blanket (one that covers all employees) or individual *fidelity bond* will protect your company against losses (such as theft or embezzlement by employees) that are not covered under any of your other policies. Be aware, however, that if the bonding company does not feel that sufficient background information is available on your employees to meet its requirements, it will likely refuse to issue either type of fidelity bond.

WARNING

As you determine the types and amount of insurance required to safeguard your foreign operations, you may decide that the expense is simply too great. This analysis needs to occur before you sign any logistics services support contract! Options then may include finding a foreign location where the risks (and, therefore, the insurance requirements) are substantially less, partnering with an existing company where the insurance costs can be shared, or reconsidering the idea of expanding into the foreign market altogether.

Knowing when your standard insurance may not be sufficient

Your insurance requirements obviously will be dictated by the foreign location you are entering into, your status as the prime contractor or a subcontractor, and the type of logistics support services you are providing. If there is a significant change in any of these elements from your domestic operations you will need more than your standard insurance.

One example of a significant modification to your standard domestic insurance may be the need for a *force majeure policy*. Much like a force majeure clause in your contract with your client or any supplier, force majeure insurance provides coverage for financial losses arising out of the inability to complete your contracted services. The coverage includes delays as well as total termination of the contract resulting from events totally outside of your company's control (such as fire, flood, epidemics, earthquake, war, and revolution). Types of losses covered by the policy include continued debt servicing, loss of income, ongoing fixed costs, spoilage, and related contingencies.

REMEMBER

It is critically important to make sure your insurance policies are very specific about what is and isn't covered, and under which country's laws claims are adjudicated. The more situations you have covered, the more expensive the policy. Most claims result in lengthy negotiations, especially if there is any question about whose rules apply. The more precise your policy is, the easier it will be to make a successful claim.

Even if your policy provides for all the events you want covered, a clause may be included that says you must prove you took all prudent actions to avoid the situation from causing you or your client damage or loss. For example, if you had sufficient notice that a major typhoon was coming in your direction and you failed to evacuate your workforce or equipment, you may find you are not covered.

If you have historically been a prime contractor for logistics support services in your domestic market and now are going to be a subcontractor in your foreign market, you may find that your insurance requirements are reduced depending on whether your new prime contractor's insurance has provisions that cover its subcontractors. But, here again, we offer a word of caution about the provisions. It is critical that you make sure the provisions are recognized in the new country where you are operating.

You should also review your standard insurance if the type of logistics support services you are providing are significantly different from those at your domestic location. For example, domestically you are insured as a facility renter, but your foreign contract requires you to own a facility to support your customer. Accordingly, you should be prepared to see a significant increase in both your coverage requirements and costs.

Be careful to review your standard insurance policies to see if the coverage is still valid when the composition of your workforce has changed to include foreign local nationals or third-country nationals. If you're not, you may have to change the composition of your foreign operation's workforce (for example, hiring other than local nationals). Be prepared to run into a major opposition if you try to hire less than the foreign country's local workforce percentage requirements. Of all the areas that will affect your insurance requirements, personnel employment insurance coverage may well be the most expensive or difficult to obtain.

Identifying national and local license and permit requirements

All countries require a business license prior to commencing operations. Depending on the country, obtaining the license or permit can be both expensive and time consuming. In a few of the more underdeveloped countries, the licenses and permits of the prime contractor are viewed as sufficient for subcontractors; but, here again, the rules can also change quickly. The primary reason for a license or permit is simple — to ensure that the company is complying with all the laws of the country and that the appropriate business taxes are being paid.

All countries have a website, controlled by the governing body for commerce or trade, that shows the requirements for obtaining business licenses and permits. Unfortunately, the laws are likely written in the primary national language. Here, again, not only is it critically important to obtain an accurate translation but also to retain a reputable legal representative who is knowledgeable about the licensing and permitting requirements.

WARNING

It is not unusual to find nongovernmental websites that discuss a specific country's business licensing, permitting, and other legal requirements. These websites are even occasionally operated by foreign legal firms. However, they may contain outdated information or misinterpretations of the law. Be sure to review them against the national websites to avoid confusion.

In some countries, you may find that in addition to the requirement for a national business license, regions may also require their own specific licenses and permits. It is through these additional licenses and permits that the region or locality receives a share of the tax revenue on your business.

TIP

You may find companies that offer a service to expedite a business license, permit, or other required legal paperwork. Many times these firms are perfectly legitimate and are under contract with the host government to ensure the paperwork is correct. Be sure to do your due diligence on any company offering such service, because for some companies the service is simply a means of obtaining a payment to which they are not entitled.

Indemnifying and Protecting Your Operations

When establishing a logistics support service operation in a new country, you need to ensure that your intellectual property, trademarks and brand, and the processes and procedures that made you successful in your domestic operations are protected to the maximum extent possible. Depending on the type of services you are providing, your status as a prime or subcontractor, and whether you are leasing equipment, you also need to ensure you indemnify yourself against losses or damages.

Establishing your intellectual property rights protection plan

For many years the national laws covering the protection of intellectual property varied greatly from country to country. As commerce entered into the global trade environment, the need for more consistency in intellectual property laws and their enforcement became obvious. The World Trade Association (WTO) Agreement on Trade-Related Aspects of Intellectual Property Rights (TRIPS), ratified in 1994, introduced standardized intellectual property protection into the multilateral trading system for the first time.

The TRIPS Agreement was intended to both equalize the way intellectual property rights are protected around the world and bring them under common international rules. It laid out minimum levels of protection that each government has to guarantee to the intellectual property of fellow WTO members. And, when there are trade disputes over intellectual property rights, the WTO's dispute settlement system is available for resolution. The types of intellectual property covered under the TRIPS Agreement include:

>> Copyrights, registrations, and related rights

>> Trademarks

>> Geographical indications (such as when a place name is used to identify a product, like "Champagne" or "Roquefort")

>> Industrial designs

>> Patents

>> Layout designs of integrated circuits

>> Undisclosed information, including trade secrets

Subsequent to the TRIPS Agreement, the WTO has negotiated additional legal texts such as the Information Technology Agreement, and other services and accession protocols.

TIP

More detailed information on the TRIPS agreement and other similar intellectual property protection tools can be found on the World Trade Organization's website at www.wto.org.

While the impact of the TRIPS agreement has been extremely positive, the agreement alone does not guarantee your intellectual property will have the same protection rights in your foreign logistics services location as it has in your domestic operations. Almost every country has its own patent and trademark laws. Persons and companies desiring a patent in a particular country must make an application for patent in that country (or region, as in the case of the Benelux), in accordance with the requirements of that country. Similarly, there may also be additional or implementing local laws that apply to the protection and enforcement of patents, trademarks, copyrights, and other forms of intellectual property.

Prior to the ratification of the TRIPS agreement, in 1970 the Patent Cooperation Treaty (PCT) streamlined the process of filing patents in more than 150 participating nations. A single patent application filed under the PCT is called an international, or PCT, application. After the review of the application by an International Searching Authority and, perhaps, an optional preliminary examination by an International Preliminary Examining Authority of the patentability of the invention, the relevant national or regional authorities issue or reject the patent application.

REMEMBER

Submission of a PCT application does not, itself, result in the award of a patent, because there is no such thing as an "international" patent. It does, however, establish the initial filing date, which then must be followed up by initiating national or regional actions to ultimately grant one or more patents.

There are also some recommended precautionary steps that companies should take when attempting to protect their intellectual property in foreign locations. These include:

>> Working with experienced and peer-acknowledged intellectual property law firms to develop an overall intellectual property protection strategy that supports protection in all your desired foreign locations

>> Developing detailed intellectual property language for licensing and subcontracting contracts

>> Conducting due diligence of potential foreign partners, especially in countries with a reputation for intellectual property theft or abuse

>> Securing and registering patents, trademarks, registrations, and copyrights in key foreign markets, including — as a defensive measure — in countries where violations are common

Protecting and enforcing your methods and operating procedures

All companies have standard operating procedures (normally written) that detail how they do business. When you are providing logistics support services in a foreign country with a local workforce, your foreign employees may not be familiar with your methods or procedures.

Obviously, the solution is a comprehensive training program. If your local employees speak a different language, your procedures need to be translated prior to their being taught to the workforce. If some of your methods or procedures include trade secrets, it is extremely important to ensure that the operating procedures are signed for and numbered, and their distribution is restricted only to those individuals with a "need to know."

Just as important as the training of your methods and procedures is the training about the penalties associated with not following the procedures or compromising your internal trade secrets. It is not uncommon to have your employees, as part of the hiring process, sign an agreement that agrees both that the employee will follow the rules of the company and will not compete against the company for a prescribed period of time after departure from the company. This can become extremely important in the event that you need to fire an employee for not following your procedures. In many countries, you can't fire an employee without reason, and having the employee's signature on the agreement (along with the documentation concerning the dismissal) will assist you if you have to prove it was a proper dismissal.

Getting and Keeping Your Permits and Licenses

Once you have received your business license and permits, you are ready to start hiring employees. If you are employing employees from outside the country of your new foreign operations, you will have to ensure that those employees obtain individual work permits. In most countries, the work permit requires written proof of a job offer that includes a contract number (if the company is working as a subcontractor or for a government institution), the hours of weekly employment, the anticipated duration of the employment (that is, whether the position is temporary or more permanent), as well as the salary and benefits the employee is expected to receive.

TIP

In countries that have a policy of ensuring their own citizens are given the opportunity to work before an individual from another country is employed, the work visa process is used as a means of monitoring the percentage of foreign workers hired under a specific contractor or contract. Other countries will have a quota system that limits the number of work visas issued, based on the type of work to be performed.

Many countries, especially those who have a socialized medical system that offers free or low-cost medical care to all residents, also require a physical as part of the work permit approval process. This is to ensure the employee is in good health prior to arriving in the country.

The process and time to obtain a work visa varies by country. It is not uncommon to have an employee working under a temporary work visa for a month or two until the work permit is approved. And, much like a driver's license, your employees will need to keep a copy of the work permit with them at all times. In most countries, work visas expire after one year, and the entire process (including a physical) must be repeated in time to avoid an underlap in work visa permissions (that is, a period of employment without a current work visa).

Depending on the type of logistics support services you are providing, you may have additional permit requirements, such as hazardous waste handling permits, medical licenses, and construction certifications. In some regions, these permits and licenses are reciprocal between countries when based on previously enacted legal agreements.

In most countries, the issuance of a work permit obligates the employee both to open a local bank account and to pay the appropriate income taxes of that country.

WARNING

It's your company's responsibility to ensure that all its employees providing logistics support services under a work permit or visa comply with all the visa or permit requirements.

Working with national and regional agencies

The best sources of information concerning the requirements for licenses and permits are the embassy websites of the country in which you intend to provide logistics support services. Based on trade and immigration agreements, the procedures may vary between countries.

Regional or national trade associations can also assist in providing general information concerning the process for obtaining permits or licenses. However, they usually only provide general information and do not directly assist you in obtaining your required documentation. There often are other companies that specialize in assisting with obtaining the correct paperwork, as well as moving the paperwork through the bureaucratic process. When it comes to obtaining a business license or permit, it is best to obtain legal counsel that specializes in that type of work in that country.

There are other websites you can access that provide good information, especially for expatriates (people temporarily or permanently residing, as immigrants, in a country other than that of their citizenship). No legal requirement governs how those websites should be maintained, so exercise caution in assuming the information is either current or accurate.

Using sponsor companies

In order to issue work permits, all countries require that either a relative or a local company sponsor the workers, with many countries only allowing the employing company to act as sponsor. The *sponsor company* (that is, the company that guarantees the individual's actions while in the host country) then becomes legally responsible to the country for the worker.

If your domestic headquarters is a large corporation already operating in the country in which you will be providing logistics support services, it may already have established its own local sponsor company. More often than not, however, larger companies use sponsor companies that already have been established specifically for that purpose.

While the services provided by a sponsor company can vary, most assist in obtaining work permits, help establish local bank accounts, provide translation services, provide housing, and often provide company vehicles. Some even have in-house legal representatives who can assist your company in keeping track of changing national laws. Remember that their contract is with the firm doing business in that country, not with the company's employees. The firm being supported pays a contracted amount per employee for the sponsor company's services. The amount charged per employee may vary significantly between sponsor companies, so be sure you understand exactly what and how much a company provides before agreeing to a lower-price firm. In this case, your sponsor company contract should be one of "best value" rather than one of "lowest cost."

TIP

A good sponsor company is worth its weight in gold. It provides support to both your company and your employees, reduces the personnel administration burden, and allows you to focus on the contractual logistics services support to your client.

Keeping up-to-date with change

The laws and regulations for conducting business in a foreign country often change frequently. It is imperative that your company has the means of keeping up both with the latest changes and even anticipated changes that have not yet been formally approved. Otherwise, you may find your operations and your employees suddenly no longer welcome in the country, with little recourse after the fact to reverse any unintended violation or breach.

Perhaps the best practice to keep up-to-date is to hire local counsel to watch what is happening in the legislature. Another excellent option is to include such a requirement in your contract with your sponsor company. If neither option is available, subscribing to a local paper or web service that monitors the regional and national government will go a long way toward keeping you in the know.

Chapter **16**

Deciding on Your Source of Manpower

In providing logistics support services, your manpower is your most essential element — and your greatest expense. When you are contemplating providing logistics support services for a client in a foreign location, there are many workforce factors to consider. Do you bring a full staff from your domestic operations or hire local nationals? Do you hire permanent employees or contract out your workforce? Are there laws in the foreign country or region governing who you can hire? And are there additional expenses associated with your workforce that you may not have experienced in your domestic operations?

In this chapter we will discuss the various types of employees, as well as the pros and cons of the use of each type. Because each country's laws related to the hiring and management of employees differ, you will need to find local experts familiar with the laws in the country or countries where you are planning to provide logistics support services.

Identifying Your Labor Pool: Internal versus External

As you prepare to provide foreign logistics support services, you have several manpower options to choose from, depending on the laws of the country where you intend to do work.

Following are the three categories of external manpower:

>> **Local nationals** (commonly referred to as LNs) are citizens of the country where the work is being performed — for example, a citizen of India working on a project in India.

>> **Expatriates** (commonly referred to as *expats*) are normally considered to be domestic employees of a multinational company or its subsidiary with a foreign assignment — for example, a citizen of India working for an Indian company in Africa.

>> **Third-country nationals** (commonly referred to as TCNs) are employees of a multinational company who work in a foreign country and do not have the citizenship of the parent company's home country or the country of employment — for example, an Indian employee working for a French company in Africa. (Note, however, that in the European Union [EU] the term "third-country national" is often used together with "foreign national" and "non-EU foreign national," to refer to individuals who are from neither the EU country in which they are currently living or staying nor other member states of the European Union.)

TIP

When it comes to work permits, visas, and other national laws, many countries do not distinguish between expatriates and third-country nationals — their laws only distinguish between their own citizens and citizens of other countries.

Understanding the labor pool options

Quite often, a company's initial preference is to bring employees from its domestic business operations because the domestic employees are familiar with its business processes and operational practices. The domestic employees also tend to be loyal to the company and require little training. That said, moving to a foreign location can be extremely traumatic for domestic employees. If they are taking their families, the move can be even more difficult. Can the spouse get a job, if desired? Can the employee and spouse get a vehicle and a driver's license? Are adequate schools or child-care facilities available? Can they retain their current personal insurance? Domestic employees also tend to be significantly more expensive, with or without their families relocating to the foreign location, as they expect to be paid not only their domestic salary but also an additional housing and relocation allowance.

Many companies' internal hiring practices do not permit the hiring of third-country nationals or local nationals for work that is conducted in a foreign location. If that practice does not apply to your company, you are then faced with the issues associated with recruiting local nationals or third-country nationals in an area you may not be familiar with, especially local labor law compliance.

For other than your domestic employees, you may choose to contract out the recruitment of that part of your workforce that is composed of expatriates, local nationals, or third-country nationals. This recruitment service can be provided by companies with the expertise to hire the type of employee you are seeking, in the foreign location where you are establishing your logistics support services operations.

Using your own workforce

The decision as to how many of your domestic employees you bring — either temporarily or permanently — to your foreign contract site is one of weighing risk versus expense. If there are intellectual property and trade secrets you want to protect, or your processes and procedures are complicated and training local nationals or third-country nationals will be time consuming, you may likely choose initially to use a greater number of your own domestic employees (that is, in a temporary duty status).

You can avoid some of the expense of long-term assignments and employee concerns over family separation by rotating your staff — just be sure continuity isn't lost when doing so. This strategy also serves to provide your domestic workforce and stakeholders a better understanding of the issues associated with your new foreign contract.

TIP

When rotating your staff, you can often obtain temporary visas (such as 30-, 60- or 90-day visas) at a lower cost than annual work visas. In some countries, other types of visas or work permits can be used instead of an official work visa. Just make sure that whatever temporary visa you get allows an individual to earn an income in that country and that the temporary income is exempt from host-country taxes.

Hiring independent contractors

Another option can be the hiring of *independent contractors.* While the definition of such an individual differs among countries, independent contractors generally can be distinguished from employees on your payroll in a number of ways. Independent contractors

>> Provide their own tools and materials

>> Can be discharged at any time, with or without cause

>> Are responsible for their own insurance, medical plans, transportation, and housing

>> Obtain their own business licenses, work visas, and other required permits

>> Pay their own taxes and all other financial obligations

>> Are paid by the job, not by the hour, as negotiated in their contract

>> Are free to come and go as they please, and — unless prohibited by their contract with you — often work for other companies at the same time as they are working for you

The more independent contractors you use, the lower your overall personnel costs are, because you only have to pay salaries (and not associated overhead costs).

TIP

It is common practice for contracts governing the use of independent personnel to contain both a nondisclosure clause and a prohibition clause that prevents the individual from working for another company while under contract to you. This is especially the case when your competitors are working in the same location.

The decision to hire your own nondomestic employees or subcontract out your workforce is again the result of an analysis of risk and cost. The risk is associated with ensuring that you retain the qualified workforce necessary to fulfill your contract. If your workforce is to be composed mostly of expatriates you can hire in your domestic location, you're more likely to be able to find and retain the employees you need. But, if the workforce will consist of a majority of local nationals or third-country nationals, you should consider contracting out the hiring and management of that portion of your workforce to ensure you can obtain and retain the number of employees you need. Additionally, your level of responsibility to all applicable foreign governments (that is, the governments issuing citizenship, as well as the host government) is reduced when your workforce is contracted to another company.

Personnel costs above and beyond direct salary expenses are another big consideration. If your overhead and operating costs are high, you may find that it is much less expensive to contract out all or part of your nondomestic workforce to another company with lower costs.

Understanding the Difference between Expatriates, Local Nationals, and Third-Country Nationals

When a logistics support services provider is fulfilling a contract in a foreign country, it is not unusual to have a mix of employees: expatriates, local nationals, and third-country nationals. The expatriates may have come from your domestic operations and know your processes and procedures. The second tier of management, or jobs that require a degree of technical expertise, may be filled with third-country nationals. It is also not unusual to see the ratios of expatriates, third-country nationals, and local nationals change significantly over time as the local nationals receive the proper training to enable them to advance in your organization.

As previously explained, local nationals are citizens of the country where you are providing your foreign logistics support services, while third-country nationals are citizens of neither the host country where the work is to be performed nor the country where your domestic headquarters is located. While on the surface that difference may seem insignificant, it makes a significant difference with respect to how they are viewed by the host country.

Most countries have laws to help ensure that their own citizens are hired as a priority over third-country nationals, whenever it is feasible. These laws can include quotas placed on the number of third-country nationals employed, either by job classification (that is, the type of work being performed) or by contract (for example, as a percentage of total employees).

TIP

The host country monitors the status of third-country nationals through the issue of work visas. If you are facing a quota situation, be sure to request work visas first for your most critical third-country national employees.

Hiring expatriates

There are several advantages to hiring expatriate employees, especially if they have worked previously in your domestic operations. Some of those advantages include:

>> Greater employee loyalty to your company and its objectives

>> Familiarity with your processes and procedures

>> Stronger ties between your foreign employees and your domestic headquarters

>> Greater domestic oversight over the foreign lower-tier management staff and employees

>> Improved training and development of the foreign staff (both LNs and TCNs)

Disadvantages in expatriate hiring

However, there are also disadvantages in using expatriate employees, in addition to the normally higher salary requirements. These include:

>> Complying with local government restrictions and quotas through the work permit process

>> Dealing with an inability of the expatriate to adapt to the culture and traditions of the foreign workplace

>> Dealing with an expatriate who lowers the standards of performance

>> Absorbing the additional cost of relocating the expatriate's family, as well as providing adequate housing, access to quality medical care, transportation, and schools

>> Preventing an expectation of further employment once the foreign contract has been completed

WARNING

It is not uncommon to experience an expatriate turnover approaching 20 percent during the life of a logistics support services contract. More often than not, this turnover is the result of an expatriate or his family's inability to adapt to their new location.

Using expatriates when providing logistics support services for governments

If your foreign logistics support services are being provided under a contract with your own government (for example, in support of your government's embassy or military), quite often some or all of your workforce will be required to have security clearances issued by your home country, and not either your host country or your employee's country of citizenship. As a result, under those circumstances expatriates from your home country will have a valid security clearance of the right level prior to starting work.

Additionally, it's not uncommon for government contracts to specify not only the security clearance requirements for your workforce, but also the national or political composition of your workforce. A recent example of this requirement is that personnel not requiring security clearances come from member nations of the European Union (EU) or the North Atlantic Treaty Organization (NATO).

Hiring local nationals

One of the most challenging aspects of hiring local nationals is simply determining how to recruit and hire them. Quite often, the common methods used for domestic employment advertising may not be either as available or, if available, as effective in your new foreign location. For example, do the foreign candidates search newspapers or job websites, or is reading job announcements posted in their village the only means of job hunting available to them? Can you describe the work sufficiently to ensure potential employees understand both the job qualifications and duty descriptions?

Another challenge comes with the completion and submission of applications and the subsequent interviews. Obviously, your domestic applications will have to be translated into the native language; subsequently, when you are conducting the interview, you will need to have interviewers who are conversant in the native language as well as familiar with local customs and traditions.

Verifying information concerning previous employment and other background material (such as education) may prove to be equally difficult. Here, also, you likely will encounter language as well as privacy barriers. Finally, the type of background information you are used to obtaining and need for full due diligence may just not exist.

TIP

Often the best approach when hiring host-country personnel to carry out a logistics support services job is to contract with a host-country employment agency, one that adds a fee percentage either based on the number of local nationals hired or the local employees' salaries over a specified time period.

Determining when third-country national hiring is the solution

So why hire third-country nationals? In a few countries, there are simply not enough citizens available for employment. For example, in Dubai only 20 percent of the population is made up of citizens of Dubai; in Kuwait, only 30 percent are Kuwaiti citizens. In other countries, the general education level is not adequate to provide sufficient local nationals for more highly technical work, especially if you or your clients require specialized permits or degrees. And, depending on the type of work, third-country nationals are often much less expensive to hire than expatriates.

There is also the issue of your company being able to get adequate insurance or bonding to support your foreign logistics support services contract. In some countries, the background documentation (both personal and security-related) is simply inadequate, which makes the hiring of third-country nationals a better option.

While many nations' citizens make up the rolls of third-country nationals, India, Pakistan, and the Philippines make up a significant percentage of a country's third-country nationals. Educated individuals from highly populated countries with limited opportunities for earning a living wage "at home" are good candidates for hiring as third-country national workers. Here again, your issue may be how to reach them if they are not already available in your domestic or foreign locations.

There are companies that specialize in the recruitment, hiring, and management of third-country nationals. These companies usually are headquartered in the country where the third-country nationals reside, and they often have a supplemental education element to teach individuals the requisite language skills and fundamental work skills (such as a level of reading and writing proficiency, mechanical expertise, or accounting) prior to your actual employment.

REMEMBER

If you are planning on outsourcing part of your personnel management function to companies that specialize in local national or third-country national labor, be sure to stipulate in the contract what currency will be used for your payment to them. In areas that experience turbulence in the valuation of currencies (such as the value of the Euro to the Kuwait dinar), it is not uncommon to allow for renegotiation of the contract when the turbulence exceeds a specified percentage (for example, plus or minus 10 percent).

Managing and Retaining Your Foreign Employees

When you hire local nationals, you're likely not obligated to provide their housing or transportation unless you're operating in a hostile environment. Nor are you concerned with their personal finance or tax payments.

Conversely, when hiring third-country nationals, you (or your contracted sponsor company) must ensure that the accommodations of the employees meet both the minimum housing requirements of the host country and all other legal requirements (for example, work permits and bank accounts). Depending on your logistics support services client, you may also have to ensure that the living and working conditions of expatriates and third-country nationals comply with the laws of their home country (that is, their home of citizenship).

Job satisfaction and employee turnover also need to be considered. Local nationals tend to remain on the job as long as they feel that their pay is commensurate with their duties and there is a possibility of upward mobility. Much like expatriates, third-country nationals have to adjust to the traditions and culture of their new workplace without a familial support network. As a result, the turnover of third-country nationals is often much higher than that of local nationals.

Local nationals expect to be paid in their national currency. In most instances this is not an issue if the payment received from your foreign client is also in the same national currency. It can become an issue, however, if the paychecks originate from your home office. In that case, you need to understand the risks associated with the fluctuation between the two currencies.

Local nationals will tend to be much more attuned to the political situation in your host country than either third-country nationals or expatriates. This can be an advantage in obtaining information concerning the nation or region that may affect your operations in the future. But, it can also prove to be a distraction if you have political disagreement in the workplace.

TIP

Do not underestimate the value of good relationships with the local community as well as with local, regional, and national governments when local nationals comprise a significant percentage of your workforce. They can go a long way toward enhancing your company's position.

Chapter **17**

Understanding Foreign Labor Laws and Requirements

When you are hiring local nationals, third-country nationals, or expatriates, be sure to comply with all the host nation's labor laws. It's important to be fully aware of the labor laws, as they are sometimes difficult to interpret and are prone to frequent change. The best option is to retain a competent local legal firm with an expertise in labor laws. Don't think you can avoid any of the labor laws. Your employees will most certainly know them as well as or better than you do.

In this chapter, we examine many of the labor laws that you may have to comply with. We discuss their impact on workforce scheduling, the need to accommodate restrictions, and how to determine the impact of the laws on your ability to successfully fulfill your logistics services support contract. We also take a look at how meeting foreign labor laws may financially impact your bottom line.

Integrating Labor Laws into Work Schedules

Labor laws vary by country, but normally address the following elements:

>> Minimum wages

>> Maximum work hours (by day and by week) and overtime considerations

>> Observance of national and regional holidays (both secular and religious)

>> Minimum age for employment (including restrictions)

>> Minimum days of vacation (paid or unpaid)

>> Compensation of employees upon release from employment (regardless of the cause)

>> Special provisions for the employment of females

>> Special provisions to accommodate religious practices

>> Special provisions for employer-funded medical costs, insurance, transportation costs, educational expenses, and child-care costs

If your logistics services contract requires you to provide simple "eight hours a day, five days a week" support, then scheduling your employees is relatively simple. (Remember that in many Muslim countries, the work week is Sunday through Thursday.) However, if your contract is to provide logistics support services for a period that either exceeds eight hours a day, includes shift work, or exceeds a five-day workweek, scheduling becomes much more difficult.

The key labor-law provisions that affect the scheduling of your workforce are those associated with the maximum allowable hours (either weekly, daily, or a combination of both), accommodation for national and regional holidays (to include those for religious observances), and the number of vacation days — both paid and unpaid — that you must provide your employees.

WARNING

Failure to abide by host country labor laws can result in significant financial penalties or even revocation of your business licenses and permits.

Complying with requirements for work hours, overtime, and vacation time

The standard workweek — that is, the work schedule period when employees are not required to be paid overtime — in most countries consists of five 8-hour days (40 total hours). Some countries — such as Columbia, India, Kuwait, and Malaysia — have legislated that the workweek can be up to 48 hours. Other countries have legislated a workweek of less than 40 hours: for example, France (35 hours), Denmark (37 hours), and Australia (38 hours). There are also many differences among nations concerning the time provisions for breaks and meals, either by amount of time allowed or by specification of a designated mealtime period.

The labor laws in most countries do not distinguish between employees paid an hourly wage and those employees on a fixed or negotiated salary (such as management). However, some countries do provide a definition of what constitutes a salaried employee that allows for a longer workweek.

Some countries define the standard workweek based on the type of work being performed. For example, the standard workweek for factory workers may be fewer than 40 hours, while the workweek for those in agriculture or the hospitality industry may be longer than 40 hours. There may also be special exceptions for those in technical fields such as medicine and information technology.

There are regions in a few countries (including China and India) that have passed their own legislation that further restrict the number of hours in a standard workweek or reduce the average week to less than five eight-hour days.

National and regional labor-law provisions for overtime also vary greatly. Many countries limit the number of overtime hours that can be worked in a week, month, and/or year. You will also find great differences in the payment for overtime hours — while 1.5 percent of the standard hourly wage is the most-often-proscribed amount, other countries place the amount at a lower percentage. In the event that an employee has to work on a national holiday, many countries require that employees be paid twice their hourly wage.

TIP

The Organisation for Economic Co-operation and Development (OECD) is an excellent source to research the average number of work hours for employees in your foreign location. Many different types of data are available on its website at www.OECD.org.

The national and regional labor laws governing the requirements for paid vacation also differ greatly by country. The typical period of paid vacation is between two and four calendar weeks and is often based on how many years an employee has worked for the company, whether the employee is a shift worker, or the type of work being performed. Many countries specify when an employee is entitled to start taking paid vacation, based on how long the employee has worked for the company.

Some countries, such as Columbia and South Africa, specify that paid vacation time must be taken over consecutive calendar days, while other countries, such as Germany and Greece, specify that vacation time excludes weekends. Some of the more interesting special provisions in the labor laws of specific countries include the following:

>> Bangladesh has a different number of vacation days for industry workers, tea plantation workers, and newspaper workers.

>> Belgium provides more vacation days for employees who work six days a week than for those working five days a week.

>> Brazil bases the number of annual paid vacation days on the number of days an employee has been absent from work.

>> France provides for 30 days of vacation (Sundays do not count), with bonus days if the employees take part of their vacation time in the "off-summer" period.

>> Hungary provides up to seven additional days of vacation based on the employee's number of children.

>> India's vacation days are different for minors and adult workers, and vary by type of employment and from state to state.

>> Italy directs the provision of a minimum of 20 workdays of vacation, plus additional personal paid time off of not more than 104 hours.

>> Pakistan has special provisions for mine workers, based on the number of days worked below ground.

>> Poland's vacation days are based on years of employment, with secondary and tertiary education partially counting toward the employment time.

>> Romania has special provisions for the handicapped and those working in dangerous conditions.

>> Singapore has no statutory minimum number of vacation days for domestic workers or employees in managerial positions.

>> The United States has no statutory minimum number of paid vacation days. According to the US Bureau of Labor Statistics, 77 percent of private employers offer paid vacation of varying length.

TIP

Foreign labor laws for paid vacation days are only minimums. In order to hire and retain employees in your foreign work location, be sure to investigate what the prevailing benefits are at that location.

The standard work hours, overtime hours, vacation time, and other special provisions cited in this chapter do not take into account those employees covered by labor unions — such as individuals in China and the European Union — who may have additional restrictions or benefits covered in a negotiated union contract. In many underdeveloped countries in Africa and South America, unions set the benefits to the employees, and the national courts in those countries defer to the contract between the union and the employer.

Paid sick leave is another factor to be aware of. While many countries require the payment of this benefit, there are also many countries that do not require employers to pay, assuming that the employee's annual leave will be used on those days the employee cannot come to work. In most cases where the payment of sick leave is mandatory, the employee is required to provide a medical slip validating the illness or injury.

Understanding work location restrictions

At times, you may have to adjust your regular work schedule because of national or local decrees. One of the most common instances is the adjustment of work schedules by two hours less per day per employee during the religious period of Ramadan in Muslim countries.

Other times, the national or local government may curtail work based on extreme weather conditions. For example, if your personnel's work site is outdoors, during periods of extreme heat their duty hours may be limited based on the temperature and you may be required to provide additional breaks.

Conversely, many times a work location may be tied to local or regional government hours, such that your employees cannot work if the local government declares a snow emergency or an evacuation due to impending hurricanes, floods, or typhoons.

There are also some countries that require a minimum percentage of handicapped local nationals in your workforce. This may necessitate special accommodations at your workplace.

Accommodating Religious Requirements

In addition to the required modification of work schedules in Muslim countries during Ramadan, there are other considerations you must be prepared to provide your employees based on their religious practices. This can include granting additional paid time off for national or religious holidays, allowing time and a place for prayer or meditation during set times of the day, scheduling limited duties on religious high holy days, allowing for the wear of religious garments, or accommodating dietary restrictions.

Accommodating national and religious holidays

Foreign national holidays are often based on a combination of significant national historical events and the prevailing religion. Therefore, they vary widely by country, with some common days such as Christmas in Christian countries and Isra' and Mi'raj in Islamic countries. The average number of national holidays runs between 8 and 15 days. On the other hand, there are other countries that do not specify employees be paid for any national holiday.

REMEMBER

The dates of a public or religious holiday can frequently change. Be sure to check the labor laws and holiday schedule in your foreign location.

The labor laws in most countries require that national (or public) holidays be observed by paying the employee either a day's wage not to work or overtime if the employee has to work. Here, too, there are exceptions. Following are some of the more unique provisions for national and public holidays:

>> In Cambodia, every employee is entitled to 27 paid public holidays.

>> In Chad, there are only 3 paid public holidays.

>> In Denmark, there is no statutory right for pay on public holidays.

>> In Germany, there is one paid public holiday (German Unity Day), but each state regulates a remaining 9 to 13 paid holidays.

>> In Greece, there are only four mandatory paid public holidays.

>> In Guyana, there are no legal provisions for pay on public holidays.

>> In India, employees are entitled to 15 to 20 paid public holidays, depending on the state.

>> In Japan, there are no provisions for pay on public holidays.

>> In Malaysia, employees are entitled to 19 paid public holidays.

>> In the Netherlands, there are no provisions for paid public holidays.

>> In Norway, there are two paid public holidays.

» In Pakistan, factory workers are entitled to 17 paid public holidays. On average, corporations provide at least 15 paid public holidays.

» In Serbia, there are nine national banking holidays and up to two additional paid holidays, depending on the religion of the employee.

» In Sweden, there are no legal provisions for pay on public holidays.

» In Switzerland, employees are entitled to between 7 and 15 paid holidays, depending on the canton (state).

» In the United Kingdom, employees do not have to be paid for holidays, as long as they are included in their overall paid vacation compensation.

» In the United States, there are no statutory paid public holidays. However, hourly employees working for federal or state customers are entitled to paid public holidays.

REMEMBER

If your logistics services support contract is for your domestic government but at a foreign location (such as an embassy), be sure to check the provisions in your contract for paid public holidays. Most embassies adhere to both their own public holidays as well as those of the host country.

There are other days that certain religions forbid work, regardless of where the employee is working. For example, the Jewish faith forbids work on Rosh Hashanah and Yom Kippur, while fundamentalist Christians are not allowed to work on Sundays or certain holy days (for example, Christmas or Easter). Normally, employers can accommodate these observances as part of the employee's paid vacation schedule. If not, the employee should be given the days off without pay.

Understanding and dealing with other religious requirements

Most countries have a law that prohibits discrimination in employment based on a person's religion, though the degree of enforcement of the law varies. In many countries, the law provides that

» Employers may not treat employees more or less favorably because of their religion.

» Employees can't be required to refrain from participating in a religious activity as a condition of employment.

» Employers must take steps to prevent religious harassment of or religious discrimination against their employees.

>> Employers must reasonably accommodate employees' regularly practiced religious observations unless doing so would impose an undue hardship on the employer or violate health or safety standards.

>> Employers may not retaliate against employees for asserting their rights under the law.

In many countries this means that employers must attempt to accommodate employees who, for religious reasons, must maintain a particular physical appearance or manner of dress in keeping with the tenets of their religion. When it comes to religious apparel, employers may insist on non-religiously proscribed dress only if it's to ensure the employee's safety.

Accommodating an employee's right to observe religious practices on the work site can be difficult. While some countries require that employers designate a specific room for prayer, most do not. However, providing an employee time to meditate or pray is a common practice as long as the employee fulfills the total daily hours of work specified in the contract.

If the employer provides food for the employees, there is an expectation that either religious dietary restrictions will be accommodated or the employee will be paid an amount equal to that of the cost of the employer-provided meals to cover employee-provided meals.

WARNING

The laws concerning the accommodation of religious beliefs and practices are "laws in progress." In many countries, during the hiring process you cannot ask the religion of a potential employee. In the event that a situation arises concerning an employee's religious practices at the work site, it's best to address and mutually resolve the situation as quickly as possible.

Understanding the Special Provisions for Employing Women and Children

If the employment of women and children is permitted by your host country, special provisions must be strictly followed. In addition to the sections of the country's labor laws concerning their employment, there usually are other national laws — such as child welfare or human trafficking legislation — that place restrictions on their employment. Your domestic country may also have ratified international labor or criminal justice agreements that you are subject to, regardless of where your foreign logistics services support contract is carried out.

Employing female workers

The number of females in the workforce has risen in most countries over the past several decades. In the logistics services support industry, women now constitute over 50 percent of the total workforce in Africa and Asia, and over 75 percent of the workforce in North and Latin America as well as the Western and Eastern European countries.

Regardless of the percentage of female employees, all countries have sections in their labor laws that pertain to their benefits and working conditions. These can include

>> Times of the day that a female employee can work

>> Paid and unpaid leave for pregnant employees and new mothers

>> Employer-provided breastfeeding and child-care facilities

The labor laws in many countries in the Middle East, South America, and Africa prohibit *requiring* women to work during the hours of darkness. Kuwait, Bahrain, Syria, and the United Arab Emirates have laws specifically prohibiting women from working at night, unless approved by the government.

The 187 countries of the United Nations' International Labour Organization (ILO) have provisions in their labor laws specific to maternity leave. The amount of leave time averages three months per child and normally begins six weeks prior to delivery. All but the United States, Swaziland, Lesotho, and Papua New Guinea have provisions for continuation of pay during the period of maternity leave. In some countries the employer pays full or partial wages, while in other countries the mother receives a stipend from both the employer and the government.

TIP

Though not as frequently, about a third of the ILO member nations also provide paid paternity leave.

In the United States, it is common practice among larger companies for the female employee to receive short-term disability benefits at a reduced wage rate for a prescribed period while not working. The short-term disability insurance premiums can be employer-paid, employee-paid, or paid by both.

Many countries also allow the employee to take additional unpaid personal leave from work, in some cases up to ten months, with the right to return to work at the same position and salary upon return.

A significant number of countries require the employer to provide a designated location for mothers to breastfeed, and many countries require the employer to host a child-care facility (or pay for an outside facility) if it has a large number of female employees.

Employing minors

All countries have defined the minimum age at which an individual can be hired for full-time employment. Some also define the minimum age for part-time or temporary employment. The average permanent employment minimum age ranges from 14 to 18 years of age, with the younger age threshold found normally in the less-industrialized countries.

The ILO has also decreed that minors (defined as those under the age of 18) shall not be employed in works and activities that, by their nature, harm the the minors' health, safety, or morals; limit their education; or involve physical, psychological, or moral hazards. There are additional restrictions for the employment of children under the age of 16.

It must be noted that while most nations are members of the ILO, the use of underage minors in the workplace is still prevalent in many parts of Africa and Asia. According to the ILO, Asia and the Pacific still have the largest numbers of child labor (almost 78 million children or 9.3 percent of the child population), but Sub-Saharan Africa continues to be the region with the highest incidence of child labor (59 million, over 21 percent of the child population).

REMEMBER

For more information on the international laws and statistics pertaining to the employment of women and minors, we recommend the ILO website at www.ilo.org/global/topics.

Addressing special provisions before they become a problem

Staying current with all labor laws in the countries in which you're providing logistics support services is imperative. It's also important to stay current with international laws, because you could be prosecuted by your own country or have your contracts terminated for violations of international laws.

Many times the application of international laws results in the subsequent definition of specific actions that an employer must take. For example, the United Nations Protocol to Prevent, Suppress and Punish Trafficking in Persons,

Especially Women and Children (the "Protocol") is currently signed by over 160 nations. As a result, many nations have interpreted the protocol to allow the right to inspect, or require you to inspect, the living quarters of your third-country national and expatriate employees to ensure they are not enabling human trafficking. The Protocol also forbids employers from withholding any employee's passport for any reason. Finally, under the Protocol many countries require employers to pay for return transportation to the employee's home country, regardless of the circumstances surrounding the return.

Compensating Your Workforce

For the purposes of this section, we define *compensation* as the wages paid directly to your employees for the services they provide you in accordance with the terms of their contract, as well as any additional sums paid (not reimbursed) to them that may be required by the labor laws of the host country.

We recognize that many company's compensation packages include additional financial benefits — often taxable — such as incentive bonuses, overseas employment allowances, vehicles, or stock options. However, most foreign labor laws do not address those forms of compensation.

Compensating for hours worked — and not worked

For starters, consider the minimum wage. Most countries have established the minimum amount a private sector employee can be paid for a set period of time. Normally, that time is on a per-hour basis, but many countries have a minimum wage set by week or month as well. The minimum wage also often differs for full-time versus part-time employees. For some, the amount is adjusted annually based on inflation, but in most countries the amount is changed only by new legislation. Over a dozen countries include a specific amount for meals as part of their minimum wage. Variations are many, so here are some of the more interesting exceptions:

>> In Australia and Kenya, the minimum wage varies by employee age, type of work, and geographic area of employee work.

>> In Austria, Denmark, Finland, Iceland, Italy, and Sweden, collective bargaining agreements set minimum wages by job classification for each industry.

- In Belgium and Ireland, the minimum is set by age and by years of employment.

- In Bolivia, Guatemala, and Puerto Rico, the laws dictate a mandatory Christmas bonus.

- In Brazil, Canada, China, India, Indonesia, Japan, Malaysia, Thailand, and Vietnam, the minimum wage is set regionally, locally, or by a combination of both.

- In Costa Rica, El Salvador, Grenada, Haiti, Mozambique, Nicaragua, and Zambia, the amount varies by industry or economic sector.

- In Cote d'Ivoire and Cypress, the rate is set by occupation.

- In the Dominican Republic, the minimum wage rate in the free trade zone is determined by the size of the company.

- In Kosovo, there are separate rates for employees under the age of 35 and those 35 and older.

- In the United States, there is a national minimum wage, but some states have legislated higher rates.

REMEMBER

Check with the local business associations where you intend to provide your logistics support services. They will know the specific minimum wages for your employees and will be aware of any pending legislation that may affect the rates in the near term. More importantly, they will know the prevailing hourly wages at your new location — which may be significantly higher than the minimum wage.

Be aware that the wages you pay your employee are only part of your financial obligation. Every country has a tax on the employer to fund social programs such as social security or national insurance programs. Normally, the tax is a set percentage of the employee's hourly or monthly wages.

So, when does your employee get paid for not working? Earlier in this chapter we discuss paid vacation time and paid holidays. Your host country's labor laws may also specify a number of paid days for sick leave or personal time, which can often be extremely generous. Many countries also require paid bereavement leave, normally only granted upon the death of an employee's immediate family member (such as a spouse, parent, or child). Note that each country defines "immediate family" differently.

Muslim countries also have provisions in their labor laws for attending the Hajj pilgrimage once in an employee's lifetime. Normally those four to five weeks are not paid leave; but in Saudi Arabia, Bahrain, and Afghanistan, at least a portion of the time off is paid by the employer.

Many countries also have provisions in their labor laws that require you to pay your employees in the event that their work has stopped entirely or in part because of exceptional circumstances or force majeure. Under those circumstances, you may be required to pay the worker's wages for the period of the stoppage, for up to 30 days. However, often you may assign the worker other similar work, or — in order to make up for the time lost — give the worker additional unpaid work hours not to exceed two hours per day for up to 30 days a year.

Finally, many countries require the employer to pay the employee a *termination indemnity,* which is a lump sum paid to an employee being terminated from employment. Depending on the host country's labor laws, the number of years of employment, and the reason for termination, this amount can even exceed the employee's annual wages.

WARNING

Terminating *any* employee providing services in a foreign country can be a complicated process. Many countries go into great detail in their laws concerning this topic by defining what are acceptable grounds for termination, when warnings to the employee need to be given, and a host of other administrative requirements. Often, regardless of the reason for termination, a termination indemnity is still required. Finally, don't think that your expatriates or your domestic employees in country supporting your foreign logistics services contract aren't covered by the foreign labor laws. You could end up being sued by them in the host country's courts.

Adjusting compensation for location and risk

In countries with high unemployment, you may be able to get by with paying minimum wages. But, be careful. If your logistics support services include any requirement for experience or technical expertise, you are going to have to compete with other companies to find a qualified local national workforce. And, if you include expatriates or third-country nationals in your workforce, you also have to adjust wages based on the work location. In some cases, it may be because you are in an urban area, where the cost of living is much higher. In other cases, it may be because you are in a rural area with fewer options for extracurricular activities.

Great differences in culture between an employee's home country and the work location often require special incentives to hire and retain employees, especially when they are separated from their families.

If your logistics support services are to be delivered in an area of moderate or extreme risk, expect to have to further incentivize your workforce. This is often done through a combination of increased salaries as well as providing additional vacation time (paid or unpaid). It may also include incentives such as higher-quality or high-security living arrangements, Internet access, gym memberships, or educational opportunities.

REMEMBER

Compensating your workforce in a foreign location generally requires a comprehensive package of incentives, all of which will vary in each of the foreign locations in which you are providing logistics support services.

5

Being Part of a Global Humanitarian & Disaster Relief Logistics Team

Get both an overview of the global humanitarian and disaster relief (H&DR) environment, and an introduction to the major international relief providers and their roles.

Gain an understanding of and appreciation for the critical role of logistics in H&DR operations.

Understand the process of determining a specific corporate response to a call for H&DR participation: to include establishing, activating, and preparing your company's logistics team for any potential deployment.

Discover the methods for provisioning, deploying, and operating an H&DR logistics support team in a seemingly unstructured and disconnected multinational, multicultural foreign environment.

Chapter **18**

Understanding Global Humanitarian and Disaster Relief Logistics

Perhaps you've responded to emergencies in your own country and feel ready to take your experience and expertise into the global arena. Or you may be a newcomer to disaster relief, propelled by a sense of corporate social responsibility to alleviate the suffering that occurs in faraway disasters. Either way, understanding the operational construct and "language" of the international humanitarian and disaster relief (H&DR) community — especially the logistics component — is essential.

In this chapter we explain the categories and scope of disasters as well as the many players involved in the conduct of relief operations, especially once the affected country asks for outside help. Both the complex lines of command and control and their specifically defined roles and responsibilities are discussed, so as to provide an understanding of the critical role logistics plays in all international H&DR efforts. Finally, we explain the planning, preparation, and infrastructure that have to be in place so that your company can be prepared to successfully respond to a United Nations (UN) call for international H&DR support.

UNDERSTANDING THE MEANING OF "DISASTER"

To be an effective contributor to any international disaster management and relief effort, it's important to understand what we mean when we use the term *disaster*. You probably think of a hurricane, flood, earthquake, or industrial accident as a "disaster." However, the international humanitarian relief community now refers to such events as *hazards* — that is, incidents that cause disasters. Regardless of whether it's called a disaster, hazard, emergency, or catastrophe, the focus of our discussion is on not only just the causative event but, more importantly, the response to the event.

Of the many definitions of *disaster* you may come across, the one we use here is from the United Nations International Strategy for Disaster Risk Reduction (UNISDR — more often referred to as the United Nations Office of Disaster Risk Reduction). Accordingly, a disaster is:

> *"A serious disruption of the functioning of a community or a society involving widespread human, material, economic, or environmental losses and impacts, which exceeds the ability of the affected community or society to cope using its own resources."*

Whether a hazard triggers a disaster at a specific location depends on the severity of the incident coupled with the affected area's resilience. Two earthquakes of identical magnitude, for example, may have very different outcomes depending on such factors as population density, building codes, and the response capabilities of the affected country.

Note: UN-hosted discussions with industry on corporate engagement in H&DR reveal that the traditional humanitarian community and the business sector often seem to be talking two different languages and have significantly different operating styles. The more you do to bridge these gaps, the easier your integration into and the more effective your contributions to international H&DR efforts are.

Defining the Scope of Humanitarian and Disaster Relief

The UN and its agencies group disasters into three categories that are roughly based on the type of hazard, the operating environment, or a combination of those factors. Those categories are *sudden onset disasters*, *slow onset disasters*, and *complex disasters*, as defined in Table 18-1.

TABLE 18-1   **UN-Defined Categories of Disasters and Their Causes**

Category	Cause
Sudden onset disasters	Suddenly-occurring natural (geophysical, hydrological, meteorological, climatological, or biological) or man-made (such as transportation or industrial) disasters
Slow onset disasters	Crises that emerge over a sustained period of time due to external triggers (such as drought-induced crop failure or illnesses)
Complex disasters	Natural or man-made disasters complicated by political or social circumstances that cause the destabilization of society

Our focus is on *sudden onset disasters*. Despite differences in their severity, sudden onset disasters have a common set of effects that drive relief needs. These include loss of life, injury, displacement, hunger, and disease. Other effects, which may complicate efforts to deliver aid, are destruction of or severe damage to roads, ports, airports, and other infrastructures. Government and foreign diplomatic facilities also may be damaged or destroyed, disrupting the very governmental and diplomatic activities required to organize and implement relief plans.

Within the category of sudden onset disasters, not all are the same in terms of the involvement of the international community. Based on those differences, the UN has adopted the three-tier classification system shown in Table 18-2.

TABLE 18-2   **UN Classification of Emergencies**

Level	Description
Level 1 (L1)	Resources on-hand are sufficient to internally handle the H&DR response.
Level 2 (L2)	Internal resources require modest external (usually local or regional) augmentation.
Level 3 (L3)	International resources are necessary to enable the affected country to respond.

Although the government of the affected country has the primary responsibility for responding to the disaster, it most often will request H&DR support from the international community to save lives and alleviate human suffering during an L3 (or sometimes an L2) emergency.

REMEMBER

Each sudden onset disaster has a unique footprint in its scale and scope that affects a country's ability to respond and, in turn, determines the emergency's classification.

Before the affected country calls for international help

It's a common trait of human nature to view any disaster as being unique and original, happening only for the very first time, or never before in that particular location, region, or country. The reality is that natural disasters often happen over and over again in the same geographical area; hurricanes and typhoons are an annual event in the Atlantic and Pacific Oceans, and earthquakes have leveled towns along the same faults for centuries. (According to UNISDR, in 2015 alone there were 346 reported natural disasters.)

It is highly probable that an affected country has experienced some major disaster in its modern history. As a result, the country may likely have in place formal government-to-government agreements that it will activate to provide a level of immediate assistance. That assistance many times is provided from outside of the region and may well be delivered by a military entity. This assistance and aid is meant to be immediate and temporary in nature, until such time that the international community is mobilized and the initial provider transitions to the longer-term relief support.

That initial pre-L3 support can be provided to the affected country by military forces under the UN's "Guidelines on the Use of Foreign Military and Civil Defence Assets in Disaster Relief" (also known as the "Oslo Guidelines"). This is due in large part both to the military's ability to quickly move personnel and equipment to the affected areas and its level of expertise in environments of uncertainty. When this support occurs, there is still close communication among the affected country, the supporting military, and the UN Office for the Coordination of Humanitarian Affairs (OCHA), which retains the primary role in the coordination of international disaster relief operations.

Transition to full international community H&DR support

The type of humanitarian aid delivered depends on the disaster conditions but follows a general pattern. Initially, the focus is on search and rescue, in order to free those trapped in the rubble or at risk from flood waters. Emergency medical care — as well as food, water, and other critical life-saving measures — arrives early in the response. Temporary shelter, hygiene kits, airport and port restoration, water treatment and sanitation facilities, emergency power, and communication services are additional examples of relief aid that follows.

While the UN shoulders a crucial role to avoid inefficient duplication of effort, mitigate gaps related to scarce assets (such as helicopters for food drops in remote areas), and arrange for innovative resources (such as porters and animals) to reach remote communities, unique circumstances arise that require even more capability and capacity.

It is important to understand that *all* H&DR support — whether initially delivered under government-to-government agreement or subsequently by the international humanitarian relief community — should be consistent with the following four widely accepted humanitarian principles:

>> **Humanity:** Human suffering must be addressed wherever it is found; the purpose of humanitarian action is to protect life and health, and ensure respect for human beings.

>> **Neutrality:** Humanitarian participants must not take sides in hostilities or engage in controversies of a political, racial, religious, or ideological nature.

>> **Impartiality:** Humanitarian action must be carried out on the basis of need alone, giving priority to the most urgent cases of distress and making no distinctions on the basis of nationality, race, gender, religious belief, class, or political opinion.

>> **Operational independence:** Humanitarian action must be autonomous from the political, economic, military, or other objectives that any organization may hold with regard to areas where humanitarian action is being implemented.

WARNING

Before the affected country formally requests that the international community at large provide H&DR support, it will make every effort to respond to the disaster using its own or negotiated resources. Your company will neither be asked to provide assistance nor welcomed *until and unless* the affected country's government officially asks the international humanitarian relief community for help.

The importance of H&DR logistics

Successful delivery of aid depends on *humanitarian and disaster relief logistics* (sometimes called humanitarian logistics, disaster logistics, or emergency logistics), which we define as getting the right people, equipment, supplies, and services to the right place at the right time at the quality and in the quantity needed.

At first glance, H&DR logistics appears to have many elements in common with commercial logistics, including sourcing of goods and services, warehousing at point of origin and destination, inventory management, transport, and distribution. Operating conditions, however, are very different. In H&DR logistics, demand is unpredictable in terms of timing and types and quantities of commodities. Once a disaster occurs, the demand for unusually large quantities of diverse products and services is sudden and urgent. At the same time, there may be severe disruptions to normal supply chains due to infrastructure damage and destruction.

The logistics support services in demand from one disaster relief operation to another generally differ only in the type and scale of needed relief. Typical H&DR logistics support includes the following:

» Movement of relief workers from point of entry to the command operations facility and into their assigned field locations

» Transport or transfer of the injured

» Evacuation of foreign nationals

» Relocation of affected population to temporary shelter

» Movement of relief supplies and equipment

» Inventory management and warehousing of relief supplies and equipment

» Provision and management of mortuary supplies and services

» Distribution of relief supplies (for example, food and water) to affected communities

» Support to other relief elements (for example, refugee and security)

Introducing the H&DR Logistics Delivery Framework

To be an effective contributor to international disaster management and humanitarian action, you should find out as much as you can about the organizational structure of the international humanitarian delivery system, the roles and responsibilities of key stakeholders, and the overall phases and key processes of the international response to disasters.

Despite differences in the way they organize their H&DR infrastructure, most countries distribute authority and responsibility between the central and lower levels of government. At the central level of the affected country, a civil authority — such as a department, ministry, or agency — typically coordinates all critical functions and sectors such as water, food, sanitation, health, logistics, and security. Lower levels of government organize their H&DR programs to mirror the national level's structure. Their programs may include organizations such as the local branches of the Red Cross or Red Crescent, other local nongovernmental organizations (NGOs), the media, and businesses ranging from small businesses to branches of transnational corporations.

An NGO is generally considered to be any non-state, nonprofit, voluntary organization. As a non-state entity, an NGO is generally independent from government influence, though it may be partially funded by governments. Many NGOs become involved in H&DR efforts.

Assessment and planning: The framework foundation

The government of the affected country has the lead for formulating a disaster response strategy. An increasing number of countries have strengthened their logistics capacity after preparing their Emergency Preparedness Plan (EPP) and, sometimes, a separate Logistics Capacity Assessment (LCA).

The EPP is a country- or region-specific plan that is developed by a potentially affected country in conjunction with OCHA, and it should be routinely updated. It includes a summary of disaster risks and their corresponding humanitarian consequences. In addition, it details the country or region's current capability to successfully implement the plan, outlines a disaster-specific response strategy, and describes coordination agreements between government, national NGOs, donors, and disaster relief agencies.

Operating under the EPP, the government of the affected state has primary responsibility for managing the disaster and organizing and coordinating aid to affected communities, though the capability and capacity to fulfill that responsibility varies from country to country.

The LCA provides an assessment of the overall capabilities in terms of strengths and weaknesses of the country's logistics infrastructure (that is, the roads, bridges, ports, and airports), as well as addressing issues such as milling capacity, quarantine procedures, and the overall telecommunications capability. The assessment then suggests potential logistics contingency responses, to include provisions for both personnel evacuation and the movement of relief goods and supplies into and throughout the country.

TIP

While engaged in humanitarian aid, you will be interacting directly or indirectly with many organizations, both from the affected country and all over the world. Understanding how the international humanitarian aid community is organized and operates will help you be a more effective contributor to response efforts.

The role of the United Nations and its components

Whenever the entire international humanitarian aid community is mobilized for emergencies, the UN leads the coordination. Within the UN the ultimate responsibility rests with the UN's Emergency Relief Coordinator (ERC), who also serves as the UN Under-Secretary-General for Humanitarian Affairs and leads the Inter-Agency Standing Committee (IASC).

Sharing the emergency response responsibility is the UN Resident Coordinator (RC) of the affected country, who in turn reports directly to the Secretary General of the UN. The RC leads the UN Country Team. While this team's primary mission is development, its activities include preparedness and mitigation activities to strengthen a country's resilience.

The IASC, as its name implies, is an inter-agency forum in which, at the time of publication, membership consists of the heads of eight full member agencies (UN operational agencies), eight standing invitees, and a consortium of NGOs meet periodically for coordination, policy development, and decision-making on humanitarian affairs. All involved in humanitarian affairs, the members (and their acronyms) are as shown in Table 18-3.

TABLE 18-3   **Inter-Agency Standing Committee (IASC) Composition**

UN Operational Agency Members		Standing Invitees	
FAO	Food and Agriculture Organization	ICRC	International Committee of the Red Cross
UNDP	UN Development Programme	ICVA	International Committee of Voluntary Agencies
UN-HABITAT	UN Human Settlements Programme	IFRC	International Federation of Red Cross/Red Crescent Societies
UNHCR	UN Refugee Agency	IOM	International Organization for Migration
UNICEF	UN Children's Fund	OHCHR	Office of the UN High Commissioner for Human Rights
UNOCHA	UN Office for the Coordination of Humanitarian Affairs	UNSRHRIDP	UN Special Rapporteur on the Human Rights of Internally Displaced Persons
WFP	World Food Programme	UNFPA	UN Population Fund
WHO	World Health Organization	World Bank	World Bank
		NGO Consortia	International Council of Voluntary Agencies (ICVA); InterAction; and the Southern Center for Human Rights (SCHR)

OCHA, as part of the IASC, supports the ERC and operates at the global, regional, and country levels. As part of its support to the UN-designated Humanitarian Coordinator's (HC) disaster relief efforts, OCHA facilitates coordination at all phases and steps of emergency response: assessing needs, agreeing on common priorities, developing strategies, mobilizing resources, promoting consistent public messaging, and monitoring progress.

OCHA has several resources for promoting coordination of effective response. Chief among these are the global clusters; the UN Disaster Assessment and Coordination (UNDAC) Team; the On-Site Operations Coordination Centre (OSOCC); the Virtual On-Site Operations Coordination Centre (VOSOCC); and various financial, information, and communication management mechanisms.

The UN adopted a cluster approach to strengthen coordination across the many international organizations that provide relief and between them and the affected country's resources. Under this approach, the IASC established 11 relief clusters, as detailed in Table 18-4. Each cluster represents a different category, or sector, of relief and has a designated lead agency. During a disaster, the ERC may activate one or more clusters to address sector-related gaps in the host country's ability to meet its humanitarian needs.

TABLE 18-4   **UN Relief Sector Clusters**

Cluster	Cluster Lead(s)
Camp Coordination & Management	IOM *and* UNHCR
Early Recovery	UNDP
Education	UNICEF *and* Save the Children
Emergency Telecommunications	WFP
Food Security	WFP *and* FAO
Health	WHO
Logistics	WFP
Nutrition	UNICEF
Protection	UNHCR
Shelter	IFRC *and* UNHCR
Water/Sanitation/Hygiene	UNICEF

In the aftermath of a disaster-triggering event, the Humanitarian Coordinator (HC) is responsible for assessing the need for and initiating international response, and designates a transportation and logistics support group responsible for port and airport clearance; commodity tracking and scheduling; local procurement of goods and equipment; vehicle allocation, management, and maintenance; driver support and payment; and storage.

In addition, the HC supports the ERC and the Humanitarian Country Team (HCT) in reaching agreement on which clusters to activate for the response.

It should be noted at this point that the Global Logistics Cluster (GLC) lead is the World Food Programme (WFP). Because one of the largest aspects of any humanitarian relief response is the receipt and distribution of food, water, and medicine that has been donated to support affected or displaced individuals, the WFP has been given the lead to oversee and coordinate not only this critical element of logistics (that is, the movement of relief goods and supplies into and throughout the country) but also the joint lead for the security of the food items being distributed.

REMEMBER

When the international relief community uses the word "logistics," it is generally only referring to the supply chain elements of receipt, storage, and distribution.

The HCT is the cornerstone of the UN's country-level humanitarian response, addressing all disasters. Its members include representatives from many UN agencies, the International Organization for Migration (IOM), international NGOs, and the International Red Cross and Red Crescent relief societies. Under the HC's leadership, the HCT is a forum designed to discuss and provide guidance on an array of country-specific humanitarian issues. All countries with a designated HC also have an HCT. If no HCT has been established, when a disaster occurs the affected country's UN RC may establish one in consultation with the UN ERC and various other UN agencies. HCTs established for specific response efforts may be disbanded once the crisis passes.

The UN Disaster Assessment and Coordination (UNDAC) team, working under the auspices of OCHA, is a standby team of volunteer emergency managers that can deploy on short notice anywhere in the world upon the request of the RC and HC, as well as the affected country.

An On-Site Operations Coordination Center (OSOCC) coordinates incoming international disaster assistance; provides a link between international relief teams and the host government; and provides a platform for cooperation, coordination, and information management among humanitarian agencies.

The Virtual On-Site Operations Coordination Center (VOSOCC) is a web-based information-sharing portal hosting the details of response operations.

Knowing and Understanding the H&DR Logistics Team

OCHA, UNDAC, the GLC, and the logistics coordination cell of the OSOCC are some of the mechanisms the UN has put in place to help the host government manage logistics response.

OCHA is charged with the overall management of emergency stockpiles, enters into support partnerships with the private sector and NGOs, works in coordination with the WFP to provide for the delivery of transportation, facilitates coordination between WFP and OCHA partners, and maintains a close relationship with the World Customs Organization to promote the adoption of measures to facilitate and expedite customs processing.

The GLC works before, during, and after emergencies to boost the international logistics community's ability to deliver humanitarian aid. The GLC produces standard tools, publishes policy documents, and operates an information-sharing platform. The Logistics Operational Guide (LOG) and the template for conducting an LCA are examples of the tools the GLC provides. The GLC also provides training, establishes and maintains surge capacity to support field activities, establishes and maintains stockpiles, and conducts LCAs for at-risk countries. Among its many activities during a response, the Logistics Cluster deploys experienced logisticians to support one or more field-level logistics clusters. It also leads the preparation of a logistics *Concept of Operations (CONOPS)*, the formal document that defines how logistics services will support relief operations. Finally, it prepares and disseminates several information products, including situation reports (SITREPS) that communicate how the response is progressing.

REMEMBER

The format, content, and timing of submission of the various agency SITREPs are not standardized, but vary from emergency to emergency depending on the requirements of the functional global cluster lead. Further, any aspect or element of a SITREP may evolve over the course of the emergency.

Logistics clusters at the field level make no assignments and do not replace or compete with other logistics actors. When gaps occur in logistics services, the cluster works with relief teams to find solutions such as innovations in resource-sharing. However, if the gaps prove to be too large, the GLC — in its role as the "provider of last resort" — can arrange for common or shared services such as transportation. Historically, participants in the in-country logistics clusters have been UN agencies, humanitarian organizations, and representatives of the affected nation's various levels of government. Corporate participation has been limited in the past, although that may change as more countries develop EPPs that cite formal roles for new networks of businesses.

Working with a wide range of humanitarian organizations, the WFP (as the lead agency for the GLC) developed the LOG as a ready resource that provides not only terminology but also details the diverse array of disaster-related logistics activities, as well as practical applications of logistics concepts in an emergency response setting.

When the in-country logistics cluster is not active, the UNDAC team may be required to support the development and implementation of a logistics program. UNDAC undertakes that responsibility consistent with the LOG. UNDAC usually provides the initial staffing for the logistics coordination cell, which often is the predecessor of the in-country logistics cluster. The cell works with the affected nation's authorities to source, procure, move, and store supplies; move affected residents and primary relief team personnel within the country; secure access points; arrange for cargo handling; and set priorities for incoming relief cargo.

Sometimes the WFP will send a Logistics Response Team (LRT) to assess the status of the disaster and determine what logistics support may be needed for the response. The LRT typically becomes responsible for starting up the in-country logistics cluster.

REMEMBER

It is important to remember that the Logistics Operational Guide is a work in progress that covers H&DR logistics from planning to the demobilization of and exit from the relief effort. It provides a common starting point from which disaster relief logistics teams coordinate and collaborate.

Identifying the Phases of Operational Response

After you develop a working knowledge of the humanitarian principles and standards that guide the structure and delivery of H&DR, you need to understand the overall process and timeline for response. Although each disaster is different, all responses generally have three phases of disaster response, after which longer-term recovery and rebuilding is undertaken.

Phase 1 starts when the Global Disaster Alert and Coordination System (GDACS) alerts the international community that an event has occurred and provides automated impact assessment information. Shortly thereafter, the government of the affected country will initiate updates via the VOSOCC, and indicate whether international assistance is needed. Key communication tools are SITREPs, which are generated and disseminated throughout the entire period of disaster response from the international community. The initial international relief teams to arrive usually are the Urban Search and Rescue (USAR) teams and Foreign Medical Teams (FMT). Either the first of those teams or OCHA staff to arrive will set up the OSOCC, beginning with the Reception and Departure Center (RDC). The RDC then coordinates the orderly arrival and departure of relief teams and cargo. Once the relief efforts have started, initial situational and operational assessments are conducted in order to lay the foundation for the next response phase.

During *Phase 2* the OSOCC undertakes a more in-depth assessment known as the Multi-Sector Cluster Initial Rapid Assessment (MIRA) to get a better understanding of the effects of the disaster, the resulting population needs, and the challenges in meeting those needs. The MIRA supports preparation of both the Preliminary Response Plan (PRP) and the Strategic Response Plan (SRP). The OSOCC distributes information in a number of different formats, provides a place for meetings, and continues to support the VOSOCC. Sometimes the OSOCC will establish sub-OSOCCs during Phase 2. Cluster staff may begin to arrive concurrent with full staffing of the OSOCC, at which point the OSOCC establishes an inter-cluster coordination mechanism. This phase generally is considered complete with the publication of the MIRA results.

Phase 3 may include issuance of the SRP, as well as the continuation of some of the response activities begun in Phase 2. In-depth cluster-specific assessments are conducted in this phase. In most cases the OSOCC will close during Phase 3, as the response transitions to longer-term recovery and rebuilding activities.

REMEMBER

Time frames for each phase are approximate, with activities from different phases often overlapping.

Chapter **19**

Defining Your H&DR Logistics Role

erhaps you're already engaged in some level of humanitarian and disaster relief (H&DR) and want to make a deeper commitment. Or, perhaps you're just beginning to get involved in H&DR. You're making this decision at an advantageous time — just when the international humanitarian relief community is looking to tap the resources, skills, management processes, and innovative approaches that reside in the private sector.

In this chapter we will discuss the steps to take in order to obtain full corporate commitment to supporting H&DR efforts as well as the various types of support your company can provide. Finally, we explain the planning, preparation, and infrastructure that have to be in place so that your company can be prepared to successfully respond to a United Nations (UN) call for international H&DR logistics support.

Making the Corporate Commitment

If you're new to H&DR and trying to decide whether to make a corporate commitment, ask yourself which of the following factors you must address before becoming part of the humanitarian relief community:

>> Do you have employees and their families, customers, or suppliers in areas that are at a high risk for disaster?

>> Have your employees advocated for participation in H&DR? Or have they supported H&DR efforts in the past, perhaps by volunteering at a disaster site or organizing a relief goods drive?

>> What future business opportunities may result from your engagement in H&DR?

>> How will engaging in H&DR, with its associated visibility, help your company's public image?

>> Would you like to help set the international humanitarian relief agenda?

These questions and their answers should serve as the starting point for developing your company's business case to engage in humanitarian relief on an ongoing basis, as well as defining the role you might play.

TIP

By reaching out to and engaging with the traditional humanitarian relief community — such as the UN and humanitarian organizations — you may find yourself invited to simulation exercises, consultations, and international conferences. This involvement will have the added benefit of elevating your visibility and planting seeds for new business opportunities.

In assessing your options for the scope and scale of your H&DR program, also give some thought to the following:

>> **Disaster management life cycle:** Take stock of your existing staff and capabilities to decide whether to engage in only some or the entire four aspects of disaster management: prevention and mitigation, preparedness, response, and recovery. Remember, though, that these aspects do not have distinct boundaries and may overlap.

>> **Category of disaster:** While all three categories of disaster — sudden onset, slow onset, and complex (see Chapter 18 for more on these category distinctions) — have some common characteristics, they also have different disaster response profiles, including business risk.

>> **Hazard type:** Your business may be more adept at providing technical and logistical expertise to respond to the effects of some hazards than others. For instance, do you have experience addressing threats to people and property

from floods, or are you more seasoned in responding to the effects of earthquakes or industrial catastrophes?

>> **Support options:** The historic role for business is to make cash donations or organize relief drives (cash or goods). More recently, however, the international humanitarian system is seeking the technical, logistics, and management expertise that resides in the private sector. That expands the options from which you can choose.

Are you better suited to one aspect of disaster management than another? To define your role, think about setting up an H&DR committee that has support from the company's highest executive levels and representation from various departments and geographic locations. Whatever role you decide on, you need to commit to an ongoing H&DR program rather than responding on an ad hoc basis to individual emergencies. The relief contributions — funds, personnel, equipment, goods, or services — make more of a difference when your company as a whole and your H&DR team in particular has the requisite training and is a formally recognized participant in the international H&DR system.

WARNING

Don't wait to take your first steps into the H&DR arena when a disaster response is ongoing — you may well become part of the problem rather than part of the solution!

How you make the corporate commitment to H&DR is similar to the approach used in crafting your company's level of national and international *corporate social responsibility* (CSR). For example, if your company's business model is grounded in business ethics that establish a self-imposed standard of protecting the environment or making positive contributions to the communities in which you operate, then becoming a member of the international H&DR community is a logical CSR initiative.

Once you have made a corporate commitment to H&DR and established a formal program, publish a document introducing and communicating the program to company staff, vendors, customers, and partners. The following are examples of what to include:

>> **H&DR vision and mission:** Clearly state your vision, mission, and objectives, and then define the measurements of success. Anchor them in your business model.

>> **Executive level commitment:** Obtain corporate commitment at the highest level not only to inspire others in the company but also to firmly establish accountability.

>> **Scope and scale of your role:** Define your specific H&DR roles and explain why they were chosen. Identify any geographic or other preferences that will guide your assessment of whether and how to respond to specific disasters.

> » **H&DR program elements:** Describe the program's organizational structure, key management systems, resource commitments, current partnerships, and the schedule for the rollout of your H&DR program.

As a company, you should give all staff members engaged in your H&DR program all the necessary training opportunities to prepare them for working in the field as well as provide the necessary corporate management, administrative, and logistics support.

Deciding What H&DR Logistics Support to Provide

There are several ways your company can provide support for a specific disaster event, or for H&DR in general. The type of support you provide may vary based on your capabilities, the magnitude and location of the disaster, and the level of response being provided by others.

Providing cash or material donations

The most common method of a company supporting humanitarian relief operations is through donations of cash or material items.

Cash donations: A straightforward "cash" donation from the company's philanthropic account is probably the least logistically complex role you can assume. You decide on the size of the donation and the recipient, such as the UN Office for the Coordination of Humanitarian Affairs (OCHA)-managed Central Emergency Response Fund (CERF) or a specific humanitarian organization.

Cash is also preferred by the organizations supporting a disaster. It both allows for flexibility, and provides for culturally, nutritionally, and environmentally beneficial aid. Most importantly, cash can be used immediately in response to a crisis and allows disaster relief organizations to purchase exactly what is needed, when it's needed. Cash gives relief organizations the means to procure supplies near the affected area, which cuts down on transportation time and cost. Monetary contributions also support local economies and ensure that businesses can operate when initial relief supplies are exhausted.

Relief item donations: Perhaps your company wants to give material donations in addition to or in lieu of cash. Opportunities to do so are rare but do come up, usually through appeals by relief organizations. In those cases, the relief organization will provide specific directions on exactly what to collect, a time frame in which to collect it, and specific directions on how to get the donations to the receiving point.

Material donations must meet *all* the following criteria; otherwise, the donation — while well–intended — burdens the relief effort it's intended to support:

>> **A credible relief organization has identified a need for the specific items it needs and wants.** Be aware that not just any relief organization can identify the need: It must be an organization that has been recognized as part of the official relief efforts.

>> **An organization in the affected country is prepared to receive, manage, and distribute the items.** The caution in the preceding bullet also applies here.

>> **The costs of transportation, shipping, warehousing, and distribution are covered.** Note that it is normally the donor's responsibility to guarantee that these costs are covered, especially those costs incurred prior to the receipt of the shipment at the reception point in the affected country; and in many cases the donor also is required to support in-country costs. The responsibility for these costs is addressed and negotiated on a donation-by-donation basis. Regardless of what the donor's share of the costs may be, *no* donation will be shipped or accepted without a firm agreement that outlines who pays for what, where, and when.

>> **Management of customs tariffs, fees, and other cross-border requirements are covered.** Unlike the previous criterion, the burden of these in-country costs often is assumed by the receiving international relief organization. Again, a firm agreement on these costs must be established prior to the actual donation.

>> **The donor has to provide documentation of meeting applicable quality assurance requirements both to the affected country government and the receiving aid organization.** In short, the donor has to show proof of the quality of its donation. More often than not, the quality has to be confirmed prior to the relief organization agreeing to the donation.

TIP

The donation of material items is made much easier if, ahead of the donation, you partner with a humanitarian organization that operates near you *and* is recognized as an international relief organization.

Taking all of that into consideration, here are a few of the many questions you need to keep in mind to determine what items you ship or services you can provide, and how you do so:

>> **Sourcing:** Are you able to send a supply of company-produced goods and services to the affected country without affecting regular customers?

>> **Transport:** Do you have either your own transportation assets or agreements with commercial carriers to move your goods from your point of origin to the port of embarkation?

>> **Packaging:** How well versed are you in international requirements for packaging and marking relief shipments?

>> **Customs:** How experienced are you in international customs clearance procedures? Do you know whether the affected country has adopted expedited customs clearance policies or has waived duties on shipments of relief goods and equipment?

>> **Forwarding:** What arrangements and experience do you have with freight forwarders, including any that will move your cargo from port to port or port to the final receipt location?

Providing relief services in the affected country

You already may have some practice in providing relief support services to domestic sudden onset disasters. While that may give you some experience, expertise, and insight into emergency response protocols, it does not automatically qualify or prepare you to work on international relief efforts.

Your own country's organizational structure for emergency management and disaster relief, as well as the terminology and processes, may vary somewhat from that of international humanitarian aid community practices. A big challenge during international relief efforts can be workers who lack training, have little experience in operating in the extreme weather and other severe conditions that are often present, or lack the necessary cultural sensitivity.

When you commit to a field service support role, you should also develop an in-depth knowledge of international humanitarian law, international human rights laws, the core humanitarian tenets, and the Code of Conduct for The International Red Cross and Red Crescent Movement and Non-Government Organizations in Disaster (http://media.ifrc.org/ifrc/who-we-are/the-movement/code-of-conduct/). Further, remember that you will have to comply with all the laws of the affected nation. Because this is a complex area, you should include international law experts on your team, either as staff or consultants.

TIP

The Code of Conduct for The International Red Cross and Red Crescent Movement and Non-Government Organizations in Disaster ("The Code of Conduct") was developed and agreed upon by eight of the world's largest disaster response agencies in the summer of 1994. Adherence to The Code of Conduct, like most professional codes, is voluntary and self-policed.

If you are already operating in foreign locations, engage with those countries' emergency management or disaster relief organizations on a regular basis to boost your readiness to support their H&DR activities. In addition, identify and collect any disaster preparedness plans, guides, and handbooks those countries have published. Further, develop and maintain an up-to-date global Continuity of Operations Plan (COOP), with country-specific annexes that take into account the pertinent government emergency management framework in all the countries in which you operate.

WARNING

Do not assume that your foreign operations can lead any disaster relief effort in their host location. Further, don't automatically assume that your foreign operations will either be guaranteed or receive priority for relief assistance if your operations are, themselves, affected by a disaster in that country. Your corporate COOP should clearly spell out what domestic corporate assistance or relief your company must provide for your affected foreign operation.

Achieving recognition by the international H&DR framework

In the aftermath of the devastating Indian Ocean and Pacific Rim tsunamis, the international humanitarian relief community's appreciation of the value of private sector resources grew. Businesses, however, experienced difficulty in figuring out how to become a part of that community. To ease the path for businesses, the UN is reaching out to businesses with guidance on how to support global disaster relief. To that end, it established the Connecting Business initiative (CBI). Check it out at www.connectingbusinessinitiative.org.

The CBI assists businesses and business associations in using existing technology networks to create platforms for disaster risk reduction, emergency preparedness, and response and recovery. It operates a global H&DR information clearinghouse that provides a clear entry point for the private sector to connect with international, national, regional, and industry business networks; gives access to resources to mobilize and support business engagement; integrates and disseminates H&DR capacity-building materials and examples of leading practices; and connects business networks both to each other and to other H&DR community members to identify and match needs at local, regional, and global levels before, during, and after disasters.

TIP

The CBI expands opportunities for businesses like yours to make in-kind contributions and create, sponsor, or participate in business networks that have formal disaster management roles, usually on a regional basis. Your participation in the CBI and other UN initiatives for private sector engagement in disaster relief will give your company both visibility and opportunities for an H&DR provider role.

Preparing Your Team: Establishing Internal Systems and Protocols

Your internal systems and protocols become more complicated as soon as you make the decision to engage more deeply in the international humanitarian relief community, particularly if deploying to the affected nation.

Adopting H&DR logistics management systems and controls

Like any other business activity, the business of H&DR depends on sound management systems. Some of them may mirror ones your business already has in place, such as:

>> Project management

>> Financial management

>> Procurement management

>> Human resources management

>> Information management (including communications and cyber security)

For all these systems, you will have to decide — in part, based on the legal and organizational structure of your H&DR program — whether you will create stand-alone H&DR networks or H&DR modules within your existing corporate management systems. If you incorporate them as add-on modules to existing systems, you may need to make some adjustments to align or adapt them both with the international humanitarian relief community and to the environment in which your team may be working.

REMEMBER

The automated data systems you use must be portable. Deployed teams must be able to use the systems in the field, preferably both online and offline. If they have been designed to depend on or integrate with domestically managed and maintained systems, make sure to develop security protocols that protect your domestic systems from external compromise that might occur during remote uploading or downloading. Finally, realize that reliable voice and data communication access and links in the affected country may be nonexistent and may well require your company to communicate via expensive or time-limited satellite-connection devices.

Developing H&DR logistics operational policies and procedures

The UN has worked with its member states, humanitarian relief organizations, corporate partners, and others to establish a framework for coordinated international logistics support to relief efforts. Through this framework, the UN facilitates coordination with the affected country's government to establish policies and protocols specific to the disaster at hand. Your job is to stay current on the evolving international H&DR logistics framework and ensure your team's protocols and checklists reflect that framework. Examples of some of the policies and protocols to be considered include the following:

>> Logistics H&DR team (CONOPS) and organizational framework (remember that your team includes both deployed and corporate personnel)

>> 24-7 situation monitoring and on-call responsibilities (to include the establishment of a "watch officer" role and procedures)

>> Alert and mobilization procedures

>> Emergency operations center (EOC) activation, operation, and deactivation procedures

>> Deployment checklists

>> Entry procedures (such as immigration and customs) for personnel and cargo

>> Disaster relief team registration and check-in protocols

>> Consumable supplies, equipment storage, and distribution management

>> Community engagement policies

>> Safety and security policies and procedures

>> Team medical monitoring and surveillance protocols

>> Protocols for interacting with other humanitarian aid elements

>> Team travel policies

>> Environmental operations policies

>> Public relations and media contact policies

Recruiting, training, and equipping the team

Now that you have your team's policies and procedures in place, your next step is to start building the team. The organizational framework you laid out in your logistics

H&DR team CONOPS identified some key positions, but you likely may need more staff to respond to the specific disaster you've been called upon to support.

Your recruiting efforts for those positions must comply with any laws and regulations that apply in the jurisdictions where you are recruiting. As soon as possible, make sure you've recruited the right people, prepared them for international assignments, and provided the administrative resources they'll need to successfully operate as members of the team (for example, dedicated human resources support personnel).

One of the biggest challenges in H&DR is relief workers who show up without formal training or experience in major international relief efforts. They are unprepared for entry formalities, aren't properly equipped, don't know the local culture or have the needed language skills, are unaccustomed to working under difficult conditions, and are unfamiliar with the organization and operation of an international disaster relief response.

Your H&DR program will need supplies and equipment both for the team members deploying to the affected area and for the personnel operating the EOC. While your EOC operation generally only requires the typical office supplies and equipment, it may need to be augmented with specialized communication devices. By contrast, some of the supplies and equipment your deployed H&DR logistics team will need depend both on their anticipated relief role and the environmental, political, and security conditions at the disaster site.

REMEMBER

You can't wait to identify and dedicate corporate assets — that is, your core H&DR logistics team members, its protocols and policies, and its corporate support resources — until you're called to participate as part of the international disaster relief community. Your team will be expected to "hit the ground running" as soon as it arrives in country.

Supporting the families of your H&DR logistics team

While membership on the H&DR logistics team is fulfilling, it also brings with it a high level of uncertainty and stress for team members and their families. Always on call 24-7, once deployed the H&DR logistics team may have unpredictable work schedules, operate under hazardous conditions (often in remote locations), and be separated from families for extended periods of time. Even those employees whose role is to provide support from a corporate office or EOC experience stress from time deadlines or heightened levels of complexity while the disaster response is in progress.

You can alleviate some of the stress and strain employees' families are experiencing by incorporating a family support plan into your H&DR program. Knowing that the company has created a support program for the team members' families will help the team focus on its tasks and diminish their concerns about what's going on at home. In addition, the family support program can make easier the reunion of team members with their families after the relief work has been completed and the team returns home.

REMEMBER

A good family support program does not end with the first deployment, because team members often rotate in and out. It should provide for the families' education on the team's roles and operation, as well as identify both company and community resources that are available to help families through pre-mobilization, mobilization, and demobilization.

Responding to the Call for Logistics Support

More often than not, your first indication that a disaster may be significant enough to warrant international relief aid will come from outside of the international humanitarian relief network — whether it be from commercial or social media sources. At this point you'll want to designate an individual to implement your watch officer procedures.

Once the disaster has been confirmed, your designated watch officer should review the information UNDAC, OCHA, and others are posting on the VOSOCC about relief needs and commitments to date. (You may or may not have yet received a GDACS alert.)

Upon the receipt of the GDACS notification, your H&DR logistics team should be placed on alert status, waiting for an official request for assistance. You are most likely to receive a formal request if you have a pre-negotiated MOA or MOU in place with the UN, one or more humanitarian relief organizations, or another entity officially recognized to participate in the relief effort. (You will need proof of the formal request in order to be allowed to enter the affected county.)

Assessing your company's ability to respond

Receipt of the official request is the prompt to assess your company's ability to respond. If you decide to respond, the H&DR logistics team will complete their deployment preparations while the company activates your EOC as well as the family support plan.

Examples of the types of questions that should be standard on your response assessment checklist include:

>> Has the disaster affected your business operations? For example, are you already operating in the affected country or in the region? If so, what impact has the disaster had on your business assets, your employees, and their families? How have your customers and suppliers been affected? Are you prepared to activate your existing COOP or H&DR plans? Have you engaged with the UN's CBI?

>> Does this disaster fit within the scope of your corporate H&DR strategy and program?

>> What is the need, as shown on the VOSOCC or ReliefWeb (www.reliefweb. int), for your products or services? What agreements do you have in place with the UN, the affected country's government, humanitarian relief organizations, or other relief providers to provide your products or services?

>> What is the security environment in the disaster area, and how willing are you to accept the physical risks to personnel and business operations?

>> What does the team know about the affected country's government, political system, geography, or logistics infrastructure? Who, if anybody, on the team speaks the country's language or understands the culture?

>> How medically ready is the team? Are any of the team members undergoing medical treatment that would preclude them from deploying?

>> How prepared are you to handle in-country emergencies (such as evacuations for medical treatment)?

>> How well trained is the team for the disaster conditions as they are known so far?

>> Does the team have all the basic supplies and equipment in working order that it needs to deploy, and are plans in place to augment those with disaster-specific items in time for mobilization to the affected country?

>> Do both the team and the EOC have the necessary protocols and specialized equipment needed to communicate?

REMEMBER

For some disasters, you may decide not to deploy your H&DR logistics team. If so, consider an alternate role, such as making a cash donation to the CERF or to the humanitarian relief organization of your choice.

Activating the H&DR Logistics Team

By this time, your watch officer has placed the H&DR Logistics Team on alert, and the company has decided to participate in the disaster relief effort by activating and deploying the team. Accordingly, the watch officer will advise all concerned parties of the decision to deploy the team.

This notification will initiate mobilization activities, to include checking the status of team equipment and supplies, operation of the company EOC, updating of team members' deployment kits, and making preliminary team travel arrangements.

Preparing for the team's deployment

All corporate parties participating in the response have been alerted. Those deploying to the affected country have received information on where to meet for their pre-mobilization briefing and other formalities.

Despite maintaining 24-7 readiness, the team as a whole, as well as individual team members, will have some last-minute preparations to make based on where they are going, the expected conditions, and the anticipated mission. Your specific disaster-modified H&DR deployment checklist will help you through these preparations.

The deploying team's personal preparations range from paying last-minute bills to modifying the contents of their pre-packed bags based on known conditions at the destination — such as climate, disease risks, and baggage allowance on in-country flights. The team also should take some time to start collectively preparing itself psychologically. For instance, team members can develop some strategies for coping with the deployment features they think will concern them the most, tap into lessons learned from any past deployments, and work out a self-care plan to bring them comfort in the field. Try to encourage including partners, spouses, children, and friends in their last-minute preparations to ease some of their anxieties.

WARNING

Don't assume your team's personal deployment bags are complete. Always run through your team's checklists to be sure. When in doubt, check then check again!

Team preparations will include posting its plans in the VOSOCC, gathering situational information from the VOSOCC, compiling as much information as possible about the affected country, and making any necessary adjustments to health and safety or other equipment and supplies. Your corporate H&DR support team should help with these tasks.

TIP

Before the team physically deploys to the affected country, check to see if the country has an up-to-date Logistics Capability Assessment (LCA) that can give the team insights into what to expect when it arrives. Confirm whether the affected country has waived or streamlined entry requirements for relief personnel and their equipment.

Providing family support for the team

Concurrent with the team's deployment preparations, your company should activate the corporate plan to provide family support to the H&DR Logistics Team. Here are some elements that are particularly important during team deployments:

>> **Briefing families before and during the deployment:** Information on the disaster, the affected country, the team's progress, and an estimated return date will be reassuring. Arrange some kid-friendly briefings to help reduce their anxiety over separation from a parent.

>> **Ensuring the hotline portal works:** Nothing is more stress-inducing for already anxious family members than to encounter broken online access or an unanswered phone when they need access to information or resources.

>> **Arranging emergency communications:** Despite excellent preparations, emergencies arise and families at home need to get in touch with team members in the field. Help families understand that during deployment, communicating with loved ones may be difficult and infrequent. Let them know, however, that there is an emergency communications mechanism in the family support program and whom to contact to use it. If necessary, provide a communications link for deployed team members to check in with their families when needed.

>> **Holding special outings and events:** Events for the team members' families or special recognition during office or corporate events can boost spirits during a sometimes anxious, lonely time.

>> **Setting up compassionate care:** Unfortunately, deployed team members occasionally are injured, fall seriously ill, or give their life to the relief effort. Have a formal process and specially trained staff for the delivery of unpleasant news. Provide the family with as much information as you can about arrangements for medical evacuation, hospital treatment, or the fallen member's return home. Facilitate the family's contact with your country's embassy or consulate in the affected country.

If your program includes an offer of practical help with day-to-day chores such as electrical repairs, mowing, or snow removal, before you make the offer, confirm that the help is available and encourage families to take advantage of it.

TIP

Make sure to address transportation and vehicle repair in your plan. The number one request for family support is help with a family vehicle that — inevitably — breaks down as soon as the team member has deployed!

Chapter **20**

Operating as Part of the H&DR Logistics Team

You've made the corporate commitment to provide a logistics disaster relief team and have an assignment — now the hard work begins!

In this chapter we discuss the steps to take in the various phases of the deployment, operations, and redeployment of your team and its equipment.

Deploying Your Humanitarian & Disaster Relief (H&DR) Logistics Team

Your team is ready to depart. Before it goes, make sure you've taken care of the following:

> » The team's mission assignment has been updated to reflect changed conditions in the affected country.

>> You've matched personnel and equipment to the mission.

>> You've finalized your plans for getting your personnel and equipment to the affected country.

Updating your mission assignment and equipment list

When you first made the corporate commitment to provide a logistics relief team, you likely establised teaming agreements with one or more relief agency partners. These agreements included a general scope of work that listed the categories of work you may be asked to support — such as requirements assessment, logistics planning, supply chain management, warehouse management, inventory control, distribution, and performance monitoring. In addition, each agreement may have identified the types of personnel and equipment you may be asked to provide.

The initial incident-specific request for support that you receive from one of your humanitarian partners will be more detailed. Terms may include a target arrival date, the estimated length of your deployment, the number of personnel and mix of skill sets needed, the equipment you're expected to provide, and cluster(s) you may be supporting. However, rapidly changing conditions in the affected country may require some last-minute adjustments to the team's role after you've accepted the initial request for help and started mobilization.

Stay in close touch with your partner in order to take mission adjustments into account when finalizing your team's roster and equipment. In addition, make sure to tap other sources for information, as communications with your partner may be challenging in the initial hours of the relief effort. Stay tuned to mainstream media, which often broadcasts round the clock, while recognizing that at the start of an incident not all reported news is accurate. If you're not already on social media, consider setting up accounts for the team.

Finally, make sure the team's familiar with all the agencies it may work with. Once it gets in country, it will be faced with an alphabet soup of agency acronyms — so a team-member drill on the United Nations (UN) players listed in Table 18-3 in Chapter 18 will help prep them.

TIP

The UN Office for the Coordination of Humanitarian Affairs (OCHA), other involved UN agencies, and many humanitarian organizations have multiple social media accounts through which they communicate real-time or near real-time incident information.

Based on the information you receive, work with your partner, as needed, to adjust the gender, linguistic, or other demographics of the team prior to its actual deployment. Similarly, revisit the team's equipment list and modify it to fit your understanding of the updated mission and in-country conditions.

For example, responders already on the scene may be reporting significant air emissions of hazardous substances, prompting you to add personal protective equipment (PPE) to your equipment list, as well as one or more individuals trained and certified in PPE use to the team. Or, you may be asked to supply additional vehicles, forklifts, or other nonequipment items.

Getting personnel and equipment to the scene

The first leg of your team's travel will be from the company's deployment location — such as corporate headquarters or a local community center — to the point of embarkation, usually a local airfield. Executing this leg may be comparatively easy, as you probably can rely on local commercial services. By contrast, seats on commercial flights may be scarce as responders flock to the affected country. Having standby arrangements in place with charter companies is advisable in order to get your team to its destination on time. Sometimes, airports in the affected country may be so damaged by the disaster as to be unusable in the early days of the relief effort, and you may need to travel first to what is known as a transit nation (TN). The UN Disaster Assessment and Coordination (UNDAC) team or OCHA may set up operations in the TN to facilitate entry and support any areas of the affected country near the border of the TN.

REMEMBER

Typically, the government of the affected country, with support from the UN, will negotiate with transit nations to admit humanitarian relief workers and cargo with a minimum of (or streamlined) bureaucratic entry paperwork.

The amount and type of equipment and supplies the team has will determine whether all of it may accompany the team or some of it will follow unaccompanied, on a separate flight or by ship. A checklist for preparing cargo to be transported separately should include, at a minimum:

>> **Verifying the destination:** Verify whether to ship the team's cargo to the affected country or a TN.

>> **Arranging for a recipient or consignee:** Line up an organization and a specific point of contact who is licensed to accept foreign goods and move them through customs.

>> **Getting your cargo to the designated airport or port:** Negotiate pre-existing arrangements for rapid response from commercial transporters. Specify equipment needed to load your cargo for overland transport to the

embarkation port, and have a backup plan if the truck arrives without that equipment. Things do go wrong!

» **Arranging for shipping:** Cargo space on ships and aircraft is scarce during an L3 or even L2 disaster. Having standby agreements in place for humanitarian shipments may give you some priority. Be sure your carrier has a good track record for handling humanitarian cargo and credentials to enter affected and transit countries.

» **Preparing your cargo:** Pack, package, and label cargo in compliance with all international transport standards, as well as those at the points of embarkation and debarkation. Find out whether the host nation has streamlined its duty, tax, and customs requirements for incoming humanitarian related cargo; and complete all required paperwork, such as cargo manifests or airway bills of lading and certificates of origin.

WARNING

International Air Transport Association (IATA) requirements for air cargo include restrictions or outright prohibitions on transport of certain dangerous cargo, and are not to be ignored. Failure to comply will put the team at risk.

In most cases, you'll arrive at the affected country's designated port of entry, although sometimes traveling through a TN may be necessary. Upon arrival, the team will first go through entry formalities and then register with the relief effort coordinators. After that, the team will begin connecting with and integrating into the relief effort and set up its base of operations.

Preparing for logistics relief efforts

After clearing immigration and customs and completing registration formalities at the Reception and Departure Center (RDC), the team will receive its briefing on the relief effort's status. Both the team and the individual team members will register. Information on the team — including title and size, phone and email for the team's point of contact, services and capacity, and humanitarian partner — and individual team members will be uploaded to the Virtual On-Site Operations Coordination Center (VOSOCC) and shared with the On-Site Operations Coordination Center (OSOCC) to populate the "who-what-where" database that helps the OSOCC get teams into the field quickly and in a coordinated way.

The RDC's briefing will bring the team up-to-date on local conditions. For instance, it will outline the relief effort's current organizational structure and the locations of key relief-effort facilities such as those for the OSOCC, host government operations center, and active clusters. The team will also receive critical safety and security information.

Once arrival and registration formalities are complete, the team will be ready to move farther into the disaster area. RDC personnel may help arrange transportation for the team, its supplies, and equipment, from its point of entry to the OSOCC. The OSOCC then will facilitate movement of teams to the field. However, if your team arrives before the OSOCC is established or fully functional and the team is supporting Urban Search and Rescue (USAR) teams or Foreign Medical Teams (FMTs), the RDC will take on the role of assigning teams to areas of operation and moving them into the field to start urgent life-saving activities.

The team should connect with as many key players as possible in the relief operation, as soon as possible. It should start with the sponsor organization for which it's providing logistics support. Its point of contact there can facilitate contact with others throughout the relief structure, including command and control, OCHA, the Logistics Cluster (LC), and other clusters it may assist during its deployment.

Unless the affected country's government is decimated and unable to function, it has the lead for command and control. The UN, generally through OCHA, facilitates coordination between the affected country and the international humanitarian relief organizations.

REMEMBER

Together with its humanitarian partner, the team will more likely coordinate through the UN structure than that of the affected country's command and control. OCHA may establish a Joint Coordination Center housed in the affected nation's designated civilian or military office.

If your country has business operations in the affected country, be sure to let local management know you've arrived and schedule a time to meet. Your local colleagues may be invaluable in guiding you on local political, social, and cultural sensitivities. Inform your embassy of your team's presence in-country to support the relief effort.

Setting up team operations

The team should get situated as soon as possible so that it's ready to accept relief assignments from its humanitarian partner(s). Setting up operations entails establishing a physical base of operations and activating the field modules of its H&DR logistics management systems and controls, including connecting to its humanitarian partner's Internet portal.

Establishing base camp

Once the team has registered and has been integrated into the relief effort, it will set up its base camp. Due to competition for limited commercial facilities, especially if some are damaged by the disaster, advance planning and agreements can boost the team's chances of having a safe, secure (perhaps even comfortable) place to live and work while deployed.

Many seasoned aid organizations have their own capability to establish base camps or have contracts with commercial entities that specialize in doing so for international relief efforts. These base camps vary in size and amenities but often include bedding, work space, canteen facilities, hygiene and sanitation, power, medical services, and Internet and communications access. In addition, they offer a relatively safe and secure environment.

TIP

When negotiating your company's original agreements with partners, try to include language specifying that they will provide the space the team needs, such as reservations for a certain number of billets in a humanitarian base camp. Be prepared to pay for some of the amenities, such as laundry or food service.

Activating the team's field-based H&DR logistics management systems and controls

Being in a base camp environment may facilitate activating the field-based modules of your Logistics Team's H&DR management systems and controls. With a reliable source of power, you'll be able to operate and recharge your laptops, giving you access to your H&DR databases. Reliable connectivity, even if hours of operation or bandwidth are limited, will enable you to transmit data from the field back to your corporate offices and conduct business in the field with your humanitarian partner.

WARNING

Whatever you do, make sure the team is prepared — and able — to operate *all* of its equipment on voltages other than those for which it was originally manufactured. Equipment designed to run on 110V may or may not be able to run on 220V with special adapters. If at all possible, acquire dual-currency operable equipment at the start, and make sure you send the team with multiple complete sets of foreign currency adapters and chargers.

Paper backup for important checklists and protocols is critical. Even if not needed at base camp, paper logs and records will inevitably need to be used at least part of the time in the field for specific missions. Some of the communities to which the team delivers relief supplies may be remote or damaged, with little or no power or Internet connectivity; and cellular and satellite system connectivity may be overloaded or nonexistent.

The team may well receive official logs and other paperwork to use on a field mission from its field team partner(s). In addition, the team needs to maintain the records required by your corporate H&DR program. Examples include field readiness checklists, daily activity and expense logs, and supply and equipment accountability and usage logs.

Conducting H&DR Logistics Operations

During any major H&DR effort, thousands of relief workers affiliated with hundreds of external organizations arrive to augment in-country resources. The result is a multinational, multicultural environment that often appears unstructured with nobody in charge. Although sharing the common objective of saving lives and alleviating suffering, many of the external and internal relief organizations have their own H&DR programs, with distinctive organizational structures, policies, and systems.

As soon as possible after the team establishes its home base — even a temporary one — it should find out all it can about the organizational structure of the humanitarian effort, with particular attention to understanding the logistics Concept of Operations (CONOPS), facing the challenges of interoperability, and making the most of mission support tools.

REMEMBER

The team's successful completion of its assigned missions and its integration into the overall relief effort depends on the level of its coordination and cooperation with all relief providers, not just the specific command and control element to which it has been assigned.

Understanding the logistics of cluster CONOPS

Logistics operations support all elements of the relief effort. Although the team may be working through the country-level LC, it can expect to support one or more of the other activated clusters. Once the team knows which clusters are operational, it needs to review the clusters' terms of reference, standard operating procedures, and organizational constructs.

As a private sector entity, how the team integrates into the LC may vary from one disaster to another. In general, clusters are open to participation from all parties involved in the humanitarian relief effort. Note, however, that the "boots on the ground" involvement of the private sector in large numbers is a relatively new phenomenon. Some clusters are more familiar than others with private-sector participation. The team should check with the humanitarian partner it's primarily supporting as well as other providers within the relief effort with which it has a relationship, so as to facilitate its integration into the cluster system.

The LC prepares a logistics Concept of Operations (CONOPS) to introduce all new logistics relief providers to how logistics services will support the relief operation. Despite slight variations in format and length from incident to incident, the CONOPS typically includes background on the disaster, a summary of logistics gaps and needs, objectives for augmenting existing capabilities, and the operating concept (known as "primary concept") for achieving those objectives. A CONOPS map shows the locations of logistics services, facilities, and assets, such as points of entry in the affected country and any neighboring TN; transit hubs and storage locations; staging areas; warehouses (fixed and temporary); fuel storage and dispensing; and road locations and hazards. Additionally, the CONOPS provides details on UN inter-agency coordination and information services as well as civil-military coordination procedures.

REMEMBER

Some non-governmental organizations (NGOs) have specific policies prohibiting working directly with military authorities. This can prove challenging as the affected country's national or regional military authorities are, themselves, deeply involved in the relief operations.

The LC periodically revises its CONOPS as the relief operation progresses, and prepares a more detailed SOP based on the CONOPS (often titled "Warehousing, Transport & Logistics Services"). Under conditions specified in the SOP, the LC may provide additional or more-detailed information on road transport, storage, World Food Programme equipment loans, emergency response airlift cargo movements, the LC Air Coordination Cell, and ocean freight services — as well as the procedures for requesting each service. The SOP will also identify the organizations that the Logistics Cluster coordinates with to facilitate the assignments and duties of relief workers.

To stay up-to-date on who will provide what — including the integration of public and private sector resources and the coordination between civil and military authorities — team members should try to attend the regularly scheduled meetings of the LC. During those meetings the LC provides the latest available information on the status of cargo handling capability and capacity, customs, staging areas, foreign military support, and road transportation.

TIP

The number of coordination meetings across the clusters can be overwhelming. If the team can't attend because it has a conflict with another meeting or it's out in the field, make sure it gets a copy of the meeting minutes to ensure it has the latest information.

Operating in different relief team structures

During the team's deployment, it may support its humanitarian partner on many different assignments. Assessments of logistics requirements, warehousing and inventory support, transportation and distribution, evacuation of communities, and specialized supply management are just a few examples. Each of the team's assignments may require different staffing levels and skill sets. As a result, the team can anticipate any one of the following arrangements:

>> The team remains intact and stand-alone.

>> The team is merged with one or more other teams to provide a larger capability.

>> Individuals are detached from the team and added to other teams to fill gaps in skills.

Regardless of the configurations of the field teams in which the team participates, it interacts with both foreign and affected country relief providers across public and private sectors from the international, national, and local communities. Establishing a climate of mutual credibility and trust is critical to accomplishing assignment objectives.

Seasoned relief workers often arrive on-scene with a head start, as a result of personal relationships forged during past relief operations or in conferences, working sessions, or other professional settings between deployments. Even if some of the team's members don't have such relationships, they still have the opportunity to cultivate them in the field. Start by visibly embracing the humanitarian principles, codes, and standards discussed in Chapter 18. Next, be attentive to the cultural norms of both the multinational relief corps and the local population. In some countries, for example, local women are prohibited from interacting with male relief workers or are embarrassed to discuss certain issues with them.

Be sensitive to the fact that the mechanisms the team members use in their "home" cultural setting to foster personal relationships — such as having a meal together — may be viewed as intrusive or even aggressive in some of the cultures from which other relief workers come.

Facing the challenges of interoperability

Despite recent advances in humanitarian relief operations, barriers remain to achieving a coherent multinational effort in any given disaster. These range from differences in policy and organizational structure to incompatibilities in safety protocols, data management, and equipment.

While in the field, the team must be prepared to interact with others whose native language is different. Even if there is a common language, different cultures attribute different meanings to the same vocabulary. Teams from other countries may operate under different safety protocols; recordkeeping standards and systems may also be different.

Your team may work with other teams whose communication equipment can't access the same frequencies, or that operate vehicles that use different fuels and refueling systems. Unless those differences are anticipated and planned for at the start of a mission or assignment, cross-team operations may be impossible to complete by sharing equipment or communication devices.

The concept of *interoperability* helps bridge many of these potential obstacles, in that it allows multiple parties to work together toward shared objectives such as saving lives, clearing debris, or delivering food. In practice, interoperability could include standardizing supplies and equipment to facilitate communications and equipment usage between teams or individuals. It could also mean developing a plan, process, or protocol that provides for the capability of different models of equipment or types of technology to interact with each other.

TIP

Simply put, interoperability should be viewed as the optimization of the team's response to the needs of the mission by ensuring that systems that are very different work better together in a predictable way, without co-opting the operation and values of the systems.

In the international humanitarian context, efforts are ongoing at both the global and field levels to apply the concept of interoperability in innovative ways. As a result, you may find some affected countries shouldering more responsibility for the relief effort than other countries to which your team may deploy. Also, if your team's role on-site includes assessment activities, they may find some data standards in place that make the sharing of information across clusters and between clusters and other organizations more effective. In addition, communication protocols — including frequency management — may be in place to enable military and civilian relief personnel to communicate with each over unclassified systems, open web-based systems, and other mechanisms.

Helping the field team execute a coherent logistics plan

The logistics relief team can support interoperability through the planning it conducts prior to starting a mission. For example, if the team's mission is to support one of the clusters in transporting needed supplies to affected communities, it should attend the field team's mission planning meetings as soon as possible. All too often, the absence of logisticians early on in the field team's planning process results in subsequent logistical bottlenecks that could have been avoided.

Prior to the start of the specific assignment, the team must verify its ultimate destination and point(s) of contact there. Upon the team's review of the instructions and details of the assigned mission, it should use both collective and individual professional judgments to assess the staffing and equipment requirements for the mission. Any and all disconnects or discrepancies found between the requirements and the team's composition and assets must be brought to the field team's attention for resolution.

Make sure that the team has the most up-to-date information on road conditions, and that it requests all geographical mapping systems and products from the LC that may be needed. The team should select a preferred route as well as any available alternatives. The team *must* develop contingency plans for unexpected road obstacles or equipment failures.

The team should establish a mission schedule and protocols including but not limited to safety; physical security for personnel, equipment, and cargo; loading and unloading vehicles; movement of cargo into storage (if needed) at their destination; and recordkeeping.

TIP

Verify that vehicles are in working order and fully fueled, with adequate plans for refueling if needed. Make sure that all team members have adequate personal supplies (such as sufficient quantities of clothing, food, water, and bedding) for the climate, terrain, and length of mission.

Before departing, identify any equipment incompatibilities and develop plans for mitigating any critical mission impacts they may pose. Compile a field team roster, with radio, cellular, or satellite phone contact information. Request military or police escort, if needed, through the Operations Center OCHA has established with the affected country's government and other partners. Finally, apprise the LC of your departure, planned route, and estimated mission schedule.

Many tools are available to support mission planning and execution, including both web-based and manual tools, such as the UN's ReliefWeb Internet site, the VOSOCC, bulletin boards at the OSOCC, and products from the LC and other clusters. If the team's sponsoring organization asks the team (or your corporate headquarters) to support the movement of supplies into the country, it would be helpful to know about the "who has what where" database, a mutual effort of OCHA and the Global Logistics Cluster Support Cell to map emergency stockpiles around the globe (www.humanitarianinfo.org/StockMap).

Participating in on-site briefings and reports

A situation report (SITREP) provides information internally to the numerous relief agencies involved in the H&DR effort, as well as externally to donors, the public, and the media concerning the status of a disaster at a given point in time. Although the format varies, a SITREP typically summarizes the key characteristics of the triggering event and its impacts, response actions to date, and planned future actions. The input from your logistics relief team, following completion of a mission, may be reflected in the SITREP.

In order to keep the media out of harm's way and provide an accurate picture of the total relief effort, OCHA will normally establish a media center. The status of your activities and missions should be sent to OCHA for it to consolidate and include in its reporting; you will not engage directly with the media.

While there may be a single, consolidated official SITREP for the release effort, it may reflect other reports prepared by activated clusters or other players.

Throughout the team's deployment, it will benefit from information in the SITREPs. Depending on the level of detail, the reports may give the team insights into areas where it may expect to deliver relief supplies; or alert it to transportation, warehousing, and other challenges.

The UN agencies and affected nation are not the only ones preparing a SITREP. Teams often prepare a SITREP to keep upper management, support personnel in the corporate Emergency Operations Center (EOC), and even customers and vendors apprised of the overall relief effort and the team's specific role, accomplishments, and challenges. Your team's SITREP can alert your management of needs the team has for more or different staffing, additional authority, supplies, or equipment.

In the early days of the relief effort, a new SITREP may be issued daily and may be accompanied by a briefing. Later, the SITREPs may be issued less frequently, as conditions stabilize.

Understanding response monitoring protocols

The Strategic Response Plan (SRP) for a relief operation sets targets for humanitarian assistance and tracks the actual assistance delivered against the targets through a process of indicators and performance measurements.

Humanitarian organizations monitor the SRP activities by collecting and analyzing data on an agreed-upon schedule. The monitoring data is publicly available and forms the basis of a periodic monitoring report. This report is an internal management tool to help assess progress against the strategic and cluster objectives and modify the relief response's direction, if necessary.

Sharing assignment execution information

Status reporting supports both situational updates and the monitoring function. In the early days of the response effort, the team may be asked to report daily on its progress, any challenges encountered, and any observations about the population's changing needs. Information the team includes may help NGO partners, the clusters and OCHA, and other relief agencies incorporate situational information such as road status, actual versus planned travel times between specific points, actual or potential bottlenecks (such as washed out bridges), warehouse and inventory statuses, and losses due to pilfering or damage. Less-frequent reporting is sufficient as the response phase progresses and begins to transition to a longer-term recovery phase.

Managing the team's internal logistics

The team's standard plans and procedures are just a foundation on which to tailor protocols and processes to a specific situation once the team is in the field. Once it arrives, the plans are situationally updated and refined. In addition to supporting field teams on specific assignments and helping the team's humanitarian partner manage its activities in-country, the team will need to manage its own supply chain and validate its readiness for assignments.

The agreement with your humanitarian partner will dictate the characteristics of the team's inventory. If your logistics team is responsible for supplying logistics support equipment (such as vehicles, forklifts, or power tools, among other items) it needs consistent, reliable supply chain arrangements in order to fulfill its mission. Even if it's not responsible for supplying heavy equipment or specialized tools, it needs to replenish team and personal supplies before deployment ends.

TIP

Be sure to have a capability to monitor the team's supplies and equipment, and plan to replenish needed items either locally or with resupplies that are sent from corporate headquarters.

Prepositioning and staging initial supplies and equipment

Prepositioning and staging of initial supplies and equipment can occur at the international, national, or regional levels depending on what the team needs, when it needs it, and whether your company has a local presence. If your company has a large or growing engagement in H&DR, you may elect to preposition equipment, spare parts, and supplies at warehouses strategically located in relation to the geographic areas you're committed to supporting. In countries where you or your humanitarian relief partners have a local presence, you may be able or choose to preposition inventory in those countries or neighboring countries.

Be sure to integrate your H&DR plan into your company's normal operational and — if included — contingency plans. Your company may also have made prepositioned contingency arrangements for each country in which you have ongoing business operations. If so, be sure to address plans for the sustainment of critical IT and communication systems equipment and parts.

Augmenting H&DR Logistics Team support agreements on-site

Regardless of whether the team brings heavy equipment to support warehousing or storage, transport, or distribution — or lighter equipment such as laptops and PPE — the team needs formalized procedures for operating and maintaining all equipment. The checklist the team used to prepare for mobilization — along with your company's inventory accounting system — will help it keep track of the equipment and parts it needs to have on hand at all times. Similarly, the team's maintenance procedures and preventive maintenance schedule will help it keep everything in working order. It's quite likely that the team's expertise needs to include special maintenance capability — such as specialized power generation or electronics diagnosis and repair — that may not be available in-country. *Don't* assume that the team can wait until equipment failure to find the needed expertise. Knowing what technical maintenance capability is available within the relief agencies should be one of the first things the team addresses and arranges for, if needed.

Concurrently, the team needs to be prepared to augment its capabilities by reaching out to local vendors. At some time during the team's deployment, it will draw on the local economy to fill its needs, whether it be for goods or services. The team must designate someone who has the appropriate authority and training to sign contracts or purchase orders, use credit cards, or make cash transfers up to specified limits. Examples of agreements the team contracting official may establish, modify, or augment in the field are for the employment of agents to receive cargo and handle customs formalities and for the leasing of storage, transport vehicles, fuel, labor, or security.

The team must *continuously* assess, reassess, and adjust its readiness posture before, during, and after each mission and assignment — and always with an eye on mission characteristics, applicable local laws and regulations, and your corporate H&DR protocols and checklists.

Remaining adaptive and agile by expecting the unexpected

No matter how carefully and thoroughly the team plans, any number of things can inevitably go wrong. For instance, it may arrive thinking it has a reservation at one of the base camps only to find that all spaces are occupied because departing teams are delayed. Or, during a mission the team may run into obstacles blocking a supposedly clear route and have to reroute or detour accordingly.

Your logistics team's contingency plans provide the ability to address most unexpected circumstances agilely and safely. Before the team deploys, it should start identifying any obstacles that could be encountered. Tap into lessons learned from past deployments to identify potential snags; or, if not previously deployed, contact another logistics relief team to gain from its experiences. With that information in hand, the team can prepare preliminary contingency plans that will be refined as the team gains more information about the evolving status of the disaster and the relief effort.

Once in-country, contingency planning continues for the larger field teams to which your company's team is assigned. For example, even if the field team's assignment is estimated to entail a half-day round trip, work with others before setting out to ensure your team will be self-sufficient in the event of vehicle breakdowns or other unexpected circumstances. The team must dress appropriately for the climate and terrain, and travel with sufficient water, food, and shelter provisions in the event it becomes stranded.

REMEMBER

A seasoned logistics relief team may find itself in a jam, even with detailed contingency plans. That's when resourcefulness comes into play: by creating entirely new solutions or adapting existing ones.

Closing out the Team's Mission: Reporting Out and Returning Home

Once the team's mission has been completed and the team has been told it is no longer required in the affected nation, the next phase of the operation begins. In the context of H&DR support, *demobilization* refers to shutting down a specific H&DR mission. It includes bringing all — or at least most — team personnel home; deciding what to do with the team's supplies, equipment, and repair parts; and winding down your corporate EOC support to the field team.

The team and the corporate EOC should start planning the team's exit strategy shortly after it arrives and gets its initial briefing on the disaster and relief effort's status. As the team gains field experience in the affected nation and participates in briefings and other information exchanges, it will be able to refine the initial demobilization strategy.

Demobilization from the field can occur in several stages or different forms, such as:

>> **Phasing down:** Partially reducing the team's in-country presence as the overall relief effort or the team's specific role winds down.

>> **Phasing out:** Completely shutting down the team's operations in an orderly way consistent with the evolution of the relief effort and arranging for the disposition of any remaining supplies and equipment and the return home of team members.

>> **Transitioning operations:** Transferring responsibility and some (or all) assets to the company's local business, to another local company, or to an international or local humanitarian relief entity that will continue to support the affected nation as part of the ongoing operations.

Your corporate H&DR policy and demobilization protocol may even specify circumstances under which part, or all, of the team remains involved as the relief effort transitions from the response phase to the recovery phase. For instance, some team members may remain in-country for some period of time to train and augment local staff. In other cases, either the affected nation's government or humanitarian organizations may ask for additional assistance, even though the UN-led international relief effort has wound down. Or, based on the team's engagement in the relief effort, new business opportunities may have emerged, and members of the deployed team will spearhead the initial phase of setting up a local business operation. Even if part of the team stays, you may deactivate the EOC and rely on long-distance support from normal corporate operating units.

When developing corporate demobilization policies and procedures, think about how the equipment and nonconsumable supplies, as well as their packaging, can be organized to reduce what must be brought back. Establish internal criteria and guidelines for triggering demobilization, and (to the extent possible) include them in your negotiated agreements with humanitarian relief organizations. These triggers may include the affected nation's decision to end international relief operations; shut down or transition the international relief operations to the recovery and rebuilding stage; or completion of the team's specific assignment.

The procedures should have a checklist that covers all aspects of the logistics support needed for each field demobilization scenario. The team (while in the field and in discussions with the corporate EOC) will select and adapt the checklist that best fits the actual demobilization approach to pursue.

Examples of the demobilization activities the team will undertake include:

>> **Base operations "housekeeping":** To comply with the "do no harm" cardinal rule of relief operations, leave all facilities in a clean, safe condition that is as good as or better than how the team found it. Use the baseline pictures the team took when it arrived as a guide.

>> **Environmental stewardship:** As part of housekeeping, be sure to address any existing or potential environmental issues associated with the team's part

of the relief effort. These may include cleanup of spilled petroleum products, disposition or redistribution of containers of unused cleaning solvents or other hazardous substances, and proper disposal of spoiled foodstuff.

>> **Equipment/facilities disposition:** The team may need to close out local leases and contracts for facilities, equipment, and vehicles and arrange for the transfer of some or all company-owned equipment.

>> **Reporting out and disconnecting from relief operations:** If the OSOCC and its RDC are still operational when the team prepares to leave, the team leader must report out before the team physically departs the country. Find out whether the team needs to provide any formal or written mission report prior to departure, or conduct any follow-up activities after it departs.

>> **Transporting personnel and equipment:** Finally, the team and the corporate EOC need to make all the necessary arrangements to get the team, all personal possessions, and its equipment home. If the team needs further assistance, the RDC may be able to help.

REMEMBER

Demobilization must comply with the affected nation's exit procedures and home country entry procedures. In almost all cases, home countries require stringent cleaning, decontamination, and inspection procedures for personnel, supplies, and equipment prior to any movement from the affected country back to the home country.

Returning versus discarding assets

Probably one of the most important demobilization decisions the team will make is what to do with its supplies, equipment, spare parts, and other leftover items. Some considerations that go into that decision include:

>> **Maintaining readiness for future deployments:** Shipping team items home, particularly if fully functioning, may support your corporate goal to be prepared to quickly respond to a the call for another H&DR mission.

>> **Reducing costs:** Returning items that are badly damaged or in severe disrepair may be costly when considering life-cycle costs, including the combined costs of shipping and repair.

>> **Complying with import/export regulations:** Leaving certain types of technology-based assets behind in an affected nation may be prohibited by your country's regulations or your own company's security protocols. Conversely, returning equipment that has been exposed to biohazards or agricultural diseases may result in officials in your country quarantining or even destroying the equipment.

For equipment that the team is returning to home base, steps similar to those followed to ship the equipment to the affected country are necessary. Make sure that the team's cargo has been packaged, labeled, and classified in accordance with all pertinent international standards. If the team's equipment and supplies are returned by air, assess whether any fall into the category of dangerous goods and be sure to comply with IATA requirements.

Damaged equipment that the team is neither taking home nor transferring to another entity must be disposed of properly in a manner compliant both with the affected nation's environmental laws and your corporate environmental stewardship policy. Your corporate H&DR program should include an environment, health, and safety component that addresses safe disposal of discarded equipment.

TIP

To avoid confusion and lost time when deciding what to do with returning assets upon demobilization, the team should make sure that when it originally arrives in the affected country (or at some opportune time during its stay in-country) it asks whether OCHA — in cooperation with the United Nations Environmental Program — has established an environmental program for the relief effort.

Improving your H&DR program: Lessons learned

An *after-action report* (AAR) is a tool often used to communicate to both the relief-effort community and the relief providers the effectiveness of a humanitarian and disaster relief effort. The AAR candidly discusses what worked and what didn't. Its aim is to lay the foundation for systemic innovations that will strengthen best practices of the international humanitarian relief community.

The organization that led the relief effort typically sponsors the preparation of an official AAR for the entire relief effort. However, participants in the relief effort may prepare their own AARs as a way to improve their organization's capability and capacity to contribute to relief efforts during future disasters. Your logistics relief team may find itself participating in an internal AAR, as well as that of your humanitarian partner.

At a minimum, the topics to address in the team's corporate AAR include:

» **Description of the humanitarian disaster:** A summary — including timelines — of the disaster-triggering incident and the scope and scale of the resulting disaster.

» **H&DR operation:** A description of the humanitarian relief effort's organizational framework, participating organizations, and response objectives.

>> **H&DR Logistics Team missions and performance:** An overview that describes the team's composition and capabilities (time-phased, if the composition changed throughout the course of the team's deployment); each of its specific missions and assignments in the affected country; the team's strengths and weaknesses; and the challenges to mission success (in terms of timeliness, efficiency, and effectiveness) it may have encountered.

>> **Recommendations:** A detailed summary of "Lessons Learned" that includes both general and specific observations on and recommendations for areas of improvement.

TIP

Your corporate H&DR program should have a protocol not only for writing the team's AAR, but also for the corporate review of the report once the team has submitted the AAR. Typical components of the AAR submission and review process include responsibility and guidelines for writing of the report (such as the report format, submission deadline, and receivers), designation of an individual to lead the corporate review, a list of review participants (both from within the team and corporate management), and review format (such as informal briefing, written report, inclusion in a "Lessons Learned" database, publication in your company's annual report, and other public information vehicles). Selection of a neutral facilitator who encourages all participants to contribute to the discussion is the key to a successful AAR.

Addressing the challenges of returning home

Your H&DR Logistics Team members and their family, friends, and colleagues eagerly look forward to being reunited at the end of the team's deployment. However, responders often discover that their return home does not go as smoothly as anticipated. Some team members become impatient with how slow the pace of life at work or home seems in comparison to the accelerated pace of the H&DR mission operation. This can easily strain personal and professional relationships.

Similarly, the work done after demobilization may seem dull and unfulfilling, in contrast to the rewards of helping those in need following a major disaster. Management should guard against misinterpreting a team member's reduced interest, attention to detail, or decreased productivity as a lack of motivation.

Recognize that the physical and emotional toll from deployment may not only result in fatigue that lasts a long time, even with what seems like an adequate amount of sleep, but it can also be a symptom of the need for medical treatment or professional support. Tap into the family support program and any other help needed to deal with this issue or any unexpected emotional reactions team members may have to daily tasks and activities.

REMEMBER

Providing logistics support to an H&DR event can be extremely rewarding. But even the most technically accomplished team can become traumatized while operating in an environment characterized by confusion, panic, and human suffering.

Getting ready for the next deployment: Training and exercising

Training between deployments keeps the team's skills fresh, integrates new members into the team, and improves the corporate H&DR program. In addition, training provides opportunities for your team members to forge new or strengthen existing relationships with other players in the international humanitarian relief community. These relationships, cultivated in advance of a deployment, support interoperability and coherent action in the accelerated pace of a multinational, multicultural relief effort.

Unfortunately, the expenses of both individual and team training can be significant. You can get the most out of your corporate H&DR training budget by developing and testing plans that combine different training methods such as:

>> **Self-paced training:** The H&DR community has available an increasing number of online training modules that can be accessed at the individual's convenience. This type of training covers numerous topics, ranging from an introduction to the principles of international H&DR, to personal preparation for deployment, to exercises in cultural sensitivity.

>> **Tabletop and virtual exercises:** This type of training has long been a cost-effective staple among disaster-management professionals. These exercises use role-play to focus on team dynamics in dealing with a fictitious incident that simulates historical or anticipated disaster-triggering events.

>> **Live exercises:** Some element of participation in live exercises is critical for your team to be fully prepared to deal with the urgency, multiple players, and constantly changing circumstances of massive disasters. Many disaster-relief agencies around the world organize, host, or participate in live exercises of varying scales. Work with your H&DR partners to identify exercises that would be particularly suitable for enhancing your team's H&DR skills, while expanding your relationships with organizations and individuals you may work with at future relief efforts.

TIP

Should your company or H&DR Logistics Team anticipate exposure to unusual disaster relief circumstances — such as extreme climates, remote locations, culturally splintered regions, or regions with security issues — look for training opportunities in those niche areas.

6

The Part of Tens

Explore the critical role logistics played in the successful global expansion of ten companies.

Draw from the lessons that companies learned when faced with major issues in entering the foreign marketplace, and understand the reasons for initial failure.

Rely on the comprehensive resources of a network of ten international organizations to help further your understanding of global logistics.

Find out how to speak the basic language of global logistics by referring to the handy glossary at the end of this part.

Chapter **21**

Ten "Stars" of Global Logistics

Many companies — large and small — have successfully expanded into the global marketplace thanks to sound logistics. While most of them experienced initial setbacks, they all had one thing in common: an expansion strategy based on a thorough understanding of the foreign locations they were entering and a logistics infrastructure solid enough to ensure successful global operations. The following are just a few of their success stories.

Amazon.com: Leveraging E-Commerce to Support a Global Logistics Enterprise

Amazon.com is a US-based electronic commerce (e-commerce) company with headquarters in Seattle, Washington. After reading a mid-1990s report about the future of the Internet, which projected a potential web commerce growth of 2,300 percent, Amazon founder Jeff Bezos created a list of 20 products that could be marketed online. From those 20, he initially settled on selling books. While the largest brick-and-mortar bookstores and mail-order catalogs at that time might offer as many as 200,000 titles, an online bookstore could offer exponentially more. Additionally, it would have a practically unlimited virtual warehouse: those of the actual publishers and distributors. In the first two months of business, Amazon sold to all 50 states and over 45 countries.

Today, Amazon.com is the largest Internet-based retailer in the world, based on total sales and market capitalization. It now sells DVDs, Blu-rays, CDs, video downloads/streaming, MP3 downloads and streaming, audiobooks, software, video games, electronics, apparel, furniture, food, toys, and jewelry. In short, any item sold via retail can be ordered from Amazon.com through its separate retail websites in the United States, the United Kingdom and Ireland, France, Canada, Germany, Italy, Spain, the Netherlands, Australia, Brazil, Japan, China, India, and Mexico.

Having a robust web-based ordering system is useless without a robust distribution system to support it: Amazon.com's phenomenal success has been its ability to rapidly deliver orders directly to the customer's doorstep, sometimes in just hours.

Amazon.com calls its warehouses "fulfillment centers." As of April 2015, Amazon had over 75 warehouses in the US alone, but the number is thought to be even greater. Further, the company has invested significantly in emerging markets, establishing four warehouses in India, nine in Germany, and more than twelve in China. Amazon recently announced its intent to invest another $20 billion (or thereabouts) to enhance and expand its distribution network in those countries.

To support its distribution, Amazon.com primarily uses United Parcel Service (UPS), FedEx, and DHL for shipments within the US and to international customers. Up to 40 percent of its shipments in certain markets use small carriers — even including delivery by individual courier. To supplement its third-party providers, Amazon.com has purchased and maintains its own growing fleet of trucks and cargo planes. It even has entered into a contract with the United States Postal Service (USPS) for weekend deliveries in the US. The expense of this direct-to-customer-focused shipping is a tremendous financial burden to the company: In the third quarter of 2016 alone, those costs were estimated to be $3.9 billion.

Always looking toward the future, Amazon.com has invested heavily in drone technology, with a goal of achieving package delivery times of less than 30 minutes in larger metropolitan markets. And in a reverse of the trend that saw a shift from brick-and-mortar to online, in October 2016 Amazon.com announced that it plans both to build convenience stores and to develop curbside pickup locations for food.

Coca-Cola: Investing in Product Sustainment in Foreign Communities

Now known as one of the most popular brand names in the world, Coca-Cola experienced early problems introducing its product into India and Africa. One of the major obstacles was dealing with the impact of plant production on the local water sources. As a result, in 2007 Coca-Cola undertook an ambitious 15-year plan to reduce and replenish the water used in its 863 global production operations.

Coca-Cola requires each plant's management to determine the sustainability of the water supply the plant shares with others in terms of quality, quantity, and the infrastructure in place that treats and distributes water. As part of the sustainability review, plant managers monitor the quality, volume, and discharge of the water the plant uses. Doing so ensures that local communities have access to sufficient amounts of uncontaminated water.

If a negative impact is identified in any aspect of operations, Coca-Cola then mandates that the plant develop and implement a Source Water Protection Plan that includes plans both for immediate and long-term water quality improvement.

In August 2016, Coca-Cola announced it had met its water replenishment goal five years early. This milestone of corporate social responsibility was achieved by implementing 248 community water partnership projects in 71 countries that focus not only on safe water supply and access but — more importantly — on watershed protection.

Though a large corporation, Coca-Cola invests in small community programs and small-scale charity projects in its foreign markets. In 1984 the Coca-Cola Foundation was launched. By the end of 2015, over $830 million in charitable contributions had been awarded — like its sponsorship of Ramadan meals for children across the Middle East, and the "Support My School" initiative to improve facilities at schools in India.

Dell: Moving Manufacturing to Capture Global Demand

Started in Michael Dell's University of Texas dorm room in 1984, Dell quickly grew to become one of the largest manufacturers and retailers of personal computers.

Its success was attributed to the company's ability to customize tech-savvy customer requirements for computers within a week of an order being placed. When Dell's market was limited to the US, Canada, and Mexico, the company was able to fill all orders from its Texas manufacturing facilities. But, as the demand for personal computers grew in other countries, Dell realized it had to develop a region-specific manufacturing capability to support new foreign markets.

Originally, Dell had exported its computers to only a few Latin American countries, including Mexico and Colombia. But it hadn't marketed in the nations that comprise Mercosur: the Latin American free-trade bloc made up of Brazil, Argentina, Uruguay, Paraguay, and Chile. Dealing with a market as vast as Mercosur, location was an extremely important consideration in the opening, in 2001, of Dell's first Latin American manufacturing operation: Porto Alegre, a city located at the south of Brazil in the state of Rio Grande do Sul, Brazil.

The site lies only a few hours' flying time from Mercosur's four major markets: Buenos Aires in Argentina, Rio de Janeiro and São Paulo in Brazil, and Santiago in Chile. Together, those four areas generate roughly half the region's wealth. More critically for Dell, most of Mercosur's computer users are concentrated in those four areas. Equally important, the 1998 privatization of Brazil's telecom systems resulted in expansion and upgrade of the nation's network, which accelerated the growth of Internet usage inside Latin America's biggest economy.

From a financial viewpoint, the computers manufactured in the new operation in Brazil enabled Dell to designate them as "100 percent locally made." As such, Dell's Brazilian-made products automatically attain duty-free access to all the nations in the Mercosur bloc. Further, since Dell's revenues in Brazil are denominated in the Brazilian currency — as are most of its operating costs — Dell is able to reduce any risks associated with foreign currency fluctuations.

There were many serious logistics issues to overcome, the most serious of which was dealing with the lengthy customs-approval delays that have been the downfall of many less experienced firms that have ventured into Latin America.

To meet this challenge, Dell put together an agreement with Brazilian tax and customs authorities to set up a "virtual" warehouse to provide high-speed clearance of the company's exports and imports. Tax and customs officials monitor the movement of Dell's goods online, making sure that the company pays the appropriate taxes and duties punctually.

International Federation of Red Cross & Red Crescent Societies: Disaster Relief

Providing global logistics services can be difficult enough when you know exactly what you have to obtain, stock, transport, and distribute in the time frame required. But, what if you have a responsibility to provide logistics support for disasters anywhere in the world, when any delay may mean additional loss of life?

The Global Logistics Service (GLS) is the logistics arm of the International Federation of Red Cross and Red Crescent Societies (IFRC). The key mission of GLS is to support the core work of the Red Cross-Red Crescent network. This network reaches 150 million people each year through 189 member national-level societies, third parties in the humanitarian relief community, and multiple foreign governments and state agencies.

In order to be able to respond quickly anywhere in the world, the GLS has a permanent network of logistics units — strategically located in Panama, Dubai (United Arab Emirates), Kuala Lumpur (Malaysia), Nairobi (Kenya), and Las Palmas (Canary Islands) — all staffed by logistics specialists. This regionalized structure ensures that GLS can quickly and efficiently source and deliver relief items and services to assist the most vulnerable.

In addition to these regional logistics units, the GLS can deploy logistics emergency response units to any disaster zone. These emergency response units support logistics operations on short notice and are deployed within hours of a disaster occurring.

On average, since 2007 the GLS has mobilized and delivered over 225 million dollars' worth of humanitarian aid annually. It holds prepositioned stock to meet the immediate needs of 450,000 people at any given time. When emergencies strike, these supplies can be delivered to affected areas anywhere in the world within 24 to 48 hours. Per month, the GLS supports 60 humanitarian operations across the world.

International Flavors & Fragrances: Integrating Multiple Supply Chains

International Flavors & Fragrances (IFF) is a major producer of flavors and fragrances that are globally marketed. It is headquartered in New York City and has creative, sales, and manufacturing facilities in 35 different countries. With $3 billion annually in sales, it serves customers in 152 countries.

IFF has an integrated supply chain — from raw material sourcing through manufacturing, quality assurance, regulatory compliance, and distribution — that enables it to provide its customers with consistent quality products on a timely and cost-effective basis. It purchases approximately 9,000 different raw materials from about 2,500 domestic and international suppliers. Approximately half of the materials it purchases are natural or crop-related items, and the other half are synthetics or chemicals. Natural ingredients are derived from flowers, fruits, and other botanical products as well as from animal products.

IFF's Vendor Code of Conduct is the cornerstone of its relationships with its vendors. IFF expects vendors to provide a safe working environment and to conduct their business with integrity. They are expected to comply with all laws, rules, regulations, and industry standards, including those concerning human rights.

IFF also participates in the Supplier Ethical Data Exchange (Sedex), the largest collaborative platform in the world for sharing supply chain data. Sedex helps drive continuous improvement in IFF's supply chain in the areas of labor standards, health and safety, environmental management, and ethical business conduct. IFF focuses its efforts with Sedex on a core set of suppliers that are critical to IFF's business, reviewing the list annually as its supply chain evolves.

Mali: Revolutionizing the Logistics of Exporting Agricultural Products

In 2005 the government of Mali — with World Bank assistance and International Development Association funding — launched the implementation of the Agricultural Competitiveness and Diversification Project (ACDP). The initiative was a six-year investment project aimed at increasing revenues from a whole set of Mali agricultural products with growing markets and strong demand. Because those product markets were mostly untapped, the ACDP is helping to diversify Mali's foreign exchange earnings that — to date — had been extremely limited: 90 percent of income had been represented by only three products (gold, cotton, and livestock).

Among the activities supported by ACDP was the scaling up of a new supply chain model for the export of fresh mangoes. The model used a new mode of shipment that combined using multi-modal transport (a combination of road, rail, and sea shipment) with refrigerated and sealed containers all the way to European ports. This new transportation model significantly reduced transit times when compared to more conventional transport routes like the classical road and sea-freight. As a result, Mali found a feasible and profitable method of delivering mangoes of excellent quality that are highly appreciated by the European importers.

In effect, ACDP initiated a revolution for the landlocked country. Before, the country was condemned to either exporting limited quantities of fruit by air-freight or letting the raw product be collected at a low price by neighboring countries' traders with market access. The project also completely changed the size of the potential market, which Mali can continue to tap into.

Although small in scale, the results of the new supply chain were significant. Shipping times to Northern Europe decreased from 25 to 12 days, product quality upon arrival in Europe was excellent, grower unit prices increased by 25 percent, and the workforce in the packing houses reached 150 (of which more than 60 percent were women) working in conditions and earning well above the national labor benchmarks. Not a bad start for one of the poorest countries in the world!

McDonald's and Starbucks: Adapting to Local Customs, Traditions, and Tastes

As you travel to cities around the world, you have likely seen one or both of two icons in the food service industry: the golden arches of McDonald's or the green mermaid logo of Starbucks. Recent statistics from their respective websites show that McDonald's has over 36,500 locations in 119 countries, while Starbucks has over 23,700 locations in over 70 countries.

Both of these companies have enjoyed success globally because of two basic principles: world-wide consistency in a standard product line coupled with a willingness to develop specific regional products based on an understanding of customs, tastes, and religious dietary restrictions.

McDonald's has been offering alcohol as part of its menu in select European countries such as Germany, France, and Portugal for years, and is now offering beer in South Korea, as well. But there is much more to its global menus than just alcohol. For example, it offers McArabia flatbread sandwiches in the Middle East, numerous vegetarian options in India, macaroons in France, and even spaghetti in South Korea.

Starbucks has also ventured into serving alcohol in its US and Canadian markets. With over 10,000 stores outside the US, Starbucks has adapted its coffees and teas to accommodate local tastes, with offerings such as Red Bean Green Tea in China, Coffee Jelly Frappuccino in the Asia Pacific region, and Toffee Mocha in Canada. It has also modified the stores' bakery products to meet local expectations, often using local suppliers.

Toyota: Streamlining the Global Management of Inventory

During Japan's post–World War II rebuilding of its industry, companies faced many issues. Japan's lack of cash made it difficult for industry to finance the big-batch, large inventory production methods common elsewhere. Japan lacks space to build big factories loaded with inventory, and the Japanese islands lack the natural resources to build products. Further, Japan had high unemployment, which meant that labor efficiency methods were not an obvious pathway to industrial success.

As a result, the Japanese learned to lean their processes. They built smaller factories in which the only materials housed in the factory were those on which work was currently being done. In this way, inventory levels were kept low, funding tied up in in-process inventories was kept to a minimum, and inventory levels were quickly consumed and replaced so that replenishment was continuous. This process of what was to become known as just-in-time (JIT) inventory revolutionized manufacturing and industry globally.

Toyota was one of the first companies to adopt JIT and continues to use it across its 53 overseas manufacturing companies operating in 28 countries and regions. Toyota's vehicles are sold today in more than 170 countries.

Lee Iococca, former president of Chrysler, cited JIT as a powerful inventory-reduction technique that saved scarce dollars during the auto manufacturer's bankruptcy. In his autobiography Iococca said, "To save money, we set up a system where parts would be shipped at the last possible moment. This is known as 'just-in-time' inventory, and it's a good way to cut significant costs. The Japanese have been doing it for years."

Volvo: Designing the Environment into Product Engineering

Volvo vehicles have long been marketed based on the company's historic reputation for safety and reliability. Volvo had been at the forefront of safety engineering well before strong government safety regulations were enacted.

Volvo's commitment to environmental activities and continuous investment to help reduce its carbon footprint goes far beyond lowering CO_2 emissions. Volvo's "clean inside and out" program represents a holistic approach to the environmental impact of the vehicle. It focuses on health, resource utilization, and the ecological consequences of the production, use, and disposal of the vehicle.

Since 2002 all new Volvo cars have been 85 percent recyclable and 95 percent recoverable. The use of recycled materials such as steel, iron, aluminum, and many other metals is common practice; metals from the catalytic convertor are reused in the manufacture of new convertors. Even the battery plastic covers become the wheel-arch liners on new cars.

In addition to responsible manufacturing, vehicle servicing is an environmentally friendly activity, as Volvo created the Volvo Exchange System where used parts are collected from dealers and remanufactured to the same quality as new parts. This program offers reconditioned Volvo-approved parts — ranging from starter motors to whole engines — that meet the same recyclability and recoverability standards.

Walmart: Pioneering the Commercial Use of RFID

It's generally said that the roots of radio frequency identification (RFID) technology can be traced back to World War II. The Germans, Japanese, Americans, and British were all using radar to warn of approaching planes while they were still miles away. The problem was there was no way to identify which planes belonged to the enemy and which were a country's own pilots returning from a mission.

Scottish physicist Sir Robert Alexander Watson-Watt developed the first active Identify Friend or Foe (IFF) system that received and sent signals air to ground that identified the aircraft as friendly. RFID works on this same basic concept in that a signal is sent to a transponder that then either reflects back a signal (passive system) or broadcasts a signal (active system).

Over the next several decades, other applications were developed that used RFID technology: the collection of tolls by automated toll-payment systems, the tracking of cows to determine which had received medicine, and the tracking of nuclear shipments within the US, to name just a few. One of the first commercial uses of RFID was in the tracking of items leaving a store to determine whether they had been purchased or stolen. Generally, however, the use of RFID was sporadic and unregulated.

In 1999 researchers at Massachusetts Institute of Technology joined with industry giants like Procter & Gamble and Gillette to establish an Auto-ID Center at the university. The term "Auto ID" referred to a broad range of existing and future technologies able to track goods, people, and information. The group's early work, to which Walmart contributed, focused on developing an RFID-based electronic product code that would allow businesses to track shipments and inventory automatically through a system of tags and sensors. It was a potential replacement for the manual scanning of bar codes, a technology that, itself, had revolutionized retail two decades earlier.

In June 2003 Walmart announced that — as the world's largest retailer — it would require its top 100 suppliers to tag pallets and cases of goods with RFID tags. Already viewed as a leader in supply-chain technology, Walmart's announcement pushed the RFID technology into the commercial world.

The start of the commercial use of RFID was difficult for Walmart due to pushback from suppliers, the cost to implement the technology, and significant technical problems. In the early days, the company's database wasn't big enough to handle the volume of data generated by the new system. But, even though Walmart had to curb its initial enthusiasm, the company continued to support the technology.

Today RFID is in use throughout the commercial world, tracking inventory from the moment a customer handles an item until a replacement item is on the shelf. It is also in use in manufacturing to keep track of production and configuration of end items. RFID uses continue to evolve, and routinely touch all of us on a daily basis.

Chapter **22**

Ten Examples of Global Logistics Gone Wrong

According to multiple industry analysts, as many as 70 percent of companies fail in their first attempt at expanding successful domestic operations into the global marketplace. While the reasons for failure are many and varied, most are built upon an ignorance of cultural and societal differences between markets.

In this chapter, we take a look at ten examples of disastrous initial attempts to go global (in no particular order). We've focused on larger corporations because their errors were more publicly visible and newsworthy. But many small and mid-sized companies have also made the same or similar errors by not benefitting from the lessons learned by industry leaders — an oversight that has brought about the death of many a company not large enough to withstand the impact of global miscalculation.

Best Buy Europe: Underestimating Cultural Differences in Technology Purchasing

Best Buy Europe was a 2008 retail joint venture created when the US-based electronics retailer Best Buy, Inc. purchased a 50 percent ownership (a £1.1 billion investment) of the UK-based mobile phone retailer Carphone Warehouse. Best Buy–branded superstores opened in the United Kingdom in 2010, with plans made for up to 200 additional superstores throughout the European Union. Four years later in 2012, with only 11 stores, Best Buy pulled the plug on the unprofitable joint venture, and Carphone Warehouse bought back Best Buy's shares for only £500 million (a 50 percent loss on original investment).

The major reason for failure was not understanding that big-box retail is not widely accepted outside of the United States. But perhaps more critically, Best Buy's understanding of technology purchasing trends was woefully inadequate. As the profit margin in electronics has grown smaller and smaller, much of the electronics retail business has moved online. Consumers around the world use the big-box stores as mere showrooms for the products offered online by multiple suppliers—many of whom are Best Buy's rivals.

Boise Cascade: Undone by Local Politics

In the 1990s Boise Cascade — a large, vertically-integrated wood-products manufacturer in the United States — decided to expand its production operations into Brazil, where it acquired timberlands and built a new mill.

Operating in Brazil, however, turned out to be much more difficult than expected because of regulatory, political, and cultural differences. Management attention, including frequent trips to Brazil, took far more time than the management of similar plants in the United States.

While Boise was able to make the business profitable after a few years, the profits were not high enough to justify the added investment needed and the disproportionate drain on top-management time to justify continued foreign operations. Boise threw in the towel in 2008, selling the Brazilian land and operations to a local paper company for $47 million — a nearly 50 percent loss on the initial land acquisition and construction costs of $90 million.

British Petroleum: Inadequate Global Operating Standards

On April 20, 2010, the British Petroleum (BP) oil drilling rig "Deepwater Horizon" (operating in the Gulf of Mexico) exploded and sank, resulting in the death of 11 platform workers. The result of the explosion was the largest accidental marine oil spill in the history of the petroleum industry, causing major devastation of not only wildlife habitats but also the local fishing and tourism industries. In 2015, BP estimated that its costs of compensation and environmental restoration as a result of the spill might exceed $54 billion.

The oil and gas industry is unusual in that it's already global: Cultural differences don't have much impact on company operations and profits, and what works in one part of the world generally works elsewhere. The same should have been true with the technical issues of drilling. Unfortunately, while the U.K.-based company applied rigid standards for its domestic offshore operations, it failed to do so in the Gulf of Mexico. There, its operating standards were weak, and oversight and control of the non-BP employees was made difficult by remoteness from headquarters.

As BP learned the hard way, any disaster in a foreign market is much harder to overcome because of the lack of "domestic market goodwill." While BP's reputation in the United Kingdom was one of being an environmentally-friendly energy company, the global perception of the company now is that of "environmental spoiler." This means that BP's corporate image and brand, which had historically been positive, will suffer for decades from its negative global impact.

Ford Motor Company: Operational Mismatches

Between 1988 and 2000, US-based Ford Motor Company acquired European boutique brands Aston Martin, Jaguar, Volvo, and Land Rover. But the automotive mammoth struggled with the luxury brands and, between 2007 and 2008, sold all of them off.

It turned out the mainstream-oriented, large-scale design and manufacturing style of Ford was a poor fit for the niche brands. Ford failed to add value to the design and logistics processes of the new models of the luxury brands.

As Ford showed in this case, just as companies can fail when they export their products to a foreign market, they can also fail when they buy an overseas company and attempt to change its processes without any understanding of the logistics of existing brands and markets.

Home Depot: Missing the Cultural Mark

Home Depot has made a fortune in the United States appealing to individuals who like to build or repair things themselves.

In 2006 Home Depot entered the Chinese market and opened 12 stores before realizing that most Chinese people have a different attitude toward home improvement.

Although China is in the midst of a huge building boom, it doesn't have the same impact as it would in North America or Europe. And it's not just that labor is cheaper in China. All those new apartment complexes and planned communities just don't need to be renovated yet.

Then there's the culture. Having work done for you is a status symbol in China. Do-it-yourself repairs are seen as a sign of being less-than-successful. Home Depot might have been better off entering the Chinese market as a wholesaler to contractors or as a retailer selling appliances and accessories for new construction.

The company closed its last seven Chinese stores in 2012, absorbing a $160 million loss.

Korean Airlines: Older Is Not Always Wiser

Between 1970 and 1999, 16 Korean Airlines aircraft were in serious accidents that resulted in the deaths of more than 700 people. In the most shocking incident, a plane was shot down in 1983, killing all 269 passengers and crew when the pilot accidentally flew into Soviet Union airspace. The carrier's miserable safety record was so bad that at one point the US Department of Defense prohibited its employees from flying on Korean Air and the US Federal Aviation Administration considered banning the airline from American airspace.

While most international failures result in companies failing to adjust to local expectations, the Korean Airlines' problem was the opposite: In expanding its global routes, the airline had failed to keep up with stricter international safety standards, partly because of its corporate culture. Because of the cultural observance of and deference to rank, flight attendants, copilots, and other crew members would not point out even the most glaring errors or maintenance deficiencies to the captain.

The airline finally brought in American experts to re-educate its flight crew workforce to address any and all operational problems and signs of equipment failure that were observed.

Nestlé: Failing to Understand the Actual Market

In the early 1970s, Swiss-based Nestlé Corporation began to aggressively market its baby formula in impoverished markets where clean water was not readily available, or where the mothers did not have the means to ensure proper sterilization of the formula and bottles. Inexplicably, the result of the company's marketing caused a much higher incidence of death among babies fed packaged formula when compared to mothers who breast-fed their newborns.

Nestlé's marketing campaign primarily targeted new mothers in hospitals, where adequate clean water and sterilized bottles were available, and the company gave incentives to hospital nurses and doctors to promote its product. As a result, the new mothers who had exchanged breast-feeding for formula fell victim to the ravages of improper sterilization.

What went wrong? Unfortunately, the company failed to understand that neither clean water nor adequate sterilization processes would be available to the new mother upon her discharge from the hospital. As a result of the increase in infant illness and deaths, Nestlé was hit with a boycott that started in 1977. The boycott has ebbed and flowed, but continues to this day in various regions around the world — including the United States, Europe, and the Far East.

The longer-term results were far ranging. In 1981 the 34th World Health Assembly adopted a resolution — specifically aimed at Nestlé — that includes the "International Code of Marketing of Breast-milk Substitutes."

SNC Lavalin: Crossing the Ethical Line

Currently facing multiple investigations into alleged wrongdoings by former executives, the Canadian engineering and construction company SNC Lavalin — a global leader in its field — is learning a hard lesson about "hanging out with the wrong crowd." In 2015 the Royal Canadian Mounted Police charged SNC Lavalin management with allegedly offering $47 million in bribes to Libyan officials in hopes of securing commercial contracts.

While the courts have yet to decide whether the millions of dollars in mysterious payments to Libya and other markets were illegal, what has hurt SNC Lavalin most is the perception that it was fraternizing with the regime of the late dictator, Muammar Gaddafi, and his family.

Although bribery and payoffs might, at first glance, be considered "the cost of doing business" in some markets, laws like Canada's Corruption of Foreign Public Officials Act make it imperative for companies to *always* comply with not only their home country's but also international trade ethics laws, even if it gives their local competitors an edge.

Target: Global Is Better Only if Your Logistics Infrastructure Can Support It

In 2011 Target announced that its first attempt at international expansion would be into the Canadian market. At the time, it seemed to make logical sense, as many Canadians were already familiar with the company from their visits to the United States. As part of the expansion, Target acquired the Canadian discount chain Zellers (now defunct) for $1.8 billion, a move hailed at the time, as it gave Target an immediate cross-country footprint and spared it the expense of building out its own stores. Target was initially forecasting a profit in its Canadian operations in only two years.

Three years later (in 2014), Target announced it would close its 132 Canadian stores and take not only a $5.4 billion write-down but also incur a total net loss of some $2 billion on the failed Canadian expansion. Why? Under the most optimistic of scenarios projected, the earliest Target Canada would make a profit would be 2021, which would be unacceptable as Target was preparing for a capital-intensive effort to expand its smaller stores in the United States.

So what happened? The reality is that most Zellers stores were unattractive, needed significant modernization, were poorly configured for Target's big-box layout, and — most critically — were located in areas not frequented by the middle-class consumers that are Target's focus. Inheriting many poor locations from a dying, low-end retailer was at the heart of the damage to Target's cheap-chic allure in Canada.

Perhaps more damaging than image was that the operation of the initial 124 stores in such a short period of time wreaked havoc with inventory planning and management, causing an enormous problem with stock-outs from the start. Shoppers had expected to see the same abundance they saw in Target's US stores. With bare shelves, Canadian shoppers couldn't buy anything, even if they wanted to.

The lesson here is that even well-established, mass-merchant brands like Target only get so many chances at international expansion. No numbers were given, but Target Canada's sales during peak holiday seasons damaged shopper loyalty and brand goodwill too significantly for Target to restore or financially recover from.

Uber: Using Technology to Circumvent Regulatory Requirements

Mobile technology has been a source of disruption in many industries. Prior to the 2010 entrance of Uber into the car-for-hire marketplace, the international taxi environment operated for decades without major competition. Uber has leveraged mobile technology to disrupt long-established local and national taxi infrastructures by offering an alternative that excels in providing convenience for passengers. Since its launch, Uber has continuously enhanced the functionality of its mobile application, thus making it easier than ever to use its services.

Uber has pursued an aggressive growth strategy, both domestically and globally. The company has expanded its operational reach to include cities in 26 different countries — but many of its successes have come only after protracted and expensive battles with regulatory powers.

In many cases Uber has found itself battling traditional local, regional, or national taxi services that often have strong political ties. As a result, Uber has been banned (or had a ban attempted) in the cities of Berlin, Delhi, and Portland, Oregon. It is also banned throughout Spain and is fighting attempted bans in Thailand and Vietnam.

Much of the opposition has come from the fact that many of Uber's drivers do not have the same transport licenses or undergo the mandatory background checks that taxi drivers do. As a result, Uber has been fined in multiple countries. Further, in some countries Uber drivers are facing tax investigations resulting from the possible failure to report income.

In January 2015, the Chinese government banned drivers of private cars from offering their services through taxi-hailing apps. It later allowed their use only under strict new rules. In the spring of 2016 Beijing police raided local Uber offices and seized thousands of iPhones and other equipment used to run the business. The city's transport commission said it suspected Uber was operating an illegal taxi service without a proper business registration. As a result, in September 2016 Uber sold its remaining assets to a local rival.

Chapter **23**

Top Ten Resources

I n this chapter, we provide what we consider to be the most comprehensive resources for your further understanding of global logistics. Several of the organizations cited — which are listed by topic — apply to more than one of the book's sections; accordingly, we've included them under the topic we thought most appropriate.

We intentionally did not include sources with a ".com" or ".net" email address. While you will find some excellent information from the websites of "for profit" entities, you will also find occasionally that the information has been presented in a way to promote the site owner's reputation or sales.

Finally, we did not specifically list any ".gov" reference. Rather, we recommend that you make use of your country's diplomatic agencies — such as embassies or trade delegations — tasked with establishing and developing trade relationships with the country you want to deal with.

Global Logistics Manufacturing and Distribution

In this section you'll find some of the more valuable resources in helping you make your decision to set up foreign manufacturing operations.

GACG — Global Anti-Counterfeiting Network

GACG (www.gacg.org) is the international network of national and regional intellectual property protection and enforcement organizations. There are currently 21 group and organizational members representing more than 40 countries. The network's common objectives are to exchange and share information, to participate in appropriate joint activities, and to cooperate in the resolution of specific intellectual property problems and challenges in their respective national or regional areas.

UN/CEFACT — United Nations Centre for Trade Facilitation and Electronic Business

Within the United Nations framework of the Economic and Social Council, the United Nations Economic Commission for Europe (UNECE) serves as the focal point for trade facilitation recommendations and electronic business standards, covering both commercial and government business processes that can foster growth in international trade and related services.

In this context, the United Nations Centre for Trade Facilitation and Electronic Business (UN/CEFACT; www.unece.org/cefact) was mandated to develop a program of work of global relevance to achieve improved worldwide coordination and cooperation. It aims to help business, trade, and administrative organizations from developed, developing, and transitioning economies to exchange products and services effectively. To this end, it focuses on simplifying national and international transactions by harmonizing processes, procedures, and information flows related to these transactions, rendering them more efficient and streamlined, with the ultimate goal of contributing to the growth of global commerce.

UN/CEFACT focuses on two main areas of activity to make international trade processes more efficient and streamlined: trade facilitation and electronic business. Trade facilitation involves the simplification of trade procedures (or the elimination of unnecessary procedures). This includes work to standardize and harmonize the core information used in trade documents, to ease the flow of information between parties by relying on appropriate information and communication technology, and to promote simplified payment systems to foster transparency, accountability, and cost-effectiveness. Electronic business, in the UN/CEFACT context, focuses on harmonizing, standardizing, and automating the exchange of information that controls the flow of goods along the international supply chain. UN/CEFACT's work on electronic business is driven by the understanding that goods cannot move faster than the processes and information that accompany them.

UN/CEFACT has produced over 30 trade facilitation recommendations and a range of electronic business standards that are used throughout the world by both governments and the private sector. They reflect best practices in trade procedures and data and documentary requirements. The International Organization for Standardization (ISO) has adopted many of them as international standards.

UNIDO — United Nations Industrial Development Organization

The primary objective of UNIDO (www.unido.org) is the promotion and acceleration of industrial development in developing countries and countries with economics in transition, and the promotion of international industrial cooperation.

UNIDO assists developing countries in the formulation of institutional, scientific, and technological policies and programs in the field of industrial development. It also analyzes trends, disseminates information, and coordinates activities in the field of industrial development. The organization acts as a forum for consultations and negotiations directed toward the industrialization of developing countries, and the implementation of development plans for sustainable industrialization in the public and private sectors.

UNIDO is one of the largest providers of trade-related development services, offering focused and neutral advice and technical cooperation in the areas of competitiveness, industrial modernization and upgrading, compliance with international trade standards, testing methods, and metrology.

WTO — World Trade Organization

There are a number of ways of looking at the World Trade Organization (www.wto.org). It is a forum for governments to negotiate trade agreements. It is a place for them to settle trade disputes. It operates a system of trade rules. Essentially, the WTO is a place where member governments try to sort out their mutual trade problems.

The WTO's negotiations have helped to open markets for trade where countries have faced trade barriers and wanted them reduced or eliminated. However, the WTO is not just about opening markets: In some circumstances its rules support maintaining trade barriers — specifically, when protecting consumers or preventing the spread of disease.

At its heart are the WTO agreements, negotiated and signed by the bulk of the world's trading nations. These documents provide the legal ground rules for international commerce. They are essentially contracts, binding governments so as to keep their trade policies within agreed limits. Although negotiated and signed by governments, the goal is to help producers of goods and services, exporters, and importers conduct their business, while allowing governments to meet social and environmental objectives.

Note: In addition to the WTO, most countries have established their own national trade organizations — and many countries also have regional and local trade organizations.

Global Logistics Services

If you've been contracted to provide global logistics services, you may find the resources of the following organizations to be helpful.

HBR — Harvard Business Review

While many internationally renowned business schools have their own periodicals, we found the *Harvard Business Review* (www.hbr.org) to be particularly valuable to companies contemplating global expansion. A 10-issues-per-year journal, it is distributed by Harvard Business Publishing, a wholly owned subsidiary of Harvard University.

HBR's articles cover a wide range of topics that are relevant to different industries, management functions, and geographic locations. The articles focus on such areas as leadership, organizational change, negotiation, strategy, operations, marketing, finance, and managing people.

ICC — International Chamber of Commerce

The ICC (www.iccwbo.org) provides a forum for businesses and other organizations to examine and better comprehend the nature and significance of the major shifts taking place in the global economy. It offers a channel for supplying business leadership to help governments manage those shifts in a collaborative manner for the benefit of the global economy as a whole.

While policy advocacy is a major part of ICC's work, everything else it does is also devoted to promoting international trade and investment, focused on making it easier for businesses to operate internationally. Drawing on the expertise and experience of its worldwide membership, ICC has, over time, developed a large array of voluntary rules, guidelines, and codes that facilitate cross-border trans-actions and help spread best practice among companies. A notable example is ICC's famous Incoterms rules — first elaborated in 1936 — which are accepted as the global standard for the interpretation of the most common terms used in con-tracts for the international sale of goods.

ICC is a leading provider of dispute resolution services for individuals, businesses, states, state entities, and international organizations seeking alternatives to court litigation. The choice of one or more ICC services as the dispute resolution method should ideally be made when businesses and governments negotiate their con-tracts and treaties. ICC provides standard and recommended clauses for this pur-pose, which can be modified to take account of the requirements of national laws and any other special requirements.

ICC's Commercial Crimes Services works closely with international law enforce-ment officials (including Interpol) to tackle piracy and commercial crime — including fraud in international trade, insurance fraud, financial instrument fraud, money laundering, shipping fraud, and product counterfeiting.

TIP

Many countries have national, regional, and local chambers of commerce that can be particularly beneficial to companies that are expanding their logistics services into new foreign locations.

OECD — Organisation for European Economic Co-operation

OECD (www.oecd.org) defines itself as a forum of countries committed to democ-racy and the market economy, providing a setting to compare policy experiences, seek answers to common problems, identify good practices, and coordinate domestic and international policies. In addition to most European countries, its members include Australia, Canada, Chile, Iceland, Israel, Japan, South Korea, Mexico, New Zealand, and the United States. It also works closely with emerging economies like the People's Republic of China, India, and Brazil; and developing economies in Africa, Asia, Latin America, and the Caribbean.

The organization's mandate covers economic, environmental, and social issues. It acts by peer pressure to improve policy and implement nonbinding instruments that can occasionally lead to binding treaties. In this work the OECD cooperates with businesses, trade unions, and other representatives of civil society. Collabo-ration at the OECD regarding taxation, for example, has fostered the growth of a global web of bilateral tax treaties.

OECD has taken a role in coordinating international action on corruption and bribery, creating the OECD Anti-Bribery Convention, which came into effect in February 1999. It has been ratified by 38 countries.

The OECD has also constituted an anti-spam task force, which submitted a detailed report with several background papers on spam problems in developing countries, best practices for Internet service providers and email marketers, and so forth. It continues to work on the information economy and the future of the Internet economy.

Global Humanitarian and Disaster Relief Logistics

The field of humanitarian and disaster relief is a complex — and often confusing — one. The organizations we discuss here are some of the major providers of disaster relief.

IFRC — The International Federation of Red Cross and Red Crescent Societies

The IFRC (www.ifrc.org) is the world's largest humanitarian organization, providing assistance without discrimination as to nationality, race, religious beliefs, class, or political opinions. Founded in 1919, the IFRC comprises the 190-member Red Cross and Red Crescent national societies, a secretariat in Geneva, and more than 60 delegations strategically located to support activities around the world. The Red Crescent is used in place of the Red Cross in many Islamic countries.

The IFRC carries out relief operations to assist victims of disasters and combines this with development work to strengthen the capacities of its member national societies. The IFRC's work focuses on four core areas: promoting humanitarian values, disaster response, disaster preparedness, and health and community care.

The Logistics Management of the IFRC is a recognized provider of humanitarian logistics services. The basic task of IFRC's humanitarian logistics comprises acquiring and delivering requested supplies and services at the places and times needed, while ensuring best value for money. In the immediate aftermath of any disaster, these supplies include items that are vital for survival, such as food, water, and temporary shelter and medicine, among others.

The volume of Logistics Management business grows in line with emerging humanitarian needs. On average, since 2007 the Logistics Management — through its global network — has yearly mobilized and delivered over 220 million Swiss francs' worth of humanitarian aid. It holds prepositioned stock capable of meeting the immediate needs of 450,000 people at any time. When emergencies strike, these supplies can be delivered to affected areas anywhere in the world within 24 to 48 hours. Per month, the Logistics Management supports 60 humanitarian operations across the world.

OCHA — United Nations Office for the Coordination of Humanitarian Affairs

OCHA (www.unocha.org) is the element of the United Nations Secretariat responsible for bringing together humanitarian actors to ensure a coherent response to emergencies. OCHA also ensures there is a framework within which each actor can contribute to the overall response effort. OCHA's mission is to mobilize and coordinate effective and principled humanitarian action in partnership with national and international actors in order to alleviate human suffering in disasters and emergencies, advocate the rights of people in need, promote preparedness and prevention, and facilitate sustainable solutions.

The OCHA website contains additional links to tools to coordinate and manage surge capacity, United Nations disaster assessment and coordination, cluster coordination, the International Search and Rescue Advisory Group, the on-site operations coordination centers and regional disaster centers, logistics support, civil-military coordination, needs assessment, and environmental emergencies.

OCHA also supports specialized digital services or portals, where relief responders can exchange information during a protracted or sudden-onset emergency in order to facilitate more efficient, effective, and coordinated response. The site is organized into information on operations, assessments, documents and maps, and the humanitarian system.

One of those portals, ReliefWeb, serves as the leading humanitarian information source on global crises and disasters, and is designed to provide humanitarian workers with timely and reliable information they need to make decisions. The site contains links to information on countries, disasters, topics, and organizations. Reports, maps, infographics, and videos are the information formats provided. In addition, the site provides information on training opportunities.

WFP — United Nations World Food Programme

The World Food Programme (www.wfp.org) is the largest humanitarian agency fighting hunger worldwide. In emergencies the WFP gets food to where it is needed, saving the lives of victims of war, civil conflict, and natural disasters. After the cause of an emergency has passed, the WFP uses food to help communities rebuild.

Due to its expertise in the field of humanitarian logistics, the WFP was chosen by the United Nations Interagency Standing Committee to be the lead agency for the Logistics Cluster. The Logistics Cluster is a mechanism responsible for coordination, information management, and — where necessary — logistics services provision to ensure an effective and efficient logistics response takes place in humanitarian emergency missions. Where there are critical gaps in a humanitarian response, WFP, as the lead agency, acts as a "provider of last resort" by offering common logistics services.

The Logistics Cluster also works to develop and improve the capacity, efficiency, and effectiveness of the logistics response in future emergencies. Preparedness training, activities, and tools are also available to benefit the entire humanitarian community through the Logistics Cluster, and represent the combined expertise of the humanitarian logistics sector.

The Logistics Cluster's website (www.logcluster.org) has links to country profiles, logistics capacity assessments, concept of operations, the "Logistics Operational Guide," training, operations support, WFP logistics, and the Relief Item Tracking Application.

Glossary

We've explored a number of concepts and used terms throughout this volume that may or may not be familiar to you. When we introduced what may have been a new concept, those terms were italicized, and we included an explanation of either the word or the concept.

We also used terminology that is often used by logistics practitioners in their day-to-day operations. When we did so, we did not break up our discussion by specifically defining fundamental logistics terms.

That said, the following terms and definitions are listed for your quick reference. Included are not only those terms that were defined in the chapters, but also some of the more fundamental logistics terms and concepts that were not specially defined. The list is not meant to be all-inclusive of either all functional aspects of the logistics enterprise, or business administration and management. Rather, it is a compilation of the terms and concepts underlying the conduct of global logistics.

Note: Generally, most of the definitions we've provided are those in general use and commonly understood: Those are not attributed. However, where we've included a definition that was developed by a particular agency or "functional proponent," we've included attribution in parentheses at the end of the definition: for example, *(The International Anti-Counterfeiting Coalition)*.

admitted insurance: Insurance policies issued by a country's specified and licensed insurance carrier.

affected country: The country where a disaster occurs.

complex disaster: Either a natural or man-made disaster, complicated by political or social circumstances that cause the destabilization of society. *(United Nations Office of Disaster Risk Reduction)*

compulsory insurance: Insurance that is required by a nation's laws.

consumables: Items that are intended to be used quickly (that is, consumed in use) and then replaced.

Continuity of Operations Plan (COOP): Also called a business resiliency plan, a COOP is the plan for creating prevention and recovery systems to deal with potential threats to company operations.

corporate social responsibility (CSR): A form of corporate regulation integrated into a business model, CSR policy functions as a self-regulatory mechanism whereby a business monitors and ensures its active compliance with the spirit of laws, ethical standards, and national or international norms.

counterfeiting: The manufacturing or distribution of goods under someone else's name without their permission. *(The International Anti-Counterfeiting Coalition)*

demobilization: The process of shutting down any effort — in this case, operations or logistics — and returning the people and their equipment to the home base.

disaster: A serious disruption of the functioning of a community or a society involving widespread human, material, economic, or environmental losses and impacts, which exceeds the ability of the affected community or society to cope using its own resources. *(United Nations Office of Disaster Risk Reduction)*

dunnage: Items or loose material used to support, brace, and protect cargo while in transit.

e-commerce: The electronic sale of items over the Internet.

environmental footprint: The total impact a company has on the environment due to the consumption of energy, water, chemicals, and other materials.

expatriates: Domestic employees of a multinational company or its subsidiary, with a foreign assignment.

external logistics: The use of outside companies for the movement of a manufacturer's material between suppliers, factories, distribution centers, and customers.

fidelity bond: A form of insurance protection that covers policyholders for losses that are incurred as a result of fraudulent acts by specified individuals. It usually insures a business for losses caused by the dishonest acts of its employees.

fifth party logistics provider (5PL): A company that guarantees the management of *networks* of supply chains, or even the entire logistics enterprise — in effect, serving as a company's corporate chief logistics officer.

first party logistics provider (1PL): The original company or manufacturer that provides all logistics services in-house for the manufacturing, selling, and servicing of its product(s).

Food and Agriculture Organization (FAO): An agency of the United Nations that leads international efforts to defeat hunger.

force majeure: A legal term defining any unforeseen condition or situation that would prevent either party from fulfilling its contractual obligation; it may be used as a legal defense for not carrying out any or all of the terms of the contract.

fourth party logistics provider (4PL): A company that guarantees and provides to the original manufacturer both the organization and full management of the manufacturer's logistics tasks. 4PL providers often manage an entire, singular supply chain.

freight on board (FOB): A term specifying at what point the seller transfers ownership of the goods to the buyer.

green logistics: A company's activities designed to measure and minimize the ecological impact of its entire range of logistics activities, throughout all aspects of its logistics chains.

humanitarian and disaster relief (H&DR) logistics: Logistics support applied to humanitarian and disaster relief efforts. This support may be accomplished through monetary support, equipment support, personnel support, or a combination of any type.

independent contractors: Personnel working under an individual term contract, and individuals who are not considered employees of the company.

integrated logistics support (ILS) plan: A plan developed by the logistics community, working closing with the product designers and systems engineers, that provides a technical basis for integrating all support elements in order to maximize the product or system's availability while optimizing the costs of logistics support throughout the life cycle. *(US Department of Defense)*

intellectual property: Intangible rights protecting the products of human intelligence and creation, such as copyrightable work, patents, trademarks, and trade secrets.

intermodal shipping: The transportation of freight in an intermodal container or vehicle, using multiple modes of transportation, without any handling of the freight itself when changing modes.

life cycle support: The composite of all considerations necessary to assure the effective and economical support of a system throughout its programmed life cycle. It includes the elements of reliability and maintainability; technical data; maintenance planning; support and test equipment; supply planning; packaging, handling, storage, and distribution; personnel; training; facilities and infrastructure; and information systems.

local nationals: Citizens of the country where the work is being performed.

localization: The process of adapting a product or marketing program for a specific region or language by adding locale-specific components and translating text. *(United Nations Economic Commission for Asia and Pacific)*

logistics: The art and science of management, engineering, and technical activities concerned with the requirements, design, and supplying and maintaining resources to support objectives, plans, and operations. *(SOLE – The International Society of Logistics)*

Logistics Cluster: A coordination mechanism, hosted by the World Food Programme, that is activated when there are response and coordination gaps in addressing humanitarian needs in order to ensure an efficient and effective emergency response. *(World Food Programme)*

logistics CONOPS: A business's concept of operations (CONOPS) detailing how it will provide logistics support for a particular mission or operation.

logistics engineering: Those support-related activities that deal primarily with system or product design and development.

logistics enterprise: The entirety of all logistics functional domains, to include logistics engineering, supply management, maintenance management, distribution and transportation, and logistics services. *(SOLE – The International Society of Logistics)*

logistics support analysis: The process of collecting and analyzing all the integrated logistics support data involved with supporting a system or product from the conceptual design, through design development, manufacturing, distributing, use, phase-out, and disposal. *(US Department of Defense)*

maintainability: The probability that a given maintenance action for an item under given usage conditions can be performed within a stated time interval when the maintenance is performed under stated conditions using stated procedures and resources. Maintainability has two categories: serviceability (the ease of conducting scheduled inspections and servicing) and reparability (the ease of restoring service after a failure). *(American Society for Quality)*

mobilization: The process of organizing and deploying a logistics team from its country of origin to the site of a disaster.

multimodal shipping: Uses different modes and involves the physical handling of the product to fit a different container or carrier unique to the next specific mode.

net realizable value: The value of what inventory is worth. It is computed by subtracting from the original inventory cost all advertising expenses, shipping and handling, and any other expenses.

nonrecurring risks: Those risks that are inherently not repeatable and are unpredictable.

obsolescence: The state or condition of being no longer in use.

phishing: The attempt to fraudulently acquire sensitive information by email.

preventive (or scheduled) maintenance: Maintenance that is regularly performed on equipment to reduce the risk of failure.

production logistics: Those logistics operations that support the manufacturing process.

provisioning: The process of determining the range and quantity of items (for example, spares and repair parts, special tools, test equipment, and support equipment) required to support and maintain an item for an initial period of service. *(US Department of Defense)*

qualitative measurements: Factors or conditions that can be observed but not numerically measured.

quantitative measurements: Measurements that are reducible to numerical values.

ransomware: A computer malware program that installs covertly on a victim's device (such as a computer or smartphone) and either holds the victim's data hostage or threatens to publish the victim's data, until such time as a ransom is paid.

recurring risks: Those repeatable risks caused by production or demand fluctuation.

reliability: The probability of a product's performing its intended function under stated conditions without failure for a given period of time. (*Society of Reliability Engineers*)

replacement value: The true cost to replace lost or damaged inventory, to include any new shipping and handling charges.

reverse engineering: The process of extracting knowledge or design information from anything man-made and reproducing it (or anything else) based on the information extracted.

reverse logistics: The process of planning, implementing, and controlling the efficient, cost-effective flow of materials, in-process inventory, finished goods, and related information from the point of consumption to the point of origin for the purpose of recapturing value or proper disposal. (*Reverse Logistics and Sustainability Council*)

second party logistics provider (2PL): A company hired by the manufacturer to serve as either a carrier, warehouse manager, or a logistics engineering firm for the operational execution of a clearly defined logistics task.

slow onset disaster: A crisis that emerges over a sustained period of time due to external triggers such as drought-induced crop failure or illnesses. (*United Nations Office of Disaster Risk Reduction*)

stock-outs: The condition of having no inventory on hand.

sudden-onset disaster: A suddenly occurring natural (geophysical, hydrological, meteorological, climatological, or biological) or man-made (such as transportation or industrial) disaster. (*United Nations Office of Disaster Risk Reduction*)

supply chain: A system of organizations, people, activities, information, and resources involved in moving a product or service from supplier to customer.

supply chain management: The planning and management of all activities involved in sourcing, procurement, conversion, and logistics management. It also includes coordination and collaboration with channel partners, which may be suppliers, intermediaries, third-party service providers, or customers. (*Council of Supply Chain Management Professionals*)

support equipment: All equipment (mobile or fixed) required to support the operation and maintenance of a material system. This includes associated multiuse end items, ground handling and maintenance equipment, tools, meteorological and calibration equipment, test equipment, and automatic test equipment. (*US Department of Defense*)

supportability: The degree to which planned logistics support (including test, measurement, and diagnostic equipment; spares and repair parts; technical data; support facilities; transportation requirements; training; manpower; and software support) allows meeting consumer user requirements. (*US Department of Defense*)

surety bond: A formal and legally enforceable contract between a company and a third party (such as a bank, a bonding company, or an insurance company) that agrees to guarantee payment or compensation to a foreign client in the event that the company fails to deliver contracted services.

sustainability and **sustainable development:** Product development that meets the needs of the present without compromising the ability of future generations to meet their own needs. *(Bruntland Report of 1987)*

tariffs (or duties): Taxes levied by governments on the value — including freight and insurance costs — of imported products.

third-country nationals: Employees of a multinational company who work in a foreign country and do not have the citizenship of the parent company's home country or the country of employment.

third party logistics provider (3PL): When the manufacturer outsources a grouping of transport and logistic activities. The 3PL service provider organizes those activities and may act as a broker and — in turn — subsequently hire additional companies for task execution.

transportation: The movement of goods from one location to another.

transportation mode: A term used to distinguish substantially different ways to perform transport. The most common modes are air, sea, and ground (which includes rail and road).

United Nations Children's Fund (UNICEF): A United Nations (UN) program that provides humanitarian and developmental assistance to children and mothers in developing countries.

United Nations Development Programme (UNDP): The United Nations global development network. UNDP advocates for change and connects countries to knowledge, experience, and resources to help people build a better life. It provides expert advice, training, and support to developing countries, with increasing emphasis on assistance to the least developed countries.

United Nations High Commissioner for Refugees (UNHCR): The United Nations program mandated to protect and support refugees at the request of a government or the UN itself and assists in their voluntary repatriation, local integration, or resettlement to a third country.

United Nations Human Settlements Programme (UN—Habitat): The United Nations agency for human settlements and sustainable urban development.

United Nations International Labour Organization (ILO): The United Nations agency dealing with international labor issues, particularly labor standards, social protection, and work opportunities for all.

United Nations Level 1 Emergency: The affected country has sufficient resources on-hand to internally handle the H&DR response. *(United Nations Office of Disaster Risk Reduction)*

United Nations Level 2 Emergency: The affected country's internal resources require modest external (usually local or regional) augmentation. *(United Nations Office of Disaster Risk Reduction)*

United Nations Level 3 Emergency: International resources are necessary to enable the affected country to respond. *(United Nations Office of Disaster Risk Reduction)*

United Nations Office for the Coordination of Humanitarian Affairs (OCHA): The part of the United Nations Secretariat responsible for bringing together humanitarian actors to ensure a coherent response to emergencies. OCHA also ensures there is a framework within which each actor can contribute to the overall response effort.

work in process: Partially fabricated components of products.

World Food Programme (WFP): The food-assistance branch of the United Nations and the world's largest humanitarian organization addressing hunger and promoting food security. It is responsible for organizing the Logistics Cluster in support of disaster relief operations.

World Health Organization (WHO): A specialized agency of the United Nations that is concerned with international public health.

Index

A

ability to respond, assessing, 239–240
acquisition logistics, 42, 71–72
"acts of man," 173
"acts of war," 173
adaptability
  importance of, 256–257
  packaging, 143–144
  products, 143–144
administration, of owning compared with leasing, 120
admitted insurance, 178, 291
affected country, 291
Afghanistan, 210–211
after-action report (AAR), 260–261
agility, 127, 256–257
Agricultural Competitiveness and Diversification Project (ACDP), 270–271
air bags, 139
airlift transportation mode, 112–117
Alexander the Great (military leader), 7
Amazon, 265–266
animal food products, 125
assessment
  of ability to respond, 239–240
  of framework, 221
  internal *vs.* external logistics support, 45–46
assets, discarding *vs.* returning, 259–260
Attainable, as a SMART goal attribute, 147
Australia, 209
Austria, 209
authority, delegations of, 87

B

Bahrain, 210–211
Bangladesh cyclone, 31
base camp, establishing, 247–248
base operations "housekeeping," 258
Belgium, 210
Best Buy Europe, 276
best practices, 70–75, 132
Bezos, Jeff (Amazon founder), 265
Bhola cyclone, 31
Boise Cascade, 276
Bolivia, 210
bonding, 179
branding, 144
Brazil, 210
"brick-and-mortar" stores, 149
British Petroleum (BP), 277
builders liability insurance, 179
bulk carriers, 117
business plans, starting small, 44–45

C

California earthquake, 32
Cambodia, 204
camp coordination and management, as a UN relief sector cluster, 223
Canada, 210
"capturing" sales, 148–149
carbon footprint, minimizing, 74–75
cargo
  center of gravity for, 125
  lashing, 139
  screening, 135–138
cargo ships, 117
cash donations, providing, 232–234
category of disaster, 230
cause, of piracy, 133–134
center of gravity, for cargo, 125
Central African Republic, 34
Central Emergency Response Fund (CERF), 232
Chad, 204

About the Authors

This volume owes its existence to the collective expertise of a number of the leaders, past and present, of SOLE – The International Society of Logistics (SOLE). It draws upon the public and private sector experiences of its four principal authors and its technical editor, all of whom have helped to shape SOLE's vision and success over the course of its more than 50 years of serving not only the field of logistics but also its worldwide practitioners.

John (Jay) J. Erb, Demonstrated Master Logistician (DML), the co-editor and primary author of Part 4, has been a career logistician for over 45 years, with 27 years in United States Army command and field logistics assignments. Currently the President of SOLE, he served as the Director of Strategic Logistics on the Joint Staff in the Pentagon (Washington, DC) upon his retirement from the Army as a Colonel. Upon leaving the Pentagon, he spent nine years with General Dynamics Information Technology as the Vice President for Integrated Support Solutions, where he oversaw logistics services projects in the United States and overseas.

Sarah R. James, DML, SOLE's Executive Director, served as the book's primary editor and author of Part 1. A past president of SOLE, she has actively promoted the development, advancement, and recognition of logisticians since 1983. No stranger to academia, she frequently serves as a guest lecturer in logistics degree programs both in the US and abroad, develops curriculum and course requirements, and authors numerous publications. Whether as a US government or private industry logistician, her multi-functional experience consistently results in not only increased operational funding but also the development of organizationally transformative programs, policies, and systems.

Joanne S. Wyman, PhD, author of Part 5, has over 30 years of experience in emergency management as a researcher, practitioner, and peer reviewer. Her early experience focused on environmental emergencies in the US. Drawing on her academic background in international relations, she expanded her portfolio to the delivery of humanitarian and disaster relief goods and services. At consulting firms — from startups to global enterprises — Dr. Wyman supported the emergency management, environmental, energy, and transportation policies and programs of multilateral organizations, government agencies, and private enterprise. SOLE's first director of its Humanitarian and Disaster Relief Application Division, she frequently represents SOLE in numerous public and private sector forums.

Philip T. Frohne, Certified Professional Logistician (CPL), is the primary author of Parts 2 and 3. As a logistics practitioner for more than 36 years, he provides logistics and maintenance engineering expertise, to include the development and conduct of technical training, for a global commercial and military aerospace corporation. The chairman of SOLE's certification qualifications review boards, he is the author of the McGraw-Hill SOLE Press volume *Quantitative Measurements for Logistics.* He frequently participates in local humanitarian and disaster relief logistics efforts as a trained community emergency response team (CERT) member and amateur radio operator.

The book's technical editor, **Dr. Lloyd H. Muller, CPL,** has over 35 years of experience in all aspects of logistics. A past president of SOLE and its current Vice President for Education, Dr. Muller has been involved in many diplomatic negotiations that gained significant benefits for both the US and many of the nations in Europe. He has taught at universities both in the US and abroad, including the University of Maryland, Embry Riddle Aeronautical University, La Verne University, and the Middle East Technical University in Ankara, Turkey. Dr. Muller currently serves as an associate professor for Florida Institute of Technology in its graduate logistics degree programs.

Dedication

This book is dedicated to all the past and present members of SOLE, the many companies and agencies SOLE has assisted since its inception, and all the logisticians who have worked tirelessly to not only advance the art and science of logistics, but also those who, on a daily basis, use logistics as a tool for global transformation.

Authors' Acknowledgments

The authors — and SOLE — would be remiss if we did not pay homage to the foresight of Dr. Wernher von Braun. It was his vision of a highly trained and professional cadre of individuals to support the emerging US space program that became the impetus for the establishment of not only SOLE but also the profession of logistics.

On a more personal note, the authors would like to acknowledge their families and friends who have encouraged them during the writing and editing of this book, and the Wiley staff who have been so supportive.

Publisher's Acknowledgments

Commissioning Editor: Annie Knight

Editorial Project Manager and Development Editor: Christina N. Guthrie

Copy Editor: Christine Pingleton

Technical Editor: Dr. Lloyd H. Muller, CPL

Production Editor: Siddique Shaik

Cover Photos: © catscandotcom/Getty Images

Take dummies with you everywhere you go!

Whether you are excited about e-books, want more from the web, must have your mobile apps, or are swept up in social media, dummies makes everything easier.

Find us online!

dummies.com

Leverage the power

Dummies is the global leader in the reference category and one of the most trusted and highly regarded brands in the world. No longer just focused on books, customers now have access to the dummies content they need in the format they want. Together we'll craft a solution that engages your customers, stands out from the competition, and helps you meet your goals.

Advertising & Sponsorships

Connect with an engaged audience on a powerful multimedia site, and position your message alongside expert how-to content. Dummies.com is a one-stop shop for free, online information and know-how curated by a team of experts.

- Targeted ads
- Video
- Email Marketing
- Microsites
- Sweepstakes sponsorship

20 MILLION PAGE VIEWS EVERY SINGLE MONTH

15 MILLION UNIQUE VISITORS PER MONTH

43% OF ALL VISITORS ACCESS THE SITE VIA THEIR MOBILE DEVICES

700,000 NEWSLETTER SUBSCRIPTIONS TO THE INBOXES OF

300,000 UNIQUE INDIVIDUALS EVERY WEEK

# of dummies

Custom Publishing

Reach a global audience in any language by creating a solution that will differentiate you from competitors, amplify your message, and encourage customers to make a buying decision.

- Apps
- Books
- eBooks
- Video
- Audio
- Webinars

Brand Licensing & Content

Leverage the strength of the world's most popular reference brand to reach new audiences and channels of distribution.

For more information, visit dummies.com/biz

PERSONAL ENRICHMENT

Staying Sharp
9781119187790
USA $26.00
CAN $31.99
UK £19.99

Facebook
9781119179030
USA $21.99
CAN $25.99
UK £16.99

Guitar
9781119293354
USA $24.99
CAN $29.99
UK £17.99

Investing
9781119293347
USA $22.99
CAN $27.99
UK £16.99

Beekeeping
9781119310068
USA $22.99
CAN $27.99
UK £16.99

Digital Photography
9781119235606
USA $24.99
CAN $29.99
UK £17.99

Meditation
9781119251163
USA $24.99
CAN $29.99
UK £17.99

Pregnancy
9781119235491
USA $26.99
CAN $31.99
UK £19.99

Samsung Galaxy S7
9781119279952
USA $24.99
CAN $29.99
UK £17.99

iPhone
9781119283133
USA $24.99
CAN $29.99
UK £17.99

Crocheting
9781119287117
USA $24.99
CAN $29.99
UK £16.99

Nutrition
9781119130246
USA $22.99
CAN $27.99
UK £16.99

PROFESSIONAL DEVELOPMENT

Windows 10
9781119311041
USA $24.99
CAN $29.99
UK £17.99

AutoCAD
9781119255796
USA $39.99
CAN $47.99
UK £27.99

Excel 2016
9781119293439
USA $26.99
CAN $31.99
UK £19.99

QuickBooks 2017
9781119281467
USA $26.99
CAN $31.99
UK £19.99

macOS Sierra
9781119280651
USA $29.99
CAN $35.99
UK £21.99

LinkedIn
9781119251132
USA $24.99
CAN $29.99
UK £17.99

Windows 10
9781119310563
USA $34.00
CAN $41.99
UK £24.99

SharePoint 2016
9781119181705
USA $29.99
CAN $35.99
UK £21.99

Fundamental Analysis
9781119263593
USA $26.99
CAN $31.99
UK £19.99

Networking
9781119257769
USA $29.99
CAN $35.99
UK £21.99

Office 2016
9781119293477
USA $26.99
CAN $31.99
UK £19.99

Office 365
9781119265313
USA $24.99
CAN $29.99
UK £17.99

Salesforce.com
9781119239314
USA $29.99
CAN $35.99
UK £21.99

Coding
9781119293323
USA $29.99
CAN $35.99
UK £21.99

dummies.com

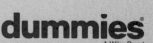

dummies
A Wiley Brand